LONDON'S POST-WAR
SMALLER CLASSES

LONDON'S POST-WAR SMALLER CLASSES

STD, TD, G436, RLH, RFW, GS, RW, XA, XF, RC

KEN BLACKER

Capital Transport

First published 2023

ISBN 978-1-85414-483-6

Published by Capital Transport Publishing Ltd
www.capitaltransport.com

Printed by Parksons Graphics

Front cover Looking unashamedly provincial in appearance, the RLH 53-seat low height double deckers made a welcome break from the intense standardisation that pervaded most of London Transport's double deck motorbus fleet for so many years. RLH 20, the highest numbered in the original batch, remained synonymous with Godstone garage and route 410 for almost 13 years before moving away to Addlestone in 1963 for the final eighteen months of its working life with London Transport. After being made redundant on 1st February 1965, it lay idle for more than three years before being exported in May 1968 to the USA. *Eric Surfleet, Southdown Enthusiasts Club*

Title page The TD class of Leyand PS1s were basic but workmanlike and reliable vehicles which could be found in many parts of London Transport's Central Bus network. They were also the last traditional half-cab single deckers in the fleet. Mann Egerton bodied TD 84 spent two years at Hornchurch garage in 1953-55 during which time its seating capacity was amended from 31 to 30. Route 248 had an end-to-end running time of only 7 minutes and linked the historically rural but rapidly developing village of Cranham, on the far eastern edge of the London urban sprawl, with railway services at Upminster.
Peter Mitchell

Opposite Demoted to bus status despite carrying the GREEN LINE fleet name, RC 7 commences a 331 short working to Standon soon after being reallocated to Hertford in August 1974. Earlier, it had been the first of this small class of AEC Reliances to receive corporate-style NBC livery, in January 1973 while still on Green Line work at Grays, losing this in favour of the approved bus colours of all-green with a central white band in August 1975. Typically of these somewhat unreliable vehicles whose periods in service were spasmodic, RC 7 saw active use for little more that seven out of the almost eleven years spent in the ownership of London Transport and London Country.
J G S Smith/The Transport Library

CONTENTS

INTRODUCTION	6
STD 112-176 – THE THIRD BATCH OF TITANS	8
LEYLAND TIGERS – THE TD CLASS	22
G 436 – A SOLITARY GUY	44
LOW-HEIGHT – THE RLH CLASS	54
LUXURY COACHES – THE RFW CLASS	80
ONE-MAN GUYS – THE GS CLASS	92
THE TWO-DOOR RELIANCES – THE RW CLASS	116
REAR-ENGINED DOUBLE DECKERS – THE XA CLASS	124
LONDON'S FIRST FLEETLINES – THE XF CLASS	148
A NEW LOOK FOR GREEN LINE – THE RC CLASS	162

INTRODUCTION

Well over forty years ago, back in 1979, I was asked by Capital Transport to write an illustrated history of the RT family of London buses which was topical at the time having just bowed out of regular use after playing a major part in London life for four momentous decades. Fortunately the book was well received and without any pre-conceived plan in mind, it was followed by others covering almost all the bus and trolleybus classes introduced by London Transport during its sometimes tumultuous existence from 1933 up to 1965, which is where this current volume terminates. The only class I have not covered from this era is the RF, which was adequately dealt with by the late Ken Glazier back in 1991, and I leave it to others to describe the MBs, SMs, DMSs and various other classes that filled the gap from the late nineteen-sixties up to 1st April 1985 when London Buses Ltd took over and London Transport finally came to an end.

London Transport will always, of course, be best remembered for the huge, highly standardised bus fleets that it created in pursuit of maximum engineering and operating efficiency, but events beyond its control dictated that small classes of non-standard vehicles would always be needed too, and this volume covers the ten such classes introduced during the first two post-war decades. These were tumultuous years when London Transport struggled with shortages of manpower which reached horrendous levels in some areas, whilst also confronting growing trade union intransigence, government interference post-nationalisation, rapidly-expanding private car ownership and falling passenger numbers.

Most of the new non-standard bus types covered in this volume came as a direct response to conditions prevailing at the time of their purchase. The STDs and TDs were a hangover from the wartime era of government-controlled ordering and allocation, fulfilling on a nationwide basis a dire need for new rolling stock at a time when new vehicles of any sort were in short supply. The RLHs, RFWs and GSs were London Transport's own response during a time of maximum standardisation to the need for small specialised fleets to cover specific types of operation and, especially in the late nineteen-fifties, they made a welcome break from the tedium that mass standardisation can bring. The RW, XA, XF and RC classes reflected London Transport's belated realisation that it was lagging behind industry trends and represented its first tentative efforts to catch up. This leaves G 436 as an anachronistic one-off whose acquisition, which ran totally contrary to normal London Transport practice, was authorised to satisfy the whim of one highly-placed but powerful member of the organisation's top management.

As in previous volumes, the information contained here has been gathered over many decades from a whole variety of sources, both official and unofficial, and it helped that from 1951 I worked for London Transport and witnessed its trials and tribulations, and its highs and lows, from the inside. I knew and rode on all the different types of vehicle described here and got to know all their foibles, with the exception of the RC coaches which I never sampled or worked with, and only heard about from others who were actively associated with them. I have included route details where appropriate to put the various stories into perspective, but these are meant only as a guide and in most cases are not claimed to be complete records of all services on which the vehicles operated. You will need to look to other sources for this information.

My grateful thanks go to everyone who has helped me over the years by supplying information, memories and photographs, all of which have helped to make this volume as complete as possible. Many, alas, are no longer with us, but at least in the compilation of this volume the fruits of their efforts linger on.

Special thanks go once again to Alan Nightingale who has helped greatly in unearthing information and photographs and who, once again, has kindly taken on the task of checking the draft of the text for the inevitable typos and grammatical errors. I have tried to make this as complete a record of each individual class as possible, but inevitably there will

By happy coincidence Leyland's standard double deck bodywork was very similar in outline to London Transport's own, and with London-style indicators at the front - including a roof-mounted route number box - the post-war STDs did not look at all out of place. Like many others of its class, STD 142 was based at Loughton garage for the whole of its working life in the capital which extended from October 1946 to February 1955. Keeping it company in Victoria bus station and just visible in the photograph are two early STLs from Forest Gate garage on route 25B.

be gaps in the accumulated knowledge and possibly the odd inaccuracies, either in interpretation or in the source material from which the information is taken, for which I apologise but have no control over.

I have enjoyed writing this series of London bus histories over a long period of years. A big 'Thank You' to you all for reading them.

KEN BLACKER

STD 112-176 – THE THIRD BATCH OF TITANS

Because of the huge early post-war clamour for new bus bodies Leyland had to arrange for construction of some to be outsourced to other manufacturers, but London's STDs were bodied at Leyland itself. The two decks of an STD are seen being married together and it is notable that both have already been fully painted and much of the window glazing is already in place. *British Commercial Vehicle Museum*

Early in October 1945 London Transport received notification of the new bus chassis that it was allocated to receive during the first six months of 1946 comprising 331 double deckers and 21 single deckers. Of the double deckers, 65 were to be PD1 type Leylands with the balance made up by 100 Daimler CWA6 and 166 RT-type AECs. At this stage, with only five months having elapsed since the end of the war in Europe, all new chassis deliveries were still controlled centrally through the Ministries of Supply and War Transport. However the same no longer applied to the provision of bodywork, and operators were now required to source their own new bodies, which was a far from easy task at a time of acute material and labour shortages. In the case of the 65 PD1s, London Transport successfully sought the help of Leyland themselves to provide bodies for the new vehicles which duly became STD 112-176 in the Board's fleet. (For completeness, it can be recorded that Park Royal built the bodies for the new Daimlers, which became D 182-281 and were described in my volume 'London's Utility Buses' (published by Capital Transport in 1997), but bodies could not be obtained at the time for the RTs which did not begin arriving until late April 1947).

Leyland's willingness to supply the 65 complete vehicles was confirmed when A B B Valentine, representing London Transport, met Henry Spurrier, Leyland's General Manager, at the factory late in October 1945. It was agreed then that, in view of the size of the order, Leyland would be prepared to make minor modifications to their standard chassis and body specifications to meet London Transport's specific requirements, and it was left to A A M Durrant to negotiate with Leyland's staff over matters of design and price.

These negotiations took place during the latter part of 1945, enabling a final specification for the new vehicles to be drawn up and to receive final approval on 7th January 1946, followed by the placing of a formal order for the 65 vehicles on 31st January. Quite minor modifications were required to the chassis specification, namely a longer exhaust pipe, blind fittings to the radiator, electrical equipment to London Transport specification and modifications to the chassis lubrication. Leyland normally supplied 11.00 x 20 tyres at the front but London Transport required 36 x 8, however Leyland's standard specification for 9.00 x 20 rear tyres was retained. More extensive modifications were required on the bodywork, totalling 24 in all, the most expensive of which were the fitment of special route indicators (including a front roof route number box), the provision of 15 standard half-drop windows instead of 10 (including ones at the upstairs front and on the front nearside bulkhead), and full lining of the interior roof on the upper deck. The agreed price per chassis was £1,460.0s.0d (against Leyland's standard one of £1,398.12s.6d), while the bodies worked out at £1,460.2s.8d (standard price £1,272.0s.0d).

At the time of placing the order it was anticipated that the first seven vehicles would be supplied during the week ended 6th July 1946, followed by further deliveries at approximately the same rate per week until the final four on week ended 24th August. During this very early post-war period delivery dates were yet to become as unpredictably haywire as they were a year or two later, and the first to be received, STD 112, was only just over seven weeks late when it arrived at Chiswick on 28th August 1946. It came four weeks ahead of the remainder which were delivered from 25th September onwards, the final arrivals (STD 168, 173, 174) being on 10th December.

By the time of their delivery the price that London Transport was required to pay for STD 112-176 had increased beyond the sums originally agreed. Since the start of 1946 all manufacturers had found that availability of labour had worsened, and to counter this a national pay increase of about 7% plus extra paid holidays had been approved by the government for engineering workers from 15th April and for vehicle bodybuilders from 20th May which, in turn, had increased the cost of raw and manufactured materials. The price per chassis for new STDs thus increased to £1,471.12s.6 with a bigger increase per body to £1,529.4s.8d, an overall rise of about 2.75% per vehicle.

When it arrived at Chiswick on 28th August, STD 112 was seen to be a much more handsome addition to the London Transport fleet than the Park Royal-bodied Daimlers that were being received at the same time, and of far superior body construction. The wooden-framed bodies on the Daimlers were obviously a development from the 'utility' styling used extensively during the war years, whereas the STDs were clearly built to full peace-time standards with their flowing lines being not so very different from those of the STLs and STDs of late pre-war vintage. In fact they were based on Leyland's standard 'Hybridge' metal-framed structure from which the manufacturer had not been prepared to deviate. The modifications were all cosmetic ones such as those mentioned earlier, plus the elimination of Leyland's traditional convex panelling below the windows, a horizontal division of the lower deck skirt panels and the use of London Transport's standard internal coloured décor in place of the usual polished wooden mouldings for window surrounds etc.

The first to be completed was STD 112 and Leyland was sufficiently proud of it to distribute this photograph widely at the time. It was taken at Worden Park, near the factory in Leyland. The eclectic mix of displays in the three front blind boxes is of interest, but in reality few of the batch were destined ever to run with a full blind display and never whilst carrying this original livery with cream upper deck window frames. *British Historic Vehicle Museum*

The rear aspect is demonstrated by STD 150 seen at work in its early days from Loughton garage on route 10A on which it arrived after a month at Potters Bar. A disappointing feature of these vehicles was the total lack of a rear blind display. They introduced to London the distinctive Leyland style of rainwater gutter above the emergency window with one end upturned and the other facing down, which was later also to be included (though subsequently discarded) on the 500 strong RTW class. *Guy Bowden collection*

Unlike the Daimlers, the STDs were painted in the latest version of the new red and cream livery, and the only real surprise was that, again in contrast to the Daimlers, no destination equipment of any sort was installed at the rear even though a full, three piece display was incorporated at the front. In later years a route number stencil was hung in the back platform window but this did not really compensate for the loss of a proper blind display. Seating was for 56, with 30 upstairs and 26 down, on the type of simple metal-framed seat commonly used at the time with chromium-plated top rail, while moquette cushion covering of the now-standard London Transport pattern was employed on both decks.

The PD1 16ft 3¼in wheelbase chassis was an almost brand new design, the first complete PD1 having only entered service with Bury Corporation as recently as March 1946. Although London Transport chose to number the vehicles in the STD class their chassis were, in fact, a complete re-design from the earlier TD4 (STD 1-100) and TD7 (STD 101-111) models in the fleet. Most notably they had a new 7.4 litre direct injection engine of 4⅜ inch bore and 5 inch stroke known as the E181 which, despite having smaller capacity than the 8.6 litre units in the earlier vehicles, theoretically developed slightly more power – 100bph and 1800rpm – and promised better fuel consumption. This engine had, in fact, been developed from a 6.2 litre unit which, modified in the war to 7.4 litre form, had been successfully used in the Leyland 'Matilda' tank. Rigidly mounted, it proved to be tough and reasonably trouble-free, but it was noticeably noisier than the famous 8.6 litre pre-war unit, producing a harsh beat that earlier STDs did not have.

Other features of the PD1 chassis design were Marles cam and roller steering, vacuum-assisted triple servo brakes, and a new 4-speed constant mesh gearbox with single, dry-plate clutch. At the front end a new and larger radiator, with its filler cap offset to the nearside to allow a wider cab, was given a chromium plated metal shell on the London vehicles although many early deliveries for provincial operators had cellulosed brass shells.

The complete vehicle, which was 14ft 4⅞in in unladen height, weighed 7tons 3cwt. Under the London Transport coding system STD 112-176 were classified 4STD3 and allocated body numbers 1336-1400. Registration numbers were issued in strict numerical sequence as HGF 990-999 (STD 112-121) and HLW 51-105 (STD 122-176), but the chassis numbers, which ranged between 460952 and 461631, were allocated in no sequence whatever and were heavily intermingled with provincial deliveries.

With the 65 new Leylands shortly to come on stream, the Bus Allocation Advisory Committee, which consisted of both management and staff representatives, sat to decide the garages and routes to which they should be allocated The Union's first priority was to diffuse areas of extreme discontent where staff action had been threatened by crews and was now imminent. One was at Palmers Green garage where staff were incensed by the removal, between October 1945 and January 1946, of their entire fleet consisting of mid to late 1930s preselector STLs and replacement by elderly

The coving panels of STD 149 had been liberally covered with advertising material by the time it was presented for its archival photographs to be taken in November 1946. Apart from the obvious difference in seat frames and coverings, the general interior finish follows closely that of the pre-war STDs, and Leyland's staff probably dusted down their old plans to help in the production of the new batch. A notable addition to the lower saloon is the bell cord, now adopted as a standard fitment on London buses, while a slightly utilitarian feature of the upper deck is the lack of side lining panels. *London Transport Museum*

Victoria garage was the first recipient of the new STDs which, after years of wartime hardship and shortages, gave a glimmer of the better times hopefully lying ahead. Newly-delivered STD 124 is at the Green Man terminus in Leytonstone. The two LTs in the distance comprise one of the newest of that class and one of the oldest. Within a few days the open staircase LTs would be swept away from route 10A with the arrival of new STDs at Loughton. *W J Haynes*

LTs, some of which were admittedly in a parlous condition. They were demanding at least a partial return of STLs, which the availability of new STDs should make possible. Another hotspot was Hanwell where Gardner-engined 'Bluebird' LTs, now reduced to nine in number, had been unwillingly tolerated for many years by drivers who detested working on them and were not prepared to do so any longer. In addition, trouble was also brewing at Croydon where staff were beginning to demand something better than their large fleet of old petrol-engined double deckers, and who particularly wanted the removal of at least some of their ex-Tilling STLs whose heavily distorted and visibly worn-out appearance was evident for everyone to see.

For its part, the management wanted to begin making inroads into the substantial fleet of open-staircase petrol-engined LT six-wheelers still fully employed in everyday service. The extreme example of this was at Loughton garage whose vehicle allocation consisted solely of open-staircase vehicles, an incredible and unique situation to be in as late as the mid-nineteen forties. Although none could go for scrap at the time because of London Transport's dire bus shortage, the worst of them could be distributed around the fleet on light duties, and with this in mind the allocation of new STDs was to be as follows:

Garage	No.	Purpose
Victoria (GM)	22	(to provide STLs for Palmers Green)
Hanwell (HW)	9	(to replace Gardner-engined LTs)
Croydon (TC)	9	(to replace an equivalent number of Tilling STLs)
Loughton (L)	17	(to begin the replacement of open-back LTs)
Potters Bar (PB)	8	(also as open-back LT replacements)

Loughton's STDs served all sorts of territory from the country roads of Essex to the central London scene at Victoria where STD 142 takes its stand time in the bus station. Again, the STD contrasts heavily with time-expired relics in the fleet such as Cricklewood's ST 183 on route 16 and the Leyton LT behind on route 38, which will be an open staircase one. Leyton's vintage LTs would continue to run alongside Loughton's new STDs until the summer of 1947 when new RTs began arriving. *S A Newman © A B Cross*

Victoria garage was the first to receive the new STDs, with STD 113, 118, 121, 123 all starting work there on 1st October 1946. Many others followed in quick succession so that the full quota of 22 was in position in just over a week, the last six being licensed for service on the 9th. So keen had London Transport been to get quick delivery of these vehicles that they had despatched their own drivers to Leyland to take delivery of nine of them in preference to waiting for the manufacturer to deliver them as would normally have been the case. Each new arrival at Victoria saw the departure of an STL to Palmers Green, and the new vehicles quickly established themselves on almost every one of Victoria's scheduled routes:

10	Victoria–Abridge
22	Putney Common–Homerton
52	Victoria–Borehamwood
77/A	Kings Cross–Tooting/Raynes Park
137	Archway–Crystal Palace

They worked indiscriminately alongside a mixture of STLs and the batch of 'utility' STDs which were unique to Victoria and never operated in service from any other garage. Only a short time had elapsed, in fact, since Victoria lost the last of its 'Hendon' STDs, and it remained the only garage in the fleet ever to run all three varieties of STD.

Attention turned next to Potters Bar, on 11th October, and Loughton on the 12th. Potters Bar received eight STDs for route 134 (Potter Bar–Pimlico) while 17 had arrived at Loughton by 22nd November for routes 10A (Leytonstone–Epping) and 38A Loughton–Victoria), in all instances replacing open-staircase LTs. Whilst the STDs were well received and proved popular at Loughton this was, apparently, not the case at Potters Bar. Compared with the petrol-engined LTs, which were flexible and speedy vehicles to drive (except when steep hills were encountered and they often quickly boiled over), the new STDs were probably found to be too slow and ponderous for a fast, busy route such as the 134, and after spending only between four and six weeks at Potters Bar, all eight were transferred overnight on 20th November to join those already at Loughton. Potters Bar's 134 allocation was fully re-stocked with open-staircase LTs, its staff happy to await the anticipated arrival of new RTs to replace them some time in 1947.

On the same day that Loughton received its last new STDs, 22nd November 1946, the first two of an eventual batch of nine were licensed at Hanwell where they were placed at work alongside STLs on route 55 (Chiswick–Greenford with a peak hour extension to Hayes). The nine Gardner-engined 'Bluebirds' that they replaced were initially delicensed but subsequently emerged on country area service at Grays, still in red livery. No work was scheduled for Hanwell's STDs on Sundays, the staff's preference being to use STLs, but at times odd ones could be found substituting for the regular stock on routes other than the 55.

Finally it was the turn of Croydon to receive an allocation of STDs which arrived between 11th and 23rd December 1946. As at Hanwell nine vehicles were received and these were scheduled to work alongside new Daimlers from Sutton garage on route 115 (Wallington–Croydon Airport). As the full allocation of nine was required for the 115 only on Sundays (Croydon's scheduled commitment being as low as six on Mondays to Friday and seven on Saturdays), it was not unusual for surplus STDs to be found covering workings on route 133 and possibly other Croydon routes too. Of the nine vehicles displaced by the new STDs, one was fit only for immediate scrapping but the other eight, all Tilling-type STLs, duly turned up – much to the amazement of many observers – on Country Bus peak hour workings from Hemel Hempstead garage, looking very strange in green livery. To appease the staff there, some were subsequently removed and allocated instead to Watford High Street and Leavesden Road garages.

The post-war STDs were destined to work from Hanwell garage for barely three years. At the Windmill Lane terminus in Greenford STD 157 shares duties with wartime Bristol B 7 which can be seen just arriving in the background. Just visible to the right of B 7 is a former ex-Tilling ST now painted in all-over red and used as a staff canteen. *J H Aston*

The STDs stayed at Croydon only until the first brand new RT became available in the summer of 1947 when, one by one, they departed as each of nine new RTs arrived, with the first leaving on 6th July and the last on 8th September. The destination for all nine was Loughton which, following its intake of new STDs in 1946 followed by those from Potters Bar, had been left with ten open staircase LTs still on its books. Augmented by a single STD transferred in from Hanwell, it was now possible to remove the last of the old LTs, rendering Loughton as an all-STD garage with the enviable record of being the only one in the whole fleet with a complete allocation of post-war rolling stock.

Generally speaking, the new STDs did not prove to be particularly popular with driving staff who found the relatively slow performance and lack of pulling power from their small engines a hindrance, especially at peak times on busy in-town routes. Their slow gear change was irritating, and the lack of engine power really showed when steep gradients were encountered. In their later years, when they were sometimes required to tackle the hill at Chingford Mount with a good load on board, it was a case of holding the vehicle noisily in first gear for the whole of the ascent and hoping for the best! On the plus side, the Leyland PD1 proved to be a sturdy and reliable workhorse, and it was the only double decker in the fleet capable of matching the 10.5mpg regularly notched up by the 435-strong fleet of G class 5-cylinder Guy Arabs. A survey taken in 1951 showed the 4STD3s to have the best fuel performance of all Leyland double deckers in the fleet, the others being the pre-war STDs at 9.9 miles per gallon, RTLs at 9.3mpg and RTWs at 8.8mpg.

Crews found other minor niggles on them too which, to its credit, London Transport's management tackled and managed to eliminate. The driver's seat was repositioned and its mechanism and cushion replaced by a modified STL pattern; the windscreen wiper motor which partly obstructed vision was reversed; a brake pedal stop bracket was fitted to alleviate the pedal striking the driver's ankle when operating the accelerator, and wooden battens were fitted inside the lower saloon ceiling to prevent excessive drumming. The latter problem was one already experienced on G class Guys with Northern Counties bodies which were also metal framed and it had arisen because, when the bodies were built, the use of plywood for lining ceilings was prohibited and aluminium had been used instead.

Croydon's flirtation with STDs was brief and lasted only until new RTs became available to replace them. STD 172 was one of those that entered service there on 11th December 1946 and it moved north to Loughton just over eight months later on 25th August 1947. It is seen at the Belmont Road terminus in Wallington about to start a circuitous 55 minute run on route 115 to Croydon Airport.
Alan B Cross

Some services became indelibly linked with the STDs and none more so than Loughton's route 20A, which was a renumbering of the 10A on 30th June 1948. STDs reigned supreme on it for more than eight years until they met their premature demise in 1955. STD 124 is still near the start of its southbound run as it sets down passengers in Epping High Street outside the once-popular Half Moon pub which is now just a memory. Across the road, behind the man smoking a cigarette, can just be seen the large bullseye sign outside the modern Epping country bus garage which outlived the STD era by eight years and closed on 21st May 1963. *C Carter*

STDs could sometimes be found working on services to which they were not officially allocated. Occasional appearances of Hanwell's STDs on routes 92 and 92A subsequently became a permanent feature, and STD 159 is seen loading up at the Empire Stadium in Wembley for a journey on route 92 just over a month before Hanwell's STDs all departed to Leyton in October 1949. *Alan B Cross*

The years 1947 and 1948 saw virtually no change in routine for most of the post-war STDs although, on 30th June 1948, route 10A at Loughton was renumbered 20 to acknowledge that it was a significant operation in its own right and much more than a mere adjunct to route 10. It was only at Hanwell garage that any real change of itinerary was involved for the STDs during this period of time, apparently at the request of the operating staff. On occasions, members of the class had been used on routes 92 and 92A instead of the 55, and acknowledgement that this had been made a permanent arrangement for the whole of Hanwell's STD allocation was contained in issue 61 of the internal "Allocation of Scheduled Buses" book dated 13th April 1949. However this arrangement was destined not to last long, and in a significant overnight move on 19th October 1949 the whole of Hanwell's STD allocation (latterly reduced to seven vehicles) was reallocated to Leyton. The spur for this had been the receipt at Hanwell of new RTWs for route 105 with a resultant reshuffling of resources within the garage, making the STDs redundant. Leyton was the most sensible new home for them to go to as, being the parent 'shed' for Loughton, its engineers were already well versed in handling them and had a stock of spare parts on hand for use whenever the vehicles came in for a major dock. Furthermore Leyton still held a sizeable number of LT six-wheelers requiring immediate replacement, and with no new RTs currently available to displace them from routes 106 (Finsbury Park–Becontree Heath) and 167 (Loughton–Barkingside), the STDs had to suffice instead, and more were received, mainly from Victoria, in December 1949 and January 1950 to bring Leyton's strength up to 17.

The first overhaul cycle for the 4STD3s was now under way, having commenced in July 1949, and resulting from this the last four to emerge from overhaul in late August and September 1950 appeared in the new standard colour scheme generally described as 'all red', in which the only cream relief was the narrow central band. The remainder were repainted in similar style at the second overhaul cycle between January 1952 and June 1953. At this overhaul some efforts were made to improve the cab environment for drivers with a number of draught-proofing measures and the reversal of the cab door handle to prevent it from catching on and tearing the driver's uniform jacket, the latter being a modification already carried out at the staffs' request on Loughton's STD 139.

At the three garages to which the 4STD3s were now allocated, the nineteen-fifties saw subtle changes occurring in their spheres of operation coinciding with the breathless and unremitting delivery of new RT family vehicles. During 1949 no fewer than 1,592 of these had entered service for the first time, and though the input rate eased off a little from 1950 onwards, the headlong rush towards the achievement of almost complete standardisation continued, with the scrapping of the tram fleet also on the agenda between 1950 and 1952. Victoria garage saw the operational scope of its STDs diminish with the arrival of new RTs on route 137 during the second half of 1950 and on routes 10 and 52 in October and November 1952. The wartime STDs had all been withdrawn from service by May 1951, and for the final stage of their operating career Victoria's post-war STDs were all scheduled to work on routes 77 and 77A. No Sunday work was scheduled for them but surprisingly, and purely by local arrangement, they made a high profile appearance on route 24 on Sundays when Victoria garage took up operation of it from 18th May 1952 onwards, firstly in place of its scheduled STLs and, from October 1952, in place of RTs. The end of STDs at Victoria came on 25th November 1953 when its share of route 77 passed to the nearly-new and largely underutilised garage at Stockwell, taking the whole Victoria allocation of STDs with it, the 77A having been converted to RT operation by now. As a result, Sunday appearances of STDs on route 24 now ceased.

Despite constant demands from its driving staff to be given an allocation of new RTs, Loughton retained its STD fleet at full strength right up to 1955, and latterly held the dubious accolade of being the only garage on the entire London Transport system never to have run RT family vehicles. On 17th October 1951 route 167 was transferred in from Leyton, still STD worked. Loughton's big day came on 2nd December 1953 when a spacious new garage opened across the road from the old

A regular slot for Leyton's STDs from October 1949 onwards was on route 106 where STD 152 – on loan from Loughton – encounters a busy traffic scene in Barking at some time in 1951. Just about to pass it in the opposite direction is one of the 'South African' SA3 class trolleybuses from Ilford depot while a Park Royal bodied Guy from Barking follows behind the STD. *Alan B Cross*

ex-LGOC property of 1923 vintage. Compared to the old premises the new Loughton garage was enormous, with room to accommodate 137 buses, a massive increase over the old building's capacity of about 40. Built in anticipation of enormous housing developments at Debden, Buckhurst Hill and Woodford which only partly materialised, the new Loughton garage was destined to remain a costly white elephant with capacity grossly in excess of operational requirements which at their maximum rose only to 48 vehicles. However, it did inaugurate one new route during the STD era, the 20A between Debden and Leytonstone, which commenced operation on 19th May 1954.

The third 4STD3 garage, Leyton, saw a complete change in its STD operation during 1951. As recorded above, route 167 moved to Loughton in October, but prior to this, from 1st August 1951, operation of STDs on route 106 had ceased. Leyton's partner garage on the 106, Hackney, received RTWs in place of STLs on this date and, not to be outdone, Leyton began using RTs. The deposed STDs were transferred to route 38A, from whence the RTs for the 106 had come, and it was a logistically sensible move anyway since Loughton's share of the 38A was already STD worked. Thereafter Leyton's allocation of STDs remained at about 13 (including engineering spares) until 19th May 1954 when the introduction of a new schedule on route 38A reduced its STD input down to a mere two buses on Mondays to Fridays only, with a balancing increase at Loughton. Thereafter Leyton was left with just three STDs on its books, two to cover its Monday to Friday service commitment and the third as a spare. During this latter phase of their existence, Leyton's STDs tended to be confined on an unofficial basis to peak hour work on route 38 (Victoria–Chingford). This was solely a Leyton garage operation and never had an official STD allocation, though appearances on it from time to time had not been uncommon ever since Leyton began running STDs.

It is interesting to record that, behind the scenes in 1951, the engineers had been examining the feasibility of converting all the non-standard post-war vehicles fitted with crash gearboxes and friction clutches to fluid transmission, possibly using scrap Wilson-type gearboxes from withdrawn STLs. The final conclusion appears to have been that, however desirable it might be from a staffing point of view, the replacement of crash gearboxes by preselectors would prove too costly and the idea was quietly dropped.

On 17th May 1953 Victoria's STD 166 stops by the aluminium 'Q' shelter in Parliament Street on a Sunday route 24 working, with Potters Bar's RT 2731 on route 29 following close behind. The era of the 'all red' livery is now well and truly entrenched and all 65 post-war STDs ended up carrying it. STD 166 had gone through its last overhaul two months earlier. *Alan B Cross*

How about a sightseeing trip to London on an STD? Loughton's STD 142 stands incongruously next to a building site to offer a half day trip on excursion L with departures at 3pm and again at 6.15. Not bad value at three shillings for adults and one and sixpence for children. STD 142 was one of several that spent their entire working lives at Loughton garage. *Peter Mitchell*

With their end now less than a year away, Loughton's STDs inaugurated new route 20A on 19th May 1954. STD 157 displays a 'To and From Epping Forest' slip board and carries a later-type polished aluminium radiator shell in place of the original chromium plated one. *Ron Wellings*

At the start of 1955 all 65 post-war STDs were still licensed for service, but their days were now numbered. The previous year had seen the withdrawal of the last pre-war STLs and STDs, while even the SRT class, which dated from as recently as 1949/50, had disappeared as their bodies were transferred to new RT chassis. Excluding experimental Routemaster RM 1, the only non-standard highbridge double deckers still operational in the entire fleet were the 4STD3s, a solitary Guy Arab, G 436, and twenty post-war STLs. With as many as 144 newly-delivered and still unused RTs and RTLs in storage, the inevitable decision was taken to dispose of all the remaining oddments.

With this in mind, a third overhaul cycle for the STDs which had begun in July 1954 was abruptly cancelled after only nine had been dealt with, STD 140 having been the last to enter the overhaul shop on 26th October 1954 from which it emerged on 22nd December.

When it came the end was swift. RTLs rendered surplus by service reductions were employed to remove all 14 of Stockwell's STDs on 16th February 1955 and Leyton's three were replaced by RTs on the same day. The position was slightly more complex at Loughton where driver training had to take place first which began on 23rd February. RTs began running from Loughton on the 26th and the last STDs were removed from service on 1st March 1955, 23 of the batch having still been available for service on the last day.

STD 122 had spent its whole working life at Victoria prior to its move to the new and imposing Stockwell premises on 25th November 1953 where it remained until the final withdrawal of STDs from route 77 on 16th February 1955. New vehicles have already taken over on the associated 77A as witnessed by the RTL standing behind STD 122 on the stand at Kings Cross. *Alan Nightingale collection*

With the end now clearly in sight and the promised RTs about to arrive, a few of Loughton's STDs surprisingly received full blind displays in their front indicator boxes for the very first time, and it suited them. STD 163, photographed swinging away from the terminus at Loughton station, remained in service until the final day of STD operation on 28th February 1955.
Ron Wellings

STDs which had operated up to the very last day at Loughton were promptly moved away for storage at Shepherds Bush garage to join all the others waiting there for the start of their journey to Yugoslavia. Seen here are STDs 169, 130, 136 and 167 one of which, STD 130, appears to have run with a full blind display in its final days. *Peter Mitchell*

All 65 STDs were sold for £305 10s 0d each to the B S E Company Ltd, a firm of export agents based in Regent Street W1 and acting on behalf of the communist state of Yugoslavia to which many older former London Transport buses had already been sent. Official sale dates varied between July 1955 and March 1956, presumably depending upon shipping arrangements under which most (if not all) went via the Tilbury–Antwerp crossing. A large number – possibly as many as half the batch – saw service in Sarajevo and others were based in Mostar, both in today's state of Bosnia Herzegovina, while yet others were recorded operating services from Split (now in Croatia). They were worked hard, their most notable input being on the 8-mile run between Sarajevo and Ilidze where more than 25 former STDs could be found, often working in pairs, on the ten-minute headway until the buses were replaced by a modern tram service.

A rumour has long circulated that an STD (believed to be STD 171) still exists in semi-preserved condition in the city of Novi Sad in today's Serbia. How rewarding it would be if one of these characterful vehicles has, indeed, been saved, and better still if it could one day return home.

The STDs still had plenty of life left in them when they arrived in Yugoslavia and they gave good service there. Soon after arrival the former STD 140 is seen departing from the premises of the Promet organisation in Split on a journey to Trogir. Still in original condition, right down to its London livery, it has yet to receive its Yugoslavian registration plates. Much later on, an unidentified vehicle is seen at the departure point in Sarajevo of the frequent service to Ilidze. Local livery is now carried and the entrance and stairway have been very neatly transposed to the European nearside to suit the rule of the road.

LEYLAND TIGERS – THE TD CLASS

Of 352 new buses scheduled for delivery to LT during the first half of 1946, the vast majority were double deckers. Only 21 single deckers were envisaged, all of the recently announced Leyland Tiger PS1 model which was only just starting to go into production. This allocation was viewed at 55 Broadway as being totally inadequate to meet London Transport's immediate needs for new single deckers, and an urgent approach to the Ministry resulted in an additional allocation of 40 AEC Regals (later increased to 50 which became the 14T12 class T 719-768) and also of an extra ten PS1s, bringing the Leyland total to 31.

It was decided to designate the new PS1 single deckers as the TD class. This meant reviving a type designation that had been in use until not so very many years earlier for an entirely different batch of vehicles whose memory was still fresh in many people's minds. The previous 195-strong TD class, consisting of Leyland TD1 and TD2 types of which the great majority were bodied as double deckers, had only ceased operating early in the war, on 30th September 1939, and the last of these had not left the fleet until as comparatively recently as June 1940. It had, in fact, been anticipated at one time that 30 of them would have remained operational for even longer, to the extent that 23 had their bodies thoroughly reconditioned in July and August 1939 in a programme that was halted prematurely and abruptly by the outbreak of war. It was the subsequent large and previously unanticipated wartime drop in vehicle requirements that had brought about their premature demise at the end of September 1939.

Scale drawings of the 1TD1 produced by Weymann prior to the start of production show the main dimensions of the bodywork. The awkward tilt of the rear destination box is clearly indicated; similar treatment of the front box would have led to a more balanced design and avoided the frowning appearance from which these vehicles suffered.

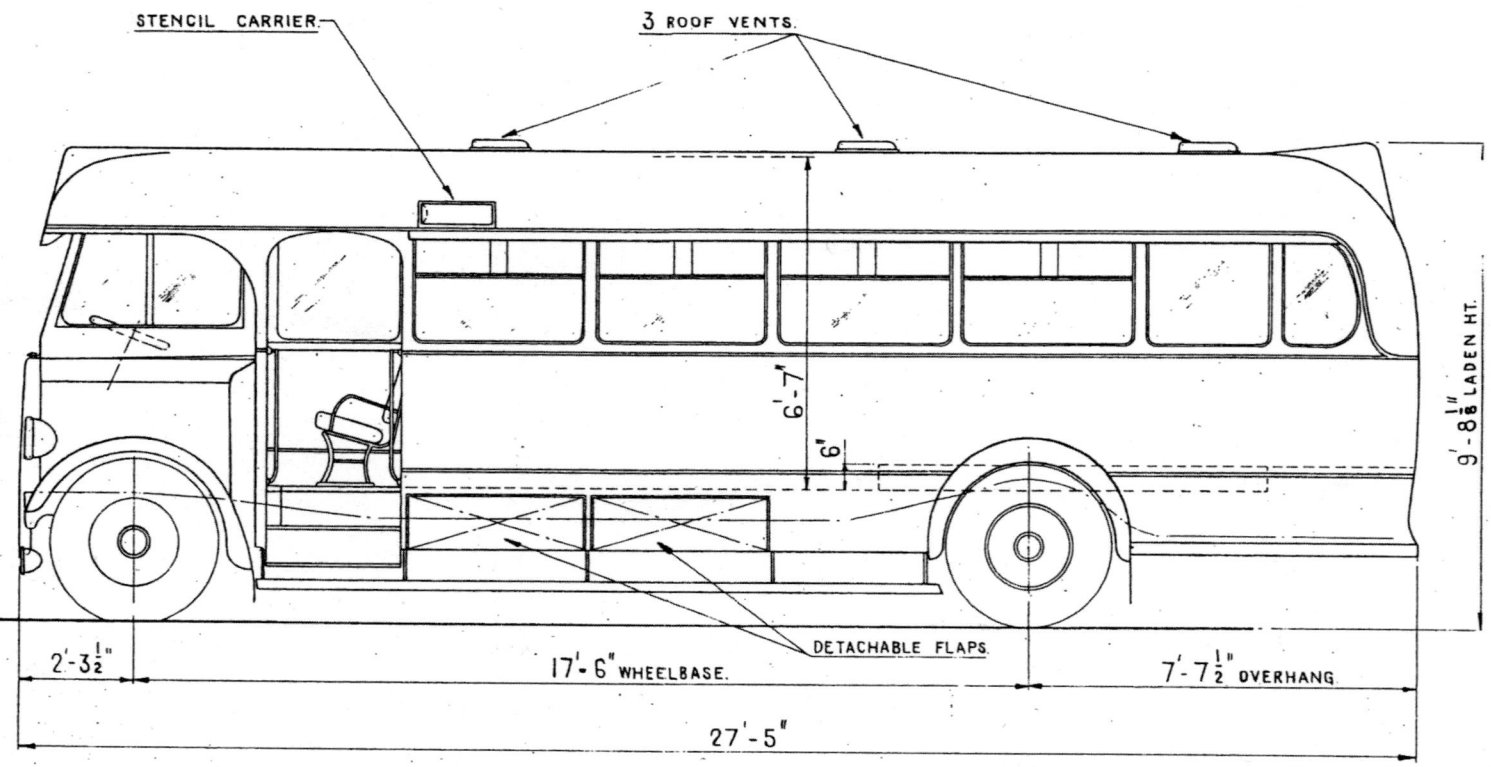

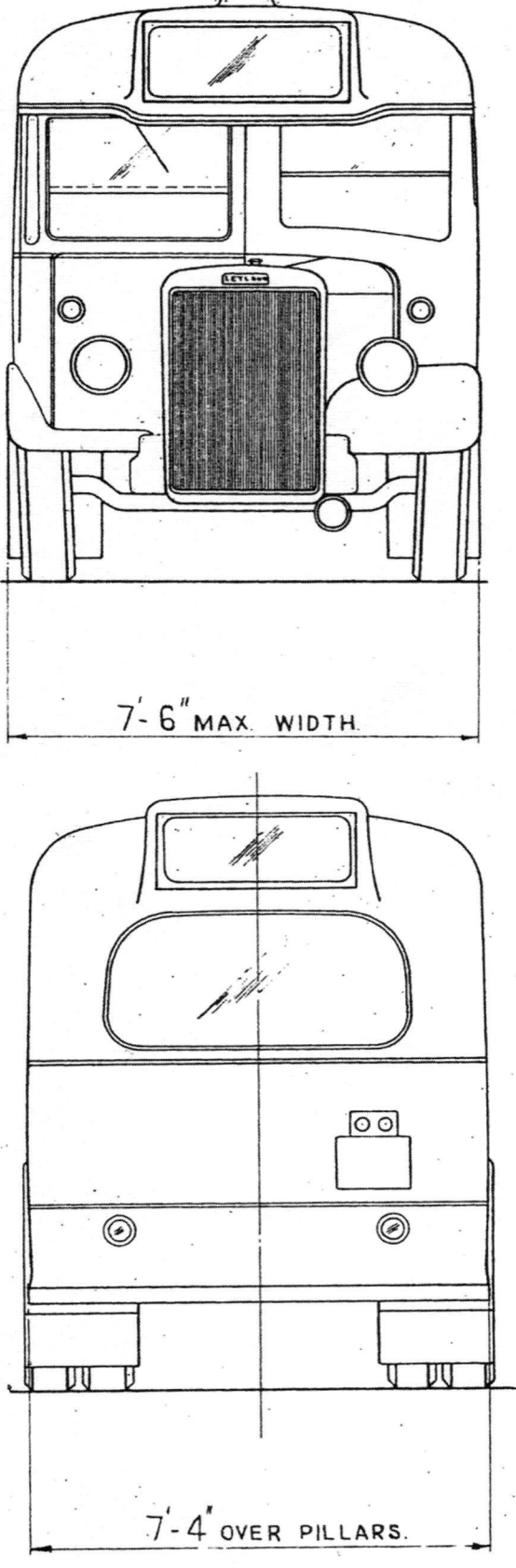

Weymann agreed to build the bodies for all 81 new single deckers provided that London Transport was prepared to accept a basic design developed by them for the British Electric Traction group that they were about to put into production. The main frame construction of the bodies was to be of timber, using oak for the underframe with steel flitch pates inserted into the cross bars, and ash for the side framing and roof hoopsticks. As far as practicable the bodies for TD 1-31 would be the same as those of T 719-768 with the obvious visible exception of the cab area where the lower-mounted radiator on the Leylands made possible a flat bottom edge to the windscreen instead of the sloping one on the Ts.

Negotiations with the manufacturers over technical aspects of the design took place in January 1946, and on 14th February Leyland submitted its finalised specification and quotation for the 31 PS1s. Exactly the same modifications from the standard design were requested as for STD 112-176 except that no deviation was made from Leyland's recommended all-round tyre size for PS1s of 9.00 x 20. The mechanical specification was, in fact, exactly the same as for the 65 STDs except for a longer wheelbase of 17ft 6ins. The cost for each chassis was to be £1,406.15s.3d to which would be added a further £8.8s.9d for delivery to the Weymann works at Addlestone. The delivery schedule provided for the first two to be sent to Addlestone during week ended 27th April 1946 and for the order to be completed by 9th November.

AEC was much quicker off the mark than Leyland in supplying their promised new chassis to London Transport with the result that all 50 of the new Regals were operational before the first TDs entered service. The Regals had begun operating in April 1946, which meant that Londoners had had plenty of time to become used to the new shape and unusual livery application of London Transport's latest single deckers before the first of the very similar looking TDs took to the road late in the same year.

Leyland's anticipated delivery dates proved to be somewhat over-optimistic and, generally speaking, the production programme ran about six months late. As a result, the first chassis were not made available until 18th September 1946 resulting in the initial deliveries of completed vehicles from Weymann being delayed until 3rd December when TD 1 and TD 2 arrived at Chiswick. Leyland was overwhelmed with work, and coupled with a requirement by government to put export contracts first, imposed a complete break in chassis deliveries between TD 13 on 1st October and the resumption of production with TD 14's chassis on 23rd November.

In appearance, the new vehicles were a mixture of Weymann influence with their outswept panels at the rear, and of BET styling in the provision of an offside emergency door rather than one at the rear as favoured by London Transport, plus the use of Rawlings 'Monovent' sliding windows in place of half drops. The latter was a feature only previously found with London Transport on 22 trolleybuses of late pre-war and wartime manufacture and on a solitary recently-delivered Guy Arab motor bus. The livery of predominantly red relieved only by thin, cream-painted mouldings above and below the windows, plus the usual black mudguards, was a precursor of the styling London Transport was to adopt for many Central single deckers in the future.

The least satisfactory aspect of the exterior design was the way in which London Transport's standard indicator boxes were incorporated. Because they did not fit satisfactorily within the rather shallow roof contour of the BET-style design, both front and rear indicators sat uncomfortably, the front one projecting downwards below the cant rail to produce a frowning effect, while the rear one projected awkwardly above the roof line of the rest of the vehicle.

Internally, only a modest effort was made to emulate current London Transport practice. The polished mahogany mouldings around the windows looked smart but very un-London-like, although the slatted wooden floor with brown cork tiles below the seats, and the cream-enamelled plywood ceiling panels were recognisable London features. The side panels were covered in green rexine and the front bulkhead in brown lino. The only bell push was at the front, a cord being fitted for passengers' use which ran the length of the saloon above the offside seats. They were built as 33-seaters, and apart from a single inward-facing seat over each wheel arch all faced forwards in pairs apart from a bench for five across the rear. In this respect the TDs differed from the Ts which had been built as 35-seaters

A factory photograph of TD 4 taken just after its completion in December 1946. It appears to be almost ready for delivery to Chiswick once the front wheel trims have been fitted. The unladen weight is shown as 6 tons 5 cwt which conflicts with official records and also with the figure of 6 tons 2 cwt ultimately displayed on the vehicles in service, and poses a question as to which was correct.

Apart from the bell cord, the seat moquette and perhaps the fareboard holder, there was not much within the Weymann bodies of TD 1-31 to hint that they were destined for London Transport. The temptation to paint over the polished wood window surrounds on overhaul, as happened with all the wartime bus deliveries, was fortunately resisted and they were retained – and occasionally revarnished – throughout their time in London although in some instances the top rail, above the windows, was painted pale green in line with the practice on a number of older pre-war types. *London Transport Museum*

with every seat facing the front, but the ones immediately above the wheel arches quickly proved unsuitable and the 50 vehicles were converted to the same configuration as the TDs at their first overhaul in 1949/50. To comply with Metropolitan Police restrictions, both classes were built without doors at the passenger entrance.

The complete vehicles weighed a not unduly heavy 6ton 2cwt unladen. London Transport's internal classification for TD 1-31 was 1TD1 and they were allocated body numbers 1305-1335 and registrations HGF 959-989, all running consecutively., Their Leyland chassis numbers were, however, far from consecutive and spanned all the way between the lowest, 461061 (TD 4), and the highest, 462837 (TD 30).

Soon after being placed into service just before Christmas 1946 the first of the batch was photographed at the Finsbury Park terminus of the busy and physically challenging route 212. A few vehicles in the batch had chromium plated windscreens when new and TD 1 was one of these. All 31 of this initial delivery of TDs were destined to operate from Muswell Hill garage for the next six years. *W J Haynes*

It was arranged that all 31 TDs would be allocated to Muswell Hill garage where they would replace almost new 14T12s which were to be redeployed at Sidcup. The main objective was to convert route 212 to TD operation. This was an unusually busy single deck operation which, though only requiring 16 minutes in end-to-end running time, required no fewer than 25 vehicles to cover the main peak-hour schedule which at its maximum saw no fewer than 48 buses per hour departing from Finsbury Park on Monday to Friday morning peaks, half travelling all the way to Muswell Hill and the remainder half way to Crouch End. For the evening peak, 43 buses per hour were scheduled throughout the whole length of the route. Any residue of surplus TDs would officially work on route 210 (Finsbury Park–Golders Green), a service normally entrusted to LT single deckers. In practice, however, LTs quite commonly appeared on the 212 for the next few years with rather more TDs working the 210 than scheduled. Regular appearances were also made on route 244 (Muswell Hill–Winchmore Hill), some journeys on which were rostered to be covered by buses primarily employed on the 212, and occasionally unscheduled appearances even occurred on Muswell Hill's fourth single deck service 251 (Arnos Grove–Burnt Oak) from time to time.

The first two members of the class (TD 3, 5) were licensed for work at Muswell Hill on 14th December 1946 after which their numbers slowly increased, the final one of all (TD 30) being licensed on 23rd June 1947, two days before the last of the Ts left for Sidcup on the 25th. The 210 and 212 were both hard-working routes which happened to include steep hill climbs, and initial performance of the TDs on them came in for criticism compared with the T types and even the old LT six-wheelers, but this was satisfactorily overcome by adjusting the rear axle ratio from 5.4 to 4.8. The 31 vehicles continued to lead an unexciting existence at Muswell Hill, with no change occurring in their routine, until their second overhaul cycle commenced in the autumn of 1952, after which redeployment at locations other than Muswell Hill finally began.

The rear end design of the Weymann body on TD 1-31 was exactly the same as that on the 14T12s. It also became a familiar feature within a number of BET fleets though none of these required the large rear indicator box that graced the London vehicles. TD 29, which was one of the last to be delivered, was photographed on 15th April 1947 and released for service the next day. *London Transport Museum*

Long before this the seeds for another 100 TDs were sown By September 1947 direct government control of new chassis allocations had ceased, and on the 3rd of that month discussions took place at Leyland over the purchase of 100 more PS1 chassis for delivery in 1948, hopefully starting in April of that year. These were urgently needed for the Central Bus fleet where 62% of its single deck rolling stock was stated to be 12 years old or more, causing a progressive decrease in the Board's ability to maintain an adequate service. Mann Egerton of Norwich had signified its willingness to produce 100 bodies based on a design produced for 30 AEC Regals that it was just about to build for the Country Bus & Coach fleet (T 769-798), but this Company was now pressing London Transport for an urgent decision as it needed to finalise its production programme for 1948 in order to set in train all the processes necessary to obtain licences and materials under the government restrictions which still prevailed at that time.

On 7th October 1947 the Board gave approval for contracts to be drawn up with Leyland and Mann Egerton, and this was the last major bus order placed by the old London Passenger Transport Board before its nationalisation on 1st January 1948. Leyland was contracted to supply 100 PS1 chassis between February and October 1948, although this arrangement was varied two months later when the contract completion date was extended to December 1948 after the manufacturer received a direction from the government to immediately increase the proportion of vehicles shipped overseas because of the urgent need to secure foreign revenue. As it happened, Leyland subsequently proved incapable of meeting even the revised delivery schedule and was actually five months late in commencing deliveries. The price finally agreed for each chassis was £1,506.3s 6d plus one shilling per mile for delivery to Norwich, while the bodies were invoiced at £1,344.15s 3d each.

The chassis specification for TD 32-131 was virtually the same as for the first batch except that the revised 4.8:1 axle ratio was specified right from the start, and a modified chassis lubrication system was included which resulted in the batch being classified by London Transport as 1/1TD2. As with the earlier batch, their chassis numbers were widely spaced, ranging from 482931 (TD 32) to 485119 (TD 129) with TDs 130 and 131 carrying 1949 series chassis numbers 490662 and 490663.

The Mann Egerton bodies were taller (at 9ft 9¾in) and heavier than the earlier Weymann batch with a deeper roof profile enabling the front and rear destination boxes to be accommodated more neatly. There was no outward swoop at the bottom of the back panels this time; normal half-drop windows were fitted instead of sliders, and the driver was provided with a sliding door instead of the hinged type. This was the first batch of post-war London single deckers to be equipped with provision for carrying semaphore-type trafficators although none were ever installed, and they were destined to be the last half-cab single deckers ever to be purchased by London Transport. The Mann Egerton TDs could easily be told apart from the original Weymann batch by their very different body style, and initially there was a further difference between them in that TD 32-131 carried the later and slightly more austere looking cast aluminium PS2 radiator shell in place of the original chromium-plated version, although these tended to get interchanged in later life.

Like the first batch, the bodies on TD 32-131 were timber framed. Mann Egerton's specification was for underframes to be in oak or ash, with side framing of ash and roofsticks of ash or birch, all treated with Cuprinol as a rot resistance measure and strengthened with steel brackets where necessary. London Transport could have been seen as taking something of a risk in ordering such a large batch of bodies from a manufacturer which had no background whatever in constructing service bus bodies and which had never previously attempted a contract of this magnitude, but in fact the bodies performed well in service, and apart from an early problem with entrance partitions breaking away from their floor framing and requiring additional angle supports (a defect also apparent on the Mann Egerton-built 15T13s), no other serious troubles were ever encountered with them.

The insides of the Mann Egerton bodies presented a much brighter and more modern appearance

With extensive use made of coloured rexine for the décor and the benefit of RT-style seats, the interiors of the Mann Egerton bodies looked far brighter and more modern than those of the Weymann batch. This photograph inside a Kingston-based vehicle carrying a fare board for routes 215 and 215A was taken after the original front offside double seat had been replaced by a single. *David Pearson*

than on the 1TD1s. All the polished woodwork was eliminated, and instead an attempt was made to emulate the colour styling used within RTs through the extensive use of rexine, using brown on the lower side panels, green on the lower halves of the window frames and pale yellow above, with cream enamelled ceilings. Once again, brown lino was used below the windows on the front bulkhead and, as on the 1TD1s, areas of the floor were covered in oak slats where passengers trod regularly. The same simple bell system was installed comprising a bell push at the front and a cord along the rest of the saloon. A big and very visible difference was the use of RT-style aluminium alloy framed seats with separate top rail. These were all forward facing, and the omission of the single, inward-facing seats over the wheel arches resulted in a reduction of two in the seating capacity which was now only 31. The employment of these heavier and more substantial seats probably contributed towards a significant increase of 8cwt in unladen weight on the Mann Egerton vehicles which weighed 6ton 10cwt.

Deliveries of complete vehicles began with the arrival of TD 32 at Chiswick from Norwich on 6th October 1948. It was evident that the same livery style had been adopted as on the earlier batch, and the new vehicles were registered JXC 225-324 with body numbers 2801-2900. Such was the parlous state of many of the T and LT type single deckers currently in use that no time was lost in getting the new TDs into service as soon as each one was received. The availability of the new TDs allowed some of the old Ts and LTs to be released to undergo a massive rebuilding programme designed to extend their lives and restore them to complete serviceability until such time as a new type of single decker built to London Transport's specification could be obtained to bring standardisation to the fleet.

A programme was drawn up for the deployment of the new TDs covering eleven Central Bus routes worked from nine garages. Unusually, no allowance was made for the provision of engineering spares to cover routine servicing or breakdowns, with the whole 131 strong class of TDs fully scheduled for work at peak times. This inevitably meant that, in the case of every one of the converted services, older vehicles continued to be seen quite frequently, and most often these were oil-engined 11T11s rebodied in the mid-nineteen thirties which still looked reasonably modern even though their chassis were twenty years old or more.

The system adopted was for a single new TD to be licensed at each garage ahead of the main batch to allow type training to take place for both drivers and engineers. Thus the first new TD in use was TD 32 which appeared at Hornchurch for staff training on 18th October 1948. The following list shows the dates between which new TDs were placed in service at each garage, although solitary service appearances may have been made by a garage's type trainer before these dates if training was completed early. The only exception to the type training procedure was Muswell Hill, whose staff were already fully conversant with the Leyland PS1.

Garage		Route	Description	Dates
Hornchurch (RD)		250	Romford–Epping	21st October to 27th October
Enfield (E)	(	205	Chingford–Hammond Street	1st November to 10th December
	(	242	Epping Forest–Potters Bar	
Hornchurch (RD)	(	247	Collier Row–Brentwood	15th December to 12th January 1949
	(	248	Upminster–Cranham	
Hanwell (HW)		211	Ealing–Ruislip	19th January to 14th February
Harrow Weald (HD)*		221	North Harrow–Pinner	16th February to 23rd February
Kingston (K)*		216	Kingston–Staines	25th February to 31st March
Muswell Hill (MH)		251	Arnos Grove–Burnt Oak	31st March to 22nd April
Kingston (K)		201	Kingston–Feltham	27th April to 25th May
Edgware (EW)	(	240	Edgware–Mill Hill East	27th May to 16th June
	(	240A	Edgware–Page Street	
Leyton (T)		236	Leyton–Stroud Green	23rd June to 10th August
Tottenham (AR)		236	Leyton–Stroud Green	11th August to 5th October

At Harrow Weald it was quite common to find a TD deputising for a low-height double decker on route 230 (Rayners Lane–Northwick Park) while Kingston TDs could commonly be found on route 213 (Kingston–Belmont) although this was never a scheduled TD operation.

The Mann Egerton bodies for the 1/1TD2s were built to a somewhat less fussy design than the earlier Weymann batch with slightly wider entrances and different pillar spacings. The inset panel immediately behind the doorway looks as though a sliding door was anticipated (as was supplied on similar bodies for the country area 15T13s) but none were fitted and the doorways always remained open. TD 39 was delivered to Chiswick on 4th November 1948 and entered service at Enfield on the 17th of that month. *Ken Blacker collection*

The deeper roof panels on the Mann Egerton bodies accommodated the destination box much more neatly than on the Weymann batch and eliminated the appearance of frowning. The sliding driver's door is evident in this 1949 view of TD 101 operating on the single deck section of route 240. TD 101 spent its whole working life at Edgware garage from May 1949 to October 1962.

The rear end of the Mann Egerton body was probably its least attractive aspect and, as this photograph shows, it did not comfortably accommodate the standard poster display. TD 65 was new to Hanwell and was still there (though the garage was now renamed Southall) in February 1952 by which time the gloss had all gone from its paintwork. *Alan B Cross*

The one hundred new TDs came into service thick and fast between October 1948 and August 1949, transforming many Central Bus operations although older single deckers still continued to appear fairly universally from time to time. Typical examples of the new fleet were Hornchurch's TD 34 of October 1948 photographed at Upminster station, Muswell Hill's TD 81 of March 1949 at Arnos Grove, and Hanwell's TD 103 of June 1949 seen in Ealing. *Alan Nightingale collection/DA Thompson/V C Jones*

The first completely new route to make use of TDs was the 243 worked from Enfield garage, which started life on 26th October 1949. TD 36, which started its working career at Enfield in October 1948 on routes 205 and 242, is on a crew changeover at Waltham Cross in April 1950. *Alan B Cross*

A year after receiving its new TDs, Enfield garage began operation on 26th October 1949 of new route 243 (Waltham Cross–Upshire) which was initially scheduled for TD operation, although there was never enough of these to go round and the official allocation was subsequently changed to pre-war Ts. In practice Ts and TDs remained intermixed on Enfield's three single deck services right through to 1953 when double deckers took over.

The allocations of TDs to garages remained fairly static for the next three years and the vehicles themselves proved to be steady and fairly reliable workhorses, a little slow and ponderous on frequent stop-start operations but capable of a fair turn of speed on country runs. Fairly early on, the two routes worked by a combination of TDs and double deckers were turned over solely to double deck operation, but this did not impact upon the number of TDs scheduled for service. When route 247 at Hornchurch went over completely to double deck operation using Guy 'utilities' on 5th April 1950 the displaced TDs were redeployed on route 238 (Emerson Park–Noak Hill), and the complete takeover of route 240 by RTs on 25th October 1951 was enabled by a projection of the 240A beyond Page Street to Mill Hill East with a corresponding increase in its TD allocation. The opening of the fine new garage at Norbiton on 14th May 1952 to relieve pressure on Kingston did not result in any of the latter's TDs being amongst the transferred rolling stock, and although route 201 moved across to Norbiton the four TDs from it remained at Kingston and were used on other services there.

Just before this, in April 1952, an interesting but abortive exercise had taken place to examine the practicability of extending the bodies of the TDs (and also the 14T12s and 15T13s) to increase their seating capacity, a process which it was hoped could be carried out without involving any chassis extension. Drawings were produced which indicated that two additional seats could, indeed be gained on Weymann-bodied vehicles (1TD1 and 14T12) and four on the Mann Egerton batches (1/1TD2 and 15T13). A general consensus emerged that the 4-seat option might prove worthwhile and that a detailed cost estimate should be obtained. Nothing further is recorded, which probably indicates that the costings obtained showed the proposal to be prohibitively expensive in relation to any modest benefits which would be gained from it.

1952 was fated to be the last year of stability for the TDs. New RFs started to flood into Central Bus service from September of that year, and it was inevitable that their arrival would have an impact on the TDs, either directly or indirectly. One of the routes destined to receive RFs was the 212 which meant that, for the first time, vehicles from the TD 1-31 batch would have to be found employment at somewhere other than Muswell Hill. In fact the first reallocations took place ahead of the 212 conversion when, upon completion of their second overhaul cycle, TDs 1 and 2 were sent to Southall (to which Hanwell (HW) had been renamed on 12th July 1950) and TDs 4 and 8 to Edgware in November and December 1952, but presumably someone in the rolling stock department at Chiswick had a change of mind, for all four were returned to Muswell Hill within a few weeks. A more permanent solution was found in February 1953 when a new policy was adopted of concentrating the 1TD1s at Loughton and Kingston.

Although Muswell Hill was the first garage to receive new red RFs, its first intake was for route 210 which meant that the conversion basically had little impact on the TDs, being mainly 6Q6s that were withdrawn from service. However a few TDs had always been present on the 210 and these were now redeployed for a short time on route 244, which became fully TD worked for the few months before it was double decked with RTs on 6th May 1953.

January 1953 found Sidcup garage in receipt of RFs, making redundant a number of 14T12s which were transferred to Southall in pursuance of a new policy of stocking route 211 with these vehicles in place of TDs. This was part of a wider scheme for concentrating all 14T12s which were expected to remain in the fleet – totalling 26 out of the original 50 – at the west London locations of Southall and Uxbridge. Southall's TD stock was gradually depleted as 14T12s came across from Sidcup, the last two departing on 14th January. A further influx of RFs at Muswell Hill in February 1953 for the 212 resulted in many 1TD1s transferring permanently to Kingston to replace Qs and 10T10s from routes 215 (Kingston–Ripley), 218 (Kingston–Staines) and 219 (Kingston–Weybridge). Additionally, a batch of seven was despatched to Loughton on 18th March to replace 10T10s from route 254 (Loughton–Buckhurst Hill). After all these vehicle movements were completed only 10 of the original 31 Weymann

The busiest of the single deck services radiating from Kingston was the 213, and though this never had an official TD allocation these vehicles appeared on it quite regularly. At Kingston bus station on 2nd February 1952 one of the newest single deckers in the Central Bus fleet, TD 75, stands alongside one of the oldest, one-time East Surry six-wheeled 'Scooter' LT 1428. *Alan B Cross*

TDs remained at Muswell Hill on routes 244 and 251. In addition to losing so many 1TD1s, Muswell Hill also lost many of the later batch, several of which were sent to Hornchurch on 11th February 1953 to convert route 252 (Romford Station–Birch Road) to TD operation. For a short while in 1953 Hornchurch's TD holding stood at its highest-ever level of 15, but a third of these were lost on 12th August of the same year when the new garage at North Street, Romford opened to provide much-needed relief to the overcrowded Hornchurch. Amongst the services and staff transferred to the new premises was single deck route 250 and the vehicles that went with it.

Although the last of the new red RFs entered service in March 1953 this did not mark the end of the year's upheavals for the TDs. A major event occurred on 6th May when all three of Enfield's single deck services were double decked following completion of strengthening work on the railway bridge at Waltham Cross. These had latterly been worked by a mixture of TDs and 10T10s. The former moved south to increase the TD fleet at Kingston to replace 10T10s still based there, and the withdrawal of these former Green Line coaches from both garages marked the end of pre-war single deckers on scheduled Central Bus operations. Henceforth any further reductions in the single deck fleet would result in the disposal of post-war vehicles starting, as already planned, with the 14T12s.

Even now, the changes for 1953 affecting the TDs were not over. On 7th October Loughton's allocation on route 254 proved to be short-lived. Staff at this garage, who appear to have been a discontented bunch, had previously complained bitterly about having to run 9T9s, and then 10T10s, on route 254, and they had now become unhappy about the TDs, the result being a promise from management that they could have the first RFs when some of these became available. This came rather sooner than expected after it had been found that, because RFs were so much faster than the older types, it had become possible to speed up the running times on routes 210 and 212, thereby reducing the resources employed on them. By this means, RFs became available for route 254, but as there was only just enough of them to meet the scheduled requirement, staff at Loughton had to accept that a single TD would remain as the engineer's spare and to provide an extra vehicle required for the Saturday schedule, a situation which prevailed right up to May 1955. However all the 1TD1s formerly employed there were sent to Kingston on 7th October and a 1/1TD2 was transferred in to serve as Loughton's permanent one-bus TD allocation.

Vehicles of the 1TD1 type began breaking away from Muswell Hill permanently in February 1953, the vehicle in this instance being TD 5 which was one of a number sent to Loughton garage to update route 254, although it only remained there for just under eight months before being reallocated to Kingston. It carries the latest style of Central Bus single deck destination blind display. Note, too, that it now also has an AEC-type pressed steel front wheel ring instead of the original Leyland cast aluminium version, a modification then being applied to all Leylands in the fleet including modern RTLs and RTWs. *Peter Mitchell*

The splendid new garage at North Street, Romford, opened on 12th August 1953 to relieve the grossly overcrowded premises at Hornchurch, and TD 124 was one of the five TDs transferred across to work route 250 which retained TDs until 1st July 1959. The slip board on the bulkhead announces a 5d minimum fare between Romford station and St John's Road, Havering.

The lack of stability that the TDs suffered in 1953 with regard to their spheres of operation followed through into 1954 when yet more changes took place. In addition, some physical modifications were also made to the vehicles themselves. During July and August all 131 had their seating capacity reduced by one through the conversion of the front offside seat from a double to a single, the purpose of this exercise being to create greater manoeuvring space in the vicinity of the entrance steps with more room for the conductor to stand when not collecting fares. Drivers benefited too, when a crash programme to install Clayton cab heaters and demisters was carried out during October. This was also the year when, in compliance with a change in the law, rear reflectors were fitted to all vehicles operating on the nation's roads.

A minor event involving just one bus was the conversion of route 238 at Hornchurch garage to RT operation on 19th May 1954, but this was balanced by the addition of a new service to the TD roster when the 215A (Kingston–Downside) was inaugurated on 3rd June operated by Kingston garage. Next, a decidedly more odd TD operation commenced on 30th June when the new 256 (Woolwich–Shooters Hill) started work. This marked the first and only time that a TD was scheduled for service in deepest south-east London, and the single vehicle required for it was based at Plumstead garage whose fleet consisted otherwise totally of RTLs. TD 71 was sent to Plumstead on 17th June for type training, including familiarisation with crash gearbox techniques, and this vehicle inaugurated the 256 although a second (TD 44) joined it from 1st July

Embellished with rear wheel discs and with the upper cream moulding overpainted in red, TD 71 presents a slightly different appearance from normal as it waits in Woolwich for the start of a short journey to Shooters Hill on new route 256 in July 1954. It was on Plumstead garage's books for only a month before double deckers took over. *G A Rixon*

to provide the necessary engineering spare. This whole operation, requiring a 100 per cent spares float, was extremely wasteful, especially as it could have been easily operated by double deckers from Plumstead's RTL allocation at much less cost as, indeed, soon began to happen unofficially when passenger demand built up to the extent that a TD was unable to cope on certain journeys. TD 71 was delicensed on 1st August 1954 and TD 44 was despatched to Hornchurch on the 4th, on which date an RTL officially took over on the 256, bringing Plumstead a record for being the shortest-lived operator of TDs at just two months.

On 1st September 1954 the policy of disposing of surplus 14T12s began to be implemented when an initial contingent of TDs was transferred into Norbiton garage to replace them on routes 201, 206 and 264 which, between them, required a total of 15 vehicles to meet the Monday to Friday peak demand. The initial intake was of eight TDs but when a further eight arrived on 1st December this marked the end of the T allocation at Norbiton. Officially the first intake was for routes 201 and 206 and the second for the 264 although in practice it seldom worked out exactly like that. Most of the second group of arrivals had come from Harrow Weald where route 221 had been replaced by an extension of double deck service 98 on 30th November. By the end of 1954 exactly half of all TDs were working in the Kingston area with 48 based at Kingston garage itself and a further 18 at Norbiton.

In theory the second intake of TDs into Norbiton should have resulted in all the many single deck services in and out of Kingston being in the hands of TDs (except for route 213 which was now worked by RFs). However, an interesting new dimension had been introduced on 8th August 1956 when three 15T13s (of the batch T 769-798) were introduced at Kingston garage, still in green livery, on route 216. With Mann Egerton bodies very similar to those on the TDs these were, in fact, very superior vehicles with preselector gears and more powerful, smoother running engines giving a performance similar to that of the RT, which quickly endeared them to staff. On the same day as Norbiton's second injection of TDs, 1st December 1956, the three green Ts were sent there too, and could normally be found on route 201 until this was taken over by RFs in January 1959. Back in the autumn of 1956 it had been London Transport's expectation that this small fleet of 15T13s at Norbiton would eventually be increased to nine, but this never happened. Instead, by July 1957, the Sales Department was angling to sell them because it could get a good price for them, but this was thwarted when Norbiton staff, backed up by the Operating Manager himself, objected and suggested that an equivalent number of TDs should be sold instead.

Both types of TD could be found working side by side at Kingston between February 1953 and February 1958 when the last two of the TD 1-31 series ran for the last time. Weymann TD 2 and Mann Egerton TD 40 stand together at Kingston and the physical differences between the two styles of body are readily apparent. *G A Rixon*

TDs began moving into Norbiton on 1st September 1954, introducing the class to route 206 for the first time, and one of the original batch of eight was TD 41. TDs at Norbiton soon became distinguishable by their repositioned route stencil holder after it had been moved from the roof to a waist height location just ahead of the running number plates. TD 41 has also acquired a chromium plated radiator shell from an earlier vehicle. *Peter Mitchell*

Not long after taking the TDs into stock, Norbiton began a programme of modifying not only some of its own but also Kingston's. Norbiton had been second (and last) garage where a self-contained docking unit was constructed separate from the main premises, in this instance in a modified laundry with a modern façade located on the other side of the main London Road. It was designated as 'parent' garage for not only Kingston but also Mortlake and Twickenham, whose vehicles now underwent their scheduled major docking routine at Norbiton. Subsequently the concept of a separate docking unit did not prove a success and the London Road premises were sold in November 1959. The modification carried out in these premises to the TDs involved moving the roof-mounted route stencil holder from its original position above the doorway to a new location just below the window in the recessed nearside saloon bay. Ostensibly done to prevent stencil carriers from damaging the washing machine, the repositioned carrier made it much easier for staff to access and, arguably, clearer for passengers to see. This work continued slowly up to about 1958, and if TDs were found at other garages carrying this modification it could be taken as a sure sign that they had been allocated to Norbiton or Kingston at some time during this period.

Although fourteen TDs joined the official Uxbridge allocation at various times between 1956 and 1959 most stayed for just a few months and only two remained for longer than a year. TD 103 was one of the exceptions to the rule, arriving at the start of December 1956 and departing for Edgware when Uxbridge finally lost its half-cab single deckers on 10th June 1959. It stands at the Uxbridge station terminus awaiting its departure time on the hourly cross-country run to Laleham. The repositioned albeit unused route stencil holder testifies that it was based at Kingston before coming to Uxbridge. *Peter Mitchell*

On 16th February 1955 route 248 was converted to double deck operation using RLHs from Hornchurch garage. Several TDs were now lying around in storage and unlicensed, mainly in North Street garage, and on 15th April 1955 six of these (TD 34, 63, 84-86, 112) were relicensed and sent on loan to the Ministry of Transport & Civil Aviation at Heston Airport. The purpose of this loan has not been established and it is not known what they were used for at Heston. Although the cessation of regular commercial flights from the Airport ceased in 1947, it was still busy with charters and training flights whilst various commercial and manufacturing activities were carried out there. These six vehicles were returned to London Transport, two at a time, over the next few months, the last returnees being TDs 84 and 86 on 19th July.

With no likelihood of the surplus TDs being required for further service it was decided to dispose of some of them starting with the lowest fleet numbers first, a clear reversal of the earlier decision to concentrate all single deck sales on the 14T12s. The third overhaul cycle for the Weymann TDs had commenced in August 1955 and this was brought to a prompt halt after only eight had been dealt with which happened, by chance, to comprise a continuous run of fleet numbers TD 1 to TD 8. The last of these to enter the works was TD 4 on 30th November 1955 whose overhaul was completed on 8th February 1956, only a few months before the first batch was offered for sale. The offer went out on 18th June 1956, but meanwhile the first permanent withdrawal from service had already taken place on 1st June when TD 12 was redeployed as a driver training bus. On 18th July agreement was reached with Millburn Motors of Glasgow to sell TD 1-7 to them for £600 apiece. Not for the first time in London Transport history, lack of internal communications between departments resulted in newly-overhauled vehicles being sold when exactly the same price could have been obtained for vehicles on which considerable sums of money had not recently been spent! At the time, these seven vehicles were still operational at Kingston, but they were all delicensed on 8th August when replacements were drafted in from various garages, and they were collected from storage at Norbiton by Millburn's during late August and September. Subsequent buyer Bird's found a ready market for them in Yugoslavia where TD 1-7 joined many other ex-London buses.

Despite the decision in late 1955 to cease overhauling the Weymann TDs, the long term future of the Mann Egerton batch looked secure and a third overhaul programme for these was put in motion in February 1957. Their first overhaul cycle had occupied from August 1951 to February 1954 and the second, which had begun in March 1954, was still only reaching the final stages and was not, in fact, concluded until May 1957. In other words, overhauling of TD 32-131 had been spaced out in such a way that it had been continuous from August 1951 onwards. As a matter of record, one body exchange had occurred during the first programme when TDs 107 and 112 exchanged bodies at some time between 9th December 1952 and 20th January 1953 when they were both in the works together, this being the only occasion when bodies were moved from one vehicle to another on the TD class. Only 12 vehicles had been submitted for their third overhaul when, after reviewing the long term prospects for the TDs once again, it was decided to bring the programme to a halt. TD 40 was the last to be sent for overhaul on 12th August 1957, emerging on 3rd October to remain unlicensed until it was once again required for service at Kingston on 1st February 1958.

A growing number of TDs were now out of service with further contraction in their usage having occurred from 1st December 1956 onwards as surplus RFs began drifting into Muswell Hill to displace this garage's last TDs which were now confined to route 251. The survivors at Muswell Hill were all of its original 1TD1 type, and when the last of these left for Kingston on 1st May 1957 it meant that the latter garage had now matched Muswell Hill in operating all 31 vehicles from the original batch, albeit not all at the same time. However this was not quite the end of TDs at Muswell Hill for odd ones of the Mann Egerton variety were now brought in from time to time to work alongside the RFs and could still occasionally be found on the 251. The last TD did not finally leave Muswell Hill until February 1958.

Hornchurch garage's route 252 may have been very short, with an end-to-end running time of only 8 minutes, but it was very frequent and busy. TD 54 worked on it from the time it was new on 1st January 1949 until it was sent to Chiswick for its second overhaul on 26th May 1954, from which it went to pastures new at Edgware and later Kingston, ending its working life on 'learner' duties in 1962/3.

1958 was destined to go down in the annals of London bus history as the year of the long and ill-advised bus strike in May and June. It resulted in the departure of large numbers of good and valuable staff and the permanent loss of a huge number of passengers, leading to the inevitable closure afterwards of several garages plus the complete withdrawal of a number of services and a significant reduction in the level of service provision on very many others. Inevitably it threw a new and unfavourable light on the future of many of the TDs.

The year started with the conversion of route 252 to RTs on 8th January, on which date Hornchurch's last four TDs departed. They were needed at Kingston to help provide replacements for more 1TD1s which were being withdrawn for sale. The availability of ten more of these had been advertised back in November 1957 and this attracted the interest of the Ceylon Transport Board which was anxious to obtain as many good quality buses as it could from London to bolster its newly nationalised fleet. In fact 14 1TD1s were eventually included in the sale at a highly lucrative price of £800 per vehicle, and these set sail – accompanied by 20 RTs and RTLs and 9 15T13 single deckers – on the MV Marian Buczek on 24th April 1958. By this date all the remaining Weymann TDs had been taken out of service in anticipation of also going to Ceylon as part of a subsequent contract which stipulated, as did all contracts with the CTB, that they should all be thoroughly serviced and guaranteed roadworthy before departure. The final operational pair, TDs 17s and 29, had been withdrawn on 1st March.

Photographs of TDs serving overseas after their departure from London are hard to find. This rarity, showing TD 28 still in full London colours including fleet number, was taken on a local service in the Ceylon capital, Colombo. It is believed to have been in Ceylon since August 1958 and to have remained in service with the Ceylon Transport Board until 1965.

When the MV Marian Buczek returned to start its next voyage to Ceylon on 11th August 1958 all ten remaining Weymann TDs should have been on board. In fact only nine were available, and in order to fulfill its part of the contract London Transport made up the shortfall by despatching the first of the Mann Egerton batch to leave the fleet, TD 57. The vehicle that should have gone but didn't was TD 30 which had been damaged in a road traffic accident in mid-May 1957 and was now in storage at Norbiton awaiting a decision on its future. It was subsequently concluded that, by repairing the vehicle, a reasonable profit could be made by selling it to Ceylon whereas it was virtually unsaleable in its existing condition. TD 30 was taken into Chiswick tram depot on 12th December 1958 for repair work to be carried out, which had been completed by 4th February 1959. Another year was to elapse, however, before it finally departed to Ceylon on 25th March 1960.

In the far west of the Central Bus area, Uxbridge garage had been allocated TDs in dribs and drabs from as early as March 1956, running alongside this garage's fleet of 14T12s on routes 222 (Uxbridge–Hounslow East) and 224/A/B (Uxbridge–Laleham/West Drayton/Stockley Estate). In fact, even before this, TDs were no strangers, these having often appeared on loan from other garages. By the end of 1956 Uxbridge had five of its own on the books, but the number fluctuated according to requirements elsewhere and by the end of 1957 Uxbridge's TD allocation had dropped to two. The position changed entirely on 26th November 1958 when, as a result of post-strike service cuts and double decking at Sidcup, sufficient RFs became available to convert route 236, the only TD service jointly worked by two garages. With more than 20 TDs being made surplus at Leyton and Tottenham, the opportunity was taken to remove all remaining 14T12s from the operational fleet. The majority (at Southall on route 211 and Uxbridge on the 222) were directly replaced by RFs, but the 224 group at Uxbridge was now turned over in its entirety to TD operation.

The final year of the decade witnessed the

Lined up in Kingston, with Bentall's garage in the background, are some of the TDs serving the local area at the start of the 1960s. The leading vehicle is TD 126 which was taken out of service on 1st September 1961. All four have been fitted with flashing trafficators and display advertising material on their roof panels. *David Pearson*

biggest drop yet in TD numbers. Eighty-six TDs were still in passenger service from five garages at the start of 1959 but this had dropped by the end of the year to only 45 still active at just two locations. The relicensing of surplus RFs brought about the big drop in TD usage on two mid-summer dates just three weeks apart. June 29th 1959 marked the end of the road for TDs at Norbiton and Uxbridge, followed on 1st July by their demise at North Street along with the first intake of RFs into Kingston where they replaced TDs from route 216. After this the only half-cab single deckers remaining in service on Central Buses were TDs at Kingston and Edgware.

A further inroad was made right at the start of 1960 when, on 6th January, the conversion of route 212 at Muswell Hill to double deckers threw up 21 surplus RFs which were immediately redeployed to replace an equivalent number of TDs at Kingston working on routes 218 and 219. This left the jointly-worked 215 and 215A as the only Kingston routes still with TDs, and these had to be retained because road conditions on the 215A between Cobham and Downside precluded the use of larger vehicles. It was now time for further batches of TDs to be sold to Ceylon. Fifty more had gone to the island during 1959; now further batches of 18 and 6 were sent on 25th March and 7th April 1960 respectively. These were the last TDs to be purchased by the Ceylon Transport Board which, over a period of two years, had absorbed a grand total of 98 into its fleet. Gross overloading, bad driving, inadequate maintenance and poor roads in Sri Lanka (as the country became known in 1972) quickly put paid to most of them, but a few could still be seen working as flat bed lorries into the nineteen-eighties.

With no immediate prospect of their replacement at hand, it was decided on 11th April 1960 to fit the remaining 26 TDs with flashing trafficators using equipment now employed as standard on RTs and other classes. TD 106 had already been dealt with as a trial run and the remainder quickly followed from April onwards. The trafficator-fitted vehicles were TD 54, 74, 86, 87, 89. 90. 95. 99-101, 103-106, 112, 114, 116, 118, 121, 123, 124, 126, 128-131.

By 1961 the remaining now heavily out-dated TDs had become something of a curiosity, but they also aroused a sense of trepidation amongst some of the driving staff through being the only vehicles in the huge Central Bus fleet still with crash gearboxes, a feature which many of the younger intake, accustomed to more modern vehicles, found tricky to handle. Their usage declined slightly in 1961 when approval was given for RFs to cover runnings on the 215 group which were not scheduled to go to Downside, resulting in Kingston's holding of TDs being decreased by a further three on 1st September.

And then there was one. From 1st March 1962 the only service still operated by TDs was the 240A for which eleven TDs remained at Edgware garage until they too were withdrawn on 10th October. On this occasion TDs 103 and 100 are present on the terminal stand at Edgware station. Also in the photograph is Enfield's RT 2648 which, through having an early post-war RT3 type body, has only two more years to run before it, too, will be disposed of.
Denis Battams

The very last TD journey of all in the late evening of 9th October 1962 was covered by TD 124, the highest numbered of the class still in service at the time. There was no real celebration to mark the end of an era, but the chalk marking on the front of TD 124 shows that the event did not pass completely unnoticed. *Capital Transport collection*

The end came in 1962. Route 215A was now cleared for operation by larger vehicles, and it became possible to replace Kingston's last four TDs with RFs on 1st March. Their departure left a void on the Kingston scene since so many of the class had made their mark there over the years; in fact only 14 out of the 131 TDs had not been allocated to Kingston garage at one time or another during the course of their London career. With Kingston now gone, Edgware's TD allocation on route 240A was all that remained until, overnight on 9th/10th October 1962, they too were swept away under an influx of RFs. The eleven vehicles still licensed on the last day of operation were TD 89, 95, 99-101, 103-105, 114, 121, 124, and it is recorded that the highest numbered of these, TD 124, was the very last of the class to return to the garage on the final night. It had the honour of being the very last traditional half-cab single decker to run in public service in London: an era was truly at an end.

For a while a few TDs could be found in mainland Britain leading a useful after-life. One such vehicle was the former TD 114 which had earlier been one of the last day survivors at Edgware. Its sale in January 1963 saw it remaining locally, and it was photographed serving as a flag bedecked coffee stall for the Elstree & Borehamwood Rotary Club. *Robert F Mack*

All that remained now was for the remaining few to be sold. The Ceylon Transport Board was not interested in obtaining any more of them so their destiny appeared to lie in the UK. A batch of six went to Bird's, the Stratford upon Avon dealer, in October 1962 and thence to various contractors, but the remainder were all disposed of in private sales during 1962 and 1963 to a range of new owners including a number of social service and religious undertakings such as the Women's Voluntary Service (which purchased three), and ended up providing private transport for youth clubs, scouts and a host of other groups. Others went, as would be expected, to contractors and other commercial organisations. An exception was TD 118 which was loaned to the Brunel College of Technology at Acton (today better known as Brunel University) on 28th November 1963 for a student trip to Moscow, returning to Chiswick on 24th November 1964 by which time it was the only TD left on London Transport's books. Sold in February 1965, it then ventured abroad again, this time to Istanbul, before adopting a more mundane role as a caravan.

Today, four TDs are thought to have survived. Foremost among them, and by far the best known, is TD 95 which is now part of the London Bus Museum's collection at Brooklands and in whose ownership it retains a fully authentic air totally redolent of the era when TDs could be found well distributed around Central Bus territory. Originally sold in December 1963 to Bromley Technical College for a trip behind the Iron Curtain to Russia, TD 95 has been in preservation since 1968. TD 118 made its appearance in restored condition in 2020 and two other survivors are rumoured to be TDs 89 and 130.

Preserved TD 95 has often been seen in action in recent years and is a fine representation of London Transport's final class of half-cab single deckers. With flashing trafficators removed and the original style of Leyland wheel nut guard restored to the front wheels, TD 95 now looks much as it did when it entered service at Kingston in May 1949 apart from carrying a later-style destination blind display. *London Bus Museum*

43

G 436 – A SOLITARY GUY

G 436 works the route on which it entered service, the short Peckham circular, on which it spent the first half of its five-year life with London Transport. Here it turns into Nunhead Lane.

This single vehicle was unquestionably the most unexpected and totally out-of-character purchase ever made by London Transport for its motor bus fleet. In the post-war era, when the emphasis was placed fully on the achievement of standardisation, and when new RT family vehicles were being delivered in massive quantities, the point of purchasing a totally non-standard one-off seemed obscure in the extreme.

The story of G 436 appears to have begun in March 1949 with a conversation between A A M Durrant and Major General J S Crawford CB, a London-based director of Guy Motors. The two were already well acquainted, having met in June 1940 on the government's wartime Tank Board charged with getting the still-unproven Churchill tank into mass production. Durrant was later appointed as director of tank design while Crawford was given the position of Deputy Director General of Armaments Production, which meant that the two inevitably worked closely together throughout the war years. It was no secret that, after the war,

Sidney Guy was disappointed that his company had failed to gain a share of the London Transport order book for new buses, having supplied no fewer than 435 Arab double deckers fitted with Gardner 5LW engines between 1942 and 1946. From an engineering standpoint G 1-435 had proved ideal in that very little ever went seriously wrong with them and their mpg figures were the best of any double deckers in the fleet. (Drivers viewed them somewhat differently, it must be admitted, but this was largely due to their perceived lack of power and the outcome might have been very different if the larger 6LW engine had been available). The latest Mark 3 version of the Arab was a rather more refined development of the wartime 'utility' models, and Crawford evidently set about trying to persuade Durrant to try it out.

Crawford's proposition was that London Transport should purchase an Arab double decker, complete with both chassis and provincial type body modified where necessary to comply with its own specific requirements, within the next six or eight weeks at a total cost no greater than that of a new RT. Further, Guy would modify another Arab chassis to accept a standard RT body, which would be made available towards the end of the year and would be loaned to London Transport free of charge. This second chassis would incorporate any variations in design which early experience with the first one may show to be desirable.

Durrant obviously went along with Crawford's proposal and produced a memorandum for the Executive recommending its acceptance. He explained that the vehicle on offer embodied most of the up-to-date features found on the RT chassis including a powerful 10.35 litre 63hp engine, fluid flywheel and Wilson-type air-operated preselective gearbox. He said that it was a "considerable advance" on the Guy vehicles currently operated and could possibly serve as an alternative source of chassis supply should this become needed. On 22nd March the Executive agreed the purchase of the first vehicle and the acceptance of the loan of a subsequent RT-style chassis, and an order was duly placed. On receipt of the order Sydney Guy himself wrote to London Transport saying: "We would say how honoured we are to be of service, and we feel sure that you will find your confidence in us is not misplaced".

The fleet number allocated to the new vehicle was, logically enough, G 436, following on from the fleet of Guy Arabs already in stock. Its chassis had much in common with the wartime Arabs except that, in developing the Arab Mk 3, Guy had copied RT practice in lowering the radiator by about six inches to 5ft at the filler cap, giving excellent vision from the cab. The distinctive forward swoop of the front mudguards which had been a feature of the Mark 2 Arab (seen in London on G 72-435) was still there, but on G 436 the radiator no longer protruded but was set back and lay flush with the cab front. This had been made possible by the use of the compact six-cylinder Meadows 6DC-630 engine with its unusual square formation of equal length 130mm bore and stroke. The very modern factory of Henry Meadows Ltd. was almost next door to Guy's premises in Wolverhampton so it was not surprising that the two companies should have co-operated, and the Meadows engine was offered by Guy as an alternative to the Gardner 5LW and 6LW between 1948 and 1951 to those operators wanting greater speed and power than the Gardner engines could achieve. Though not widely used in passenger vehicles, this engine could also be found on Scammell, ERF and Dodge lorries and also on marine craft and crawler tractors.

It was arranged that for London service the three-point mounted 6DC-630 engine would be downrated to 115bhp at 1,800rpm. Standard features of the 16ft 3in wheelbase Arab 3 chassis were incorporated in G 436 including the centrally-mounted gearbox, Westinghouse air pressure brakes, Marles double roller type steering, automatic RP lubrication, and a back axle ratio of 5.6:1. Special London Transport requirements incorporated during the construction phase included all the cab instruments, head side and fog lamps, lubrication pipes, and even the driver's seat cushion and squab.

G 436 was sold to London Transport as an 'all Guy' product, the bodywork having also been constructed at Wolverhampton. The latter was, in fact, only an assembly and finishing job on the part of Guy who had concluded an agreement in

1947 with Park Royal to market and build the latter's standard metal framed bodywork on Arab chassis under licence using framework, metal pressings and other material supplied by them. Some 75 body shells were fitted-out by Guy under this arrangement between 1948 and 1950. Guy did not attempt to stamp any distinctive identifying features of their own on these bodies which so closely resembled a standard Park Royal product that it was not possible to tell the two apart. Park Royal's patented frame design was used on the lower deck structure and employed T-shaped steel side pillars with the prong of the T facing into the saloon, an arrangement which meant that conventional flat lining pieces could not be used for the window surrounds which were instead covered by rounded pressed-aluminium mouldings covered in rexine. This feature had, in fact, already become well established in London on 175 STLs and 25 N2 class trolleybuses supplied by Park Royal before the war, and was repeated on G 436.

London Transport's special requirements featured more heavily on the bodywork than they did on the mechanical specification and its influential chief draughtsman, Philip Lunghi, visited the Wolverhampton factory and worked with Guy's staff to finalise an agreed specification. For the exterior, London Transport specified the provisioning and positioning of all mouldings and lights and required the use of its own standard driving mirrors and the inclusion of its own standard battery booster socket below the driver's entry step. It requested an unusual and unique two-piece side-by-side destination and route number display at the front with single screens at the side and rear, plus the use of standard RT-type route number carriers under the driver's canopy and on the offside staircase panel.

General arrangement drawings of G 436 prepared at Chiswick based on Park Royal plans, showing basic dimensions and all the special items required by London Transport. The figure of 14ft 3ins shown for its overall height refers to the vehicle in fully laden condition; when unladen it was estimated to have a height of 14ft 6½ins.

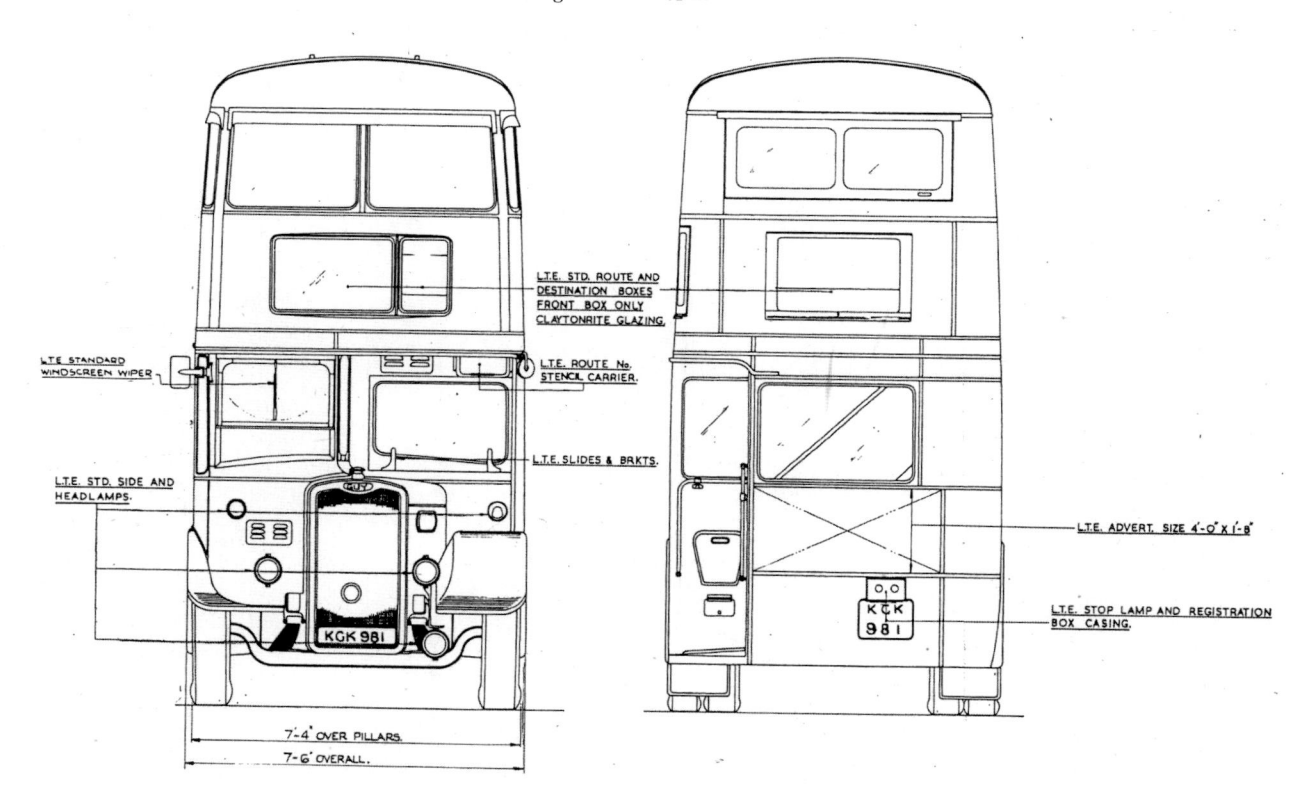

47

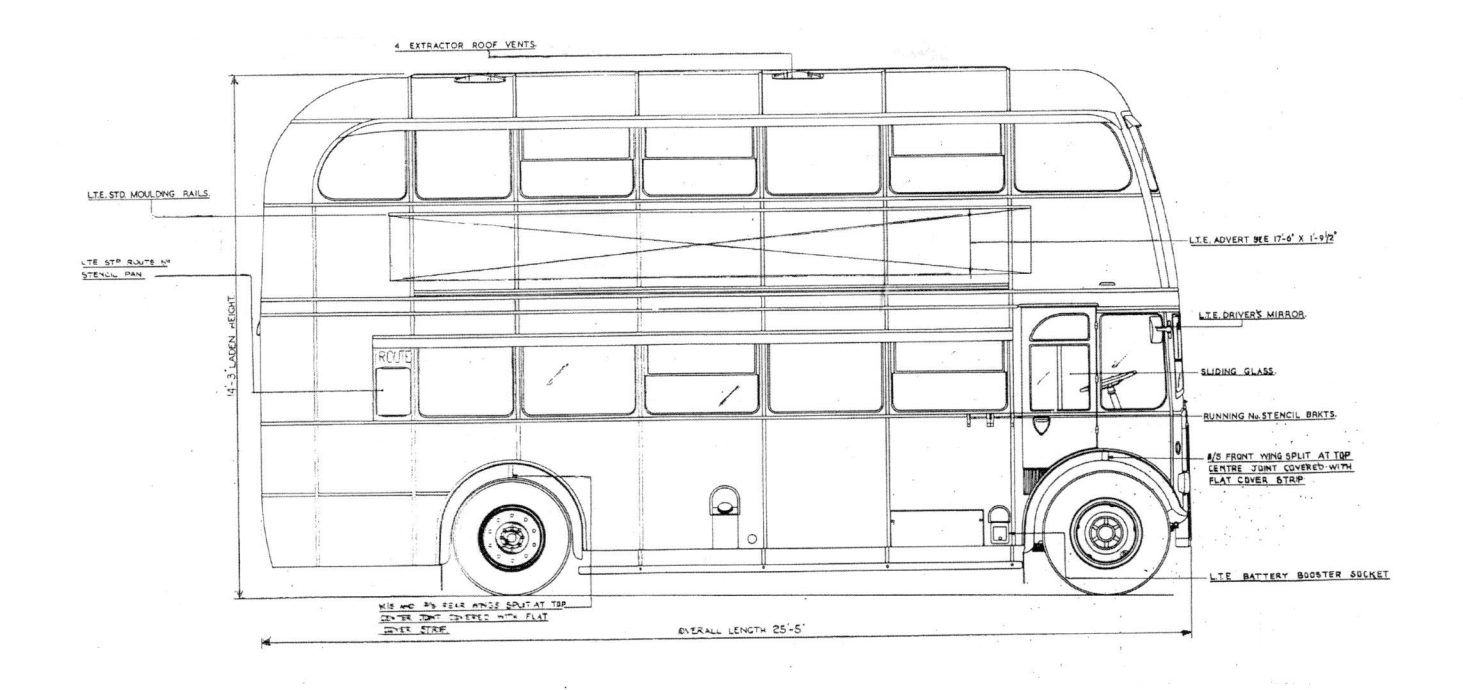

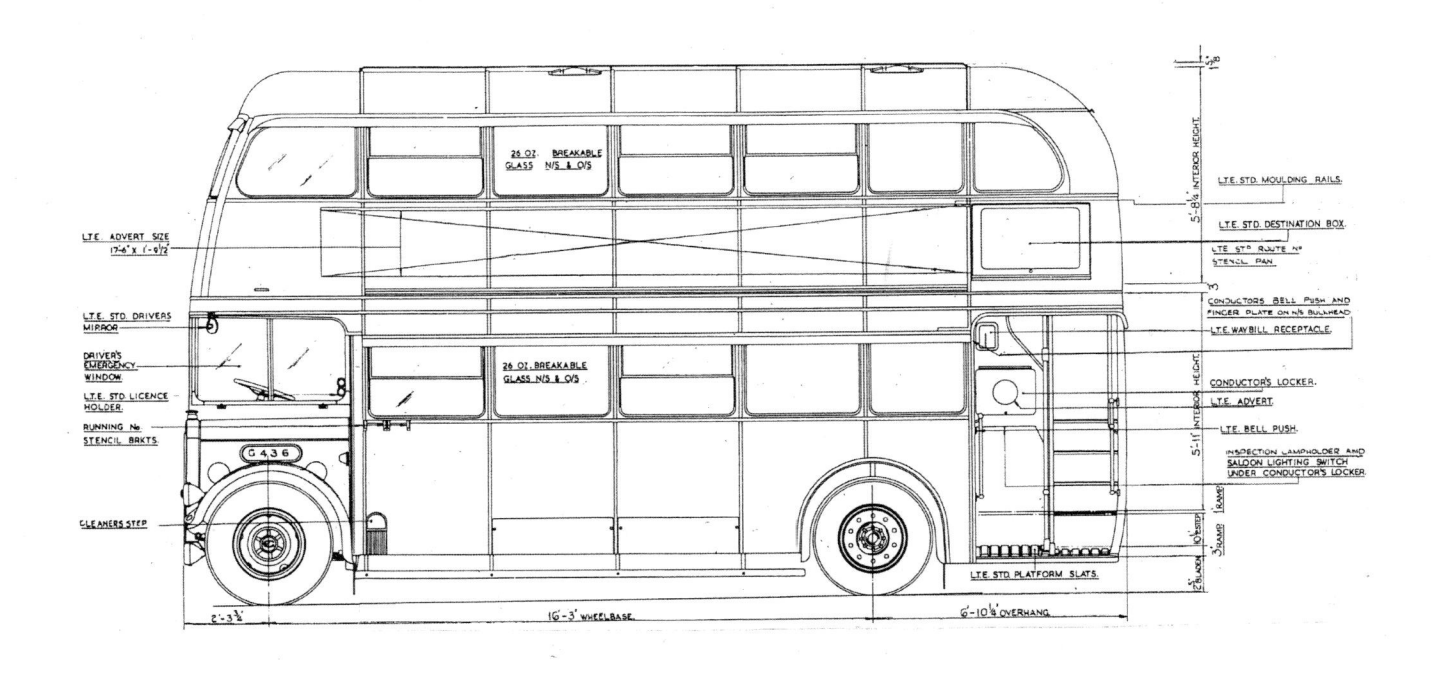

Interior views of G 436 reveal an unmistakable London Transport 'look' brought about by the colour scheme, the use of familiar upholstery, and the incorporation of standard RT fittings such as the bell cord, lower bulkhead advertisement panel, and fareboard holder. In contrast, the seat frames are provincial in style while the single-skinned upper deck ceiling and domes fall below the London standard and the ventilation arrangements on each deck look very utilitarian. *John C Gillham © Tony Peters*

Internally the décor was to be as close to RT standard as possible except on the bulkheads which were covered in ribbed rubber. The bells and buzzers were to be exactly to LT standard, and a standard fare card frame was to be fitted as were a conductor's locker and waybill receptacle. Floor slats, tread plates and drain ferrules were also to London Transport specification. In the driver's cab the windscreen wiper, fire extinguisher and holder, emergency saw, grab handles, and horn button were all standard London fittings. It was also specified that all paints and rexines would be sourced from RT stock held at Park Royal.

Interestingly, London Transport was happy to accept certain reductions from its customary high standard of internal finish such as unlined side panels and a single-skinned upper deck ceiling. The Widney 'Aero' half-drop windows were the last ones to be fitted to any London bus to have pinch grips rather than winding mechanisms, while plain glass instead of half-drops was considered adequate for the upstairs front windows. The lack of internal lining panels would have helped to keep the weight down but even so, for a standard 56-seater, G 436 was by no means a lightweight at 7 tons 17cwt unladen.

G 436 stands outside the experimental shop at Chiswick shortly after its arrival with London Transport on 11th November 1949, still carrying trade plates and with the manufacturer's label still in the window. Five weeks of testing lie ahead before being passed out for service. Standing behind is an RT chassis with mock-up 8ft wide body shell. *G E Baddeley*

For comparison, a completely standard Meadows-engined Arab III with Guy body is shown to illustrate how little G 436 deviated from the original specification, the main visible differences being purely cosmetic ones related to some of the horizontal mouldings for livery purposes and the inclusion of London Transport's offside route number plate holder. This particular vehicle, HWU 438, was photographed in Doncaster and was one of a pair owned by Samuel Morgan of Armthorpe. *Ken Blacker*

The rear aspect was not particularly attractive on this type of body, with the emergency exit being set at an unusually high level while the tumble-home at the bottom was quite pronounced and more reminiscent of pre-war design practice. The young conductor, with bell punch machine ready for action and his cap at a jaunty angle, awaits passengers at the Lord Hill terminus. *Alan B Cross*

The final specification for the new vehicle was agreed between the two parties in late September 1949, allowing manufacture to commence immediately. The registration number KGK 981 had already been reserved for it, while Chiswick allocated body number 5401 and the internal classification 4G3. Its Guy chassis number was FD36223. The completed vehicle was delivered from Wolverhampton to Chiswick on 11th November 1949 and immediately taken into LT stock.

The invoice, when it arrived, was for £4,180, which was immediately examined to determine whether or not it was reasonable in relation to the original decision that the cost of G 436 should not exceed the price paid for a standard RT vehicle. After experiencing some difficulty in determining exactly how much each individual RT cost when orders for them were always placed in bulk, it was subsequently decided that the price of each individual Park Royal bodied RT equated to £4,157. As G 436 was a one-off whereas RTs were built in huge quantities with all the accompanying benefits of economy of scale, it was finally decided that Guy's bill was very reasonable and should be paid in full.

G 436 was now installed at Chiswick, still unlicensed but undergoing the usual multitude of tests to which any new class of vehicle was always subjected. It was perhaps time to now discuss with Guy the second half of the project, ie the provision of a modified Arab chassis on which a standard RT body could be mounted. In fact, the trail runs dead here. No records have been found to show that this matter was ever followed up, either by London Transport or by Guy, and the reason for the abandonment of the project has never come to light. G 436 duly entered service, but without the subsequent planned follow-up there seems to have been little point in its doing so, and it soon became clear that Guy's hopes of breaking into the London double deck bus market would never be realised.

The question of which garage G 436 should operate from was not entirely straightforward since, with an unladen height of 14ft 6½ins, there were several Central Bus garages from which it was precluded from entering. It was finally licensed for service on 18th January 1950 at Old Kent Road and, judging by the choice of route on which it was to operate, the deduction can only be made that there was no intention to exploit the vehicle's obvious potential for fast running or for its hill-climbing prowess. Route 173, from which it did not stray, was a mundane, flat, urban, frying-pan type operation between Peckham and Nunhead, with a circular routeing at its outer end and a running time of 26 minutes to complete the whole loop from Peckham back to Peckham.

Reallocation of route 173 took G 436 to Nunhead garage on 2nd May 1951. Still looking dent-free and well cared for, it is seen in Peckham High Street on 14th July 1952 with only two months left to go before it moved away from the 173. *Alan B Cross*

The 173 quickly gained a notoriety for having such an unusual (for London) bus working on it, and the loud roar with a hint of a whine from the Meadows engine became a feature of the streetscape around Nunhead and district. G 436 was certainly not a quiet vehicle and sometimes it could be heard approaching before it could be seen.

G 436 stayed at Old Kent Road garage for almost 1½ years, but on 2nd May 1951 the new Peckham garage opened with a resultant reshuffle of local operations including the transfer of responsibility for route 173 to Nunhead garage on Mondays to Fridays along with part of the Saturday schedule (the other half of which was worked from Peckham along with the whole Sunday service). G 436 was destined to remain on the 173, but now working from Nunhead and with no Sunday work. At the same time the Peckham end of the service was cut back from its old terminus at the Lord Hill pub to the forecourt of the new garage. From 14th May 1952 Nunhead's operation on the 173, along with that of G 436, was reduced to Monday to Friday only.

With little point in keeping G 436 on a five-day week operation, and perhaps also in the face of a little hostility from the Nunhead crews, it was agreed between management and the Transport & General Workers' Union that a new home should be found for it in the northern suburbs of London at Enfield garage. This agreement was reached in June 1952 but in fact the bus was not transferred until 12th September. Enfield had formerly been a major operator of 'utility' Guy Arabs, most of which had now been withdrawn and sold, and whether it was by accident or design will probably never be known, but G 436 arrived at Enfield on the very same day that the last of its older Guys was withdrawn from service, thus maintaining an unbroken Guy presence there for a little while longer. Its scheduled operation was on route 121, a short 16-minute run from Ponders End to Chingford which it usually worked on Mondays to Saturdays, leaving the service solely to RTs on Sundays. From its Ponders End terminus, which was actually in the forecourt of Enfield garage, it was a flat run across the Lea Valley followed by a steep climb up to Chingford, and G 436 became renowned for seemingly flying effortlessly up the gradient of Kings Head Hill while, in the hands of some of Enfield's drivers, it sometimes seemed to achieve breakneck speeds across the flatness of the Lea Valley too.

With RTs all around it, both inside and outside the premises, G 436 stands on the forecourt of the new bus garage which served as the Peckham terminus of route 173 instead of the Lord Hill pub during the vehicle's sixteen month spell working from Nunhead. Unlike most other London Transport double deckers, it never carried advertisements alongside the destination boxes at the front or back. *F G Reynolds*

After moving to Enfield garage and the rather remote route 121 in September 1952 G 436 largely fell off the radar and its comings and goings were recorded much less frequently by photographers. Standing alongside it outside Enfield garage on Christmas morning 1952 is STD 44, one of the vehicles that had helped to oust the previous generation of Guy Arabs from Enfield earlier in the year. *Allen T Smith © A B Cross*

G 436's existence at Enfield was uneventful, and it was never seen operating on any of that garage's routes other than the 121. On 1st January 1953 it was delicensed and taken into Chiswick for its first and only overhaul from which it emerged on 23rd February ready to be relicensed for service back at Enfield on 1st March. No structural changes are known to have taken place during the overhaul except that it emerged now fitted with a cab heater and demister. Adoption of the latest 'all red' livery without cream relief around the upper deck windows now gave it a slightly more sombre appearance. There is nothing more to record except that on 16th February 1955 it was delicensed, its London Transport service at an end after little more than five years.

After a period of storage, latterly at Shepherds Bush, G 436 was sold on 14th July 1955 for the same price as the STDs to the B S E Company of Regent Street W1 for further service in Yugoslavia alongside STD 112-176. No record has emerged of its movements while in Yugoslavia.

G 436 emerged from its first and only overhaul on 23rd February 1953 carrying the latest style of livery but otherwise externally unaltered. The newly-overhauled vehicle standing next to it in Chiswick Works is tower wagon 733J, temporarily minus its tower, which once served in the double deck fleet as STL 9. *Michael Rooum collection*

LOW-HEIGHT – THE RLH CLASS

Newly arrived at Chiswick on 12th May 1950 and with its trade plate still attached, RLH 1 ushers in a new era of low height double deckers. This was a time of massive change within the London Transport fleet as witnessed by the vehicles in this scene. Apart from the brand new RLH, an LT single decker is present having just returned from a major rebuilding by Marshall's of Cambridge with what amounts to almost a completely new body, while the two STLs have probably come to the end of their days. *G E Baddeley*

In the early post-war years London Transport's stock of low-height double deckers was miniscule in size compared with the main double deck fleet and consisted of just 50 vehicles. These comprised 8 venerable STs dating right back to 1930, 12 front-entrance 8.8-litre engined STLs built in 1934 (the highly distinctive 'Godstones'), 20 conventional STLs rebodied at Chiswick in 1943 and 10 'utility' Daimlers dating from 1943 and 1945. It was planned for all 50 to remain in service until 1954 when they would be replaced by a new standardised fleet of custom-built vehicles, and in order to achieve this considerable expense had already been incurred on the eight oldest vehicles in reconditioning their bodywork, and it was planned to replace their petrol engines with overhauled 7.7 diesels taken from withdrawn STLs during 1949/50. Suddenly, in July 1949, the future outlook changed.

On the 17th of that month a letter was despatched from Tilling headquarters at Crewe House in Curzon Street notifying London Transport that 55 vehicles ordered by the Midland General Omnibus Company and imminently due for construction had been deemed surplus to requirements, and asking if London Transport might be interested in acquiring any of them. The vehicles on offer comprised 35 single deck Leyland PS1s and 20 double deck AEC Regents, all with Weymann bodywork, and the execution of the orders for their construction had been delayed pending a decision on their future.

The reason that so many brand new buses had suddenly become surplus to requirements at a time of dire vehicle shortage was an unusual one. Midland General, along with its associated companies Mansfield District and Notts & Derby Traction (the latter solely a trolleybus operator), were subsidiaries of the Midland Counties Electricity Supply Company which held all their shares. This was, in turn, a wholly-owned subsidiary of the construction conglomerate Balfour Beatty & Co Ltd. Under the Electricity Act 1947 the Midland Counties Electricity Supply Company was nationalised with effect from 1st April 1948 along with the rest of the electricity supply industry, coming under the aegis of the East Midlands Electricity Board. The three transport companies thus found themselves under state ownership and answerable, initially, to the Electricity Board. A more logical line of management was subsequently established when they were placed under the wing of the Tilling Group Management Board along with all the Tilling road transport assets which had themselves come into state ownership in November 1948.

The Tilling management obviously took a close look at its new acquisitions and quickly came to the conclusion that the 55 vehicles currently on order for Midland General were not needed. The reasoning behind this has not been disclosed but presumably it was either because the Company's fleet was already of such a young age profile that – based on Tilling's rather more frugal standards – future enhancement could not be justified, or because its financial situation was considered to be such that it could not bear the imposition of yet more new rolling stock. The orders for the new vehicles had, in fact, been placed by Balfour Beatty on behalf of Midland General on 17th March 1948, only a fortnight before the latter was due to be nationalised and removed from Balfour Beatty's control, but the contracts were considered inviolate and could not be cancelled.

London Transport lost no time in reviewing the offer, and though it immediately decided that it had no need for the 35 single deckers (which had, in any case, been promptly snapped up by Crosville Motor Services), Durrant and the operating managers agreed that good use could be made of the 20 AEC Regents if these could be bodied in lowbridge format. The 20 vehicles had, in fact, been ordered with 14 highbridge and 6 lowbridge bodies, but Weymann had already confirmed that it was not too late to amend the order to 20 lowbridge if desired.

On 13th August London Transport wrote to Tilling's to confirm that it would accept the 20 AEC Regents which, at the time, were due for delivery between October and December 1949 although this target later slipped by several months. Tongue in cheek, Tilling's were asked if, in the event of London Transport subsequently deciding to buy a complete fleet of new standardised low-height double deckers, they would be prepared to buy back the 20 Midland General ones, only to be informed that it would be "very difficult" to give any such undertaking. An unavoidable proviso of the agreement to take the 20 vehicles was that they would have to be purchased by someone else first – possibly the Road Passenger Executive – as London Transport was already fully committed to its 1949 quota of new buses within the Ministry of Supply allocation, which prevented it from buying any more directly from the manufacturers. This matter was still outstanding when talks between London Transport, AEC and Weymann commenced in earnest over the exact specification for the new buses. Negotiations to modify both body and chassis specifications to suit London Transport's particular requirements began in September 1949 and were not finalised with the manufacturers until mid-November. Meanwhile the RLH (Regent Low Height) title was adopted and the vehicles were given the internal classification 1RLH1.

The contract with AEC was for the supply of 'provincial' type Regent III chassis of the 9612E model with fluid flywheel and preselector gearbox, an arrangement with which London Transport was fully familiar on the RT model and had adopted as its post-war standard. The obvious and very visible difference between the 9612 range and the RT lay in the use on the former of a much taller radiator with higher bonnet line and a consequent reduction in the driver's forward and nearside visibility. This was done to accommodate an oil bath air cleaner on top of the engine which London Transport did not regard as necessary on the RT but was happy to accept on the Midland General vehicles, which were fitted with the AEC A208 9.6 litre engine.

Photographed when brand new, Midland General's no. 426 was one of the batch from which the RLHs were diverted. In their eye-catching blue and cream livery adorned by a handsome fleet crest, these were striking-looking vehicles. No. 426 demonstrates some of the bodywork features that London Transport discarded for its RLHs including the separately-mounted side lights, the ventilators in the front dome and, most notably, the three-piece front destination display which was similar in function to that used by London Transport on its RTs but was rejected for the RLHs. *John Cockshott*

In finalising the specification, certain special features previously ordered by Midland General and specific to their requirements were deleted, while London Transport also requested the omission of front and rear stabilisers which were a standard part of the Regent III design. This brought the new RLHs in line with London Transport's RTs, the inevitable result being a heavier ride similar to that of the RT and noticeably inferior to that of a standard Regent III, especially on bumpy road surfaces or at speed in country districts. London Transport's own features replacing standard Regent III ones included a 3RT steering column with worm and nut steering, its own design of front axle springs, provision of a towing hook at the nearside front, and various lighting arrangements of its own design including the side and fog lamps.

The basic features of the low height body specification agreed between Midland General and Weymann remained unchanged. These provided for a 53-seat 4-bay body (with 27 seats upstairs and 26 down) based on MCW's patented riveted construction, with sunken offside upper saloon gangway permitting a low overall unladen height of about 13ft 4ins (official versions vary). Midland General had specified elimination of the outswept lower panelling normally installed by Weymann at that time as a styling feature, and they had also specified the installation of Widney Mk I sliding side windows in place of half-drops, the only examples of the latter being in the two upstairs front windows and worked by pinch grips. London Transport retained all these Midland General features but eliminated the installation of saloon heaters from both decks and also the sound insulation material from the lower deck front bulkhead. It also deleted ventilator slots from the front dome and arranged for the offside side light to be built into the front dash instead of projecting from the side of the driver's cab which had been Midland General's preference. The latter's standard front and rear destination display consisted of a three-screen arrangement at the front and two at the back, not dissimilar to London Transport's own standard specification on the RT, but for some long-forgotten reason London Transport opted for a much simpler arrangement consisting of a single box at the front and side with nothing at all at the rear except for a route number stencil bracket fitted centrally on the outside top of the platform window.

ALL COMMUNICATIONS TO BE ADDRESSED TO THE COMPANY.

DIRECTORS:
G. CARDWELL.
SIR JOSEPH NALL, D.S.O.
J. N. VALLANCE.
W. VANE MORLAND.
R. H. WILSON.

THE MIDLAND GENERAL OMNIBUS COMPANY LIMITED

REGISTERED OFFICE:
STATION ROAD,
LANGLEY MILL.
NOTTINGHAM.
TELEPHONE No.
LANGLEY MILL, 261 (4 LINES.)
GENERAL, LANGLEY MILL.
NOTTINGHAM.

YOUR REF.....................

OUR REF. JM/AR/MG

LANGLEY MILL, NOTTINGHAM.
13th July, 1950.

Mr. Shave,
London Transport Executive,
Griffith House,
280, Marylebone Road, S.W.1.

Dear Sir,

We enclose herewith our invoice for £83,013.3.4d., in respect of the 20 A.E.C. Low Bridge Double Deck vehicles with Weymann bodies, which we understand have now all been delivered.

Yours faithfully,

[signature]

SECRETARY

Midland General wrote to London Transport on 13th July 1950 invoicing for the cost of the RLHs and this is the covering letter accompanying that invoice. All twenty vehicles had already entered service with London Transport by then. It is not known when the bill was finally paid to formally transfer ownership.

Other standard London Transport requirements included its own bells and buzzers and also a bell cord on the nearside of the lower deck, a fare board frame on the staircase panel, a conductor's ticket rack and waybill container, cork-covered floor boards with hardwood slats on all wearing surfaces, external advertisement mouldings and an extra moulding to accommodate the central cream band. The seats were, of course, upholstered in standard London Transport materials: moquette with leathercloth edging on the cushions and squabs and green rexine on the backs. The driver's seat was also a standard London Transport fitment.

Construction of the chassis began at Southall early in 1950, a few weeks later than originally promised, and the first one to be completed (RLH 2) was delivered to Weymann's factory on 8th March. A block of chassis numbers was allocated to them, 9612E5025-5044, but these were not carried in sequence with the fleet numbers. Immediately prior to constructing the chassis for RLH 1-20 AEC had, in fact, built ten chassis that had originally been part of the same order which Midland General had been allowed to retain and which duly became nos. 421-430 in its fleet (registered ONU 630-639). The same applied at Weymann who proceeded to build all 30 bodies as a single batch. The Midland General vehicles received Weymann body numbers 4338-4347 and the London vehicles followed immediately on from these as 4348-4367 (none of which was supplied in strict numerical order to either operator). London Transport's own body numbers for RLH 1-20 were 7099-7118 (in that order) and a block of matching registration numbers was reserved as KYY 501-520.

The first completed vehicle was RLH 1, which arrived at Chiswick on 12th May 1950, and the remainder came in a fairly steady stream between 18th May and 5th July. As all 20 were intended for service with the Country Bus & Coach department they all carried the very latest version of the green and cream livery with no cream relief around the upper deck windows, which Weymann had begun applying to new RTs in April 1950.

Just before manufacturing commenced the Tilling management decided that, in order to meet London Transport's inability to purchase the vehicles directly from the manufacturers, they would be bought initially by Midland General itself even though all 20 were being delivered direct to London Transport. Midland General would then pass ownership to London Transport and invoice them accordingly, which they did on 13th July 1950, just over a week after the last of the batch had been delivered. The final cost for each individual bus was £4,150.13s.2d comprised of £1,814.0s.6d for the chassis, £2,183.0s.0d for the body and a surcharge of £153.12s.8d. The latter sum was, in fact, commission payable to Balfour Beatty, it having been that Company's standard practice to charge a commission of about 3.8% on any order for new buses or trolleybuses which it placed on behalf of its operating companies.

The brand new, shining RLHs made a big and very favourable impression when they first entered service. This was only to be expected when the vehicles they replaced dated back to 1930 and 1934, and however well kept the latter were, there was no disguising their age. Not only did the exteriors of the RLHs look modern and curvaceous, their interiors were welcoming too. Or at least the lower deck was; the upper saloon with its rows of bench seats (six for four passengers and a back one for three) was not to everyone's taste, and the finish was a little spartan with a single-skinned ceiling and unlined side panels. Large amounts of polished woodwork around the windows, and also along the ceiling on the lower deck, gave an air of semi-opulence and bore absolutely no resemblance to the RT with which so many passengers were now familiar. The seats, with their gently arched, chromium plated top rails, looked welcoming too. The back of all the offside ones on the lower deck and on all the rows of four upstairs bore the blunt warning 'CAUTION LOW ROOF' and along the whole length of the lower saloon on the radiused panel of the sunken portion of ceiling was a prominent, 1 inch wide red line to remind passengers to duck down or hit their head. The new model tipped the scales at 7tons 10cwt unladen, and sounding much like an RT with its 9.6 litre engine matched to a back axle ratio of 5⅙:1, the RLH ran well and certainly brought a much-needed performance boost to the services on which it was now scheduled to run.

London Transport used RLH 10 as the subject for its archive photographs of the class, which included interior scenes taken in June 1950. Whilst the lower deck was furnished to a high standard, the lack of side and roof lining panels was evident on the upper deck, and the biggest drawback was that the seats upstairs were sited too high relative to the windows for passengers to obtain good outward visibility. *London Transport Museum*

Although a few standard London Transport features are apparent, such as the seat moquette and bell cord running the length of the lower saloon, most of the scene that met the eye was pure Weymann. A particular Weymann feature of the early post war years was the curvature of the front bulkhead windows at both top and bottom. *London Transport Museum*

By pure coincidence the number of new RLHs matched exactly the quantity of elderly and officially time-expired vehicles in the lowbridge fleet. Furthermore the 8 STs and 12 'Godstone' STLs were all 48-seaters, so the 20 RLHs provided an immediate 10% increase in carrying capacity. It was only to be expected that route 336 (Chesham–Watford), which was home for most of the oldest vehicles, would be the first to receive the new intake. Despite extensive bodywork rebuilding the STs on the 336 were grossly outmoded and still displayed a long-abandoned arrangement of two sunken gangways on the upper deck, one on each side, and were probably the last vehicles in regular service anywhere in the country to do so. From February 1949 onwards they had been helped out by brand new Bristol/ECW K types diverted directly to London Transport under a loan agreement with the Tilling management. RLH 1-5 were all licensed at Amersham on 25th May 1950 and ran alongside a dwindling number of STs and the odd Bristol for a few days. One last new vehicle, RLH 6, arrived on 7th June. Meanwhile the last Bristols left Amersham on 31st May preparatory to being despatched to their rightful owner, and the final ST departed from there on 23rd June.

It is hard, so long after the event, to convey fully the impact that the sleek and brand new RLHs brought to route 336 after it had been dominated for so many years by seemingly ancient STs. Amersham's RLH 2 is seen in Watford town centre glistening with newness soon after entering service in May 1950.

59

The rear end of the bodywork, as demonstrated by RLH 2, was disappointing in having no built-in destination display, which was a particularly surprising omission as the original Midland General specification had included a two-screen layout not unlike London Transport's standard arrangement on the RT family. The route stencil in the back window hardly compensated adequately for this omission and soon fell out of use anyway in Country Bus service. *Alan B Cross*

It had been a long-standing arrangement lasting for many years that while six of the lowbridge STs would be based at Amersham the other two would work at Addlestone where they were used on the jointly-worked 436 (Staines–Woking) and 461 (Staines–Walton), latterly alongside vehicles of the wartime-rebodied STL19 class. The decision was taken to displace not only the two STs but also the complete fleet of STLs from the 436 and 461, and to implement this RLH 7-15 were licensed as a complete batch at Addlestone on 22nd June 1950. The two STs were delicensed on the very next day, and the STLs were removed over a period of time to work from Godstone garage on route 410 (Bromley–Reigate).

The final five RLHs (RLH 16-20) joined the recently arrived ex-Addlestone STLs at Godstone on the 410, and they were licensed there between 1st and 6th July. Before this the 410 had been the stamping ground for the characterful and highly distinctive 'Godstone' STLs which, like the STs at Amersham, had latterly been augmented by a few hired Bristols. However, as at Amersham, the last Bristols left on 31st May which meant that they had gone before the first of the RLHs arrived. Henceforth route 410 was worked by a mixture of RLHs and STL19s, along with various highbridge STLs on Saturday short workings which kept clear of the restricted Godstone–Westerham section with its low bridge at Oxted.

The new RLHs proved instantly successful both with crews and passengers. The latter might have been expected to complain about the exceptionally poor visibility from the upper saloon where the bench seats were placed unduly high in relation to the window line meaning that passengers had to lower their heads to see where they were going, but this never seems to have become a bone of contention.

The only complaints appear to have been about strong draughts caused by the six 'Ashanco' extractor ventilators fitted in the upper deck ceiling and it is thought that, although no official action was ever deemed to be feasible to alleviate the problem, local action was taken in some cases to block up some of these ventilators.

It was standard London Transport practice at the time to post advertising material on newly-received buses as quickly as possible, and generally within a few days, instantly dulling the impression of newness. The highest numbered vehicle in the original batch, RLH 20, joined four others on route 410 in July 1950 which they shared with STLs until further new RLHs arrived in 1952. *F G Reynolds*

The Country Bus & Coach department obviously found the twelve now-delicensed 'Godstone' STLs too good to waste. According to their own estimation the Weymann-built metal-framed bodies of 1934 were still almost as good as new, and it was decided to put them back to work, while at the same time bringing forward a long-awaited plan to revive through operation between Staines and Guildford which had been severed in the war when the northern portion of the 436 was double decked. A major revision of services based at Addlestone took place on 27th September 1950 and saw the 436 revert to its Staines–Guildford format, replacing 4Q4s from the southern section, latterly numbered 438, between Woking and Guildford. A network of lowbridge double deck operation was established which retained route 461 as it was but now included 436A (Woking–Ripley, now extended through to Staines) and 463 (Walton–Woking, extended to Guildford). Guildford garage now commenced operation of lowbridge double deckers using six of the surplus STLs, while the other six went to Addlestone. Route 461A (Walton–Ottershaw) was henceforth also interworked using low height buses although, like the 463, normal height double deckers could now be used on it. At Addlestone garage, RLHs were now officially scheduled to work 436/A and 461/A with STLs on the 463, but in practice these demarcation lines were not strictly maintained, while Guildford's 'Godstones' were scheduled to run alongside Addlestone's RLHs on the 436.

Even with all twelve 'Godstone' STLs relicensed, the availability position in regard to lowbridge double deckers was once again tight and it became necessary to also start putting some of the STs back into service with the first returning to Addlestone on 27th September. For the next two years routes such as the 436 were a delight to travel on because you never knew whether your bus was going to be a brand new RLH, a truly characterful if somewhat mournful-sounding front-entrance STL, or even an ancient ST. A similar position applied at Godstone from the same date when, for the very first time, this garage received a lowbridge ST to join its RLHs and STL19s on route 410.

Such was the success of the RLHs that, by mid-1951, high level consideration was already being given to the prospect of purchasing more vehicles of the same type to eliminate all other vehicles from the lowbridge fleet by as early as 1952. The original hope of retaining many of the older vehicles in service until 1954 was, of necessity, abandoned. Many had bodies of wartime construction which would require extensive repair work to keep them operational for that length of time, and this could not be justified financially. Four of the wartime Daimlers were now in very poor condition and one of the STs had already been taken permanently out of service. After establishing the future needs of both operating departments, including a possible increase in the scope of lowbridge double deck operation, it was decided that 56 more RLHs would be required, with the assumption that procurement of these would be a simple matter of transferring them from the RT building programme for 1952.

Both manufacturers were approached, and while AEC saw no problem in changing production of 56 chassis from RT to provincial type Regent III, Weymann was unable to help. It had already committed itself to material allocations for RTs but, more importantly, a serious contractual problem would arise as Park Royal was also party to a joint agreement whereby each manufacturer supplied a stipulated proportion of RT bodies. This agreement could not be varied until the existing contract expired at the end of September 1952, which would delay delivery of the new RLHs until well into 1953 and would be too late to meet London Transport's needs. The British Transport Commission now decreed that Eastern Coach Works (which, like London Transport, was in the nationalised sector), should be asked to supply the bodies.

A meeting was held with J W Shirley, Director and General Manager of ECW, on 10th September, who reported that the Lowestoft factory's capacity was already totally absorbed for the whole of 1952. Another state-owned source, the Ulster Transport Authority, was then 'recommended', with the claim that UTA could manufacture bodies cheaper than other people. This idea met heavy resistance from the Executive's senior officers who felt that no attempt should be made to buy from someone so far away of whom they had no experience. In any event, technical liaison would be very difficult and, even if the bodies were indeed cheaper, the transportation charges to and from Ulster, plus the additional costs involved in inspection and technical liaison, would almost certainly override any price saving.

Lengthy negotiations during the second half of 1951 ultimately resulted in the RLH fleet growing to a total of 76 units. Most of the second batch were needed to replace older lowbridge vehicles, but a few surplus ones were initially put to other uses including three which were employed at East Grinstead on single deck route 424 from 1st November 1952. RLH 44, seen here when brand new, was the first to move away, in July 1954, and all three had been re-employed at other garages by February 1956.

The BTC next stipulated that bodywork for the new RLHs should go out to tender, and offers were duly issued to three likely candidates. These were opened on 26th November 1951 and were as follows:

	On provincial type chassis	On RT type chassis
MCW (Weymann's)	£2,125	£2,275
Park Royal Vehicles	£2,195	£2,355
Saunders-Roe (Anglesey)	£2,490	£2,600

It was a fortunate outcome for London Transport that the lowest tender was from Weymann as this meant that the 56 new vehicles could be as close as possible in specification to the earlier batch. For standardisation, it was decided to continue using the AEC Regent provincial type chassis rather than the RT type for the lowbridge fleet, with the promise of chassis deliveries between July and October 1952 and the hope that all 56 completed vehicles would be in stock by the end of the year. Five years after it first went into production, the Regent III was now an immensely successful model generally regarded as the most refined vehicle on the double deck market, and the 56 new vehicles for London Transport would be the latest variant of this model designated the 9613E. In most major respects this was similar to the earlier 9612E chassis of RLH 1-20 and London Transport's specification for the new batch included all the same of its own modifications as before. The engine was also a later model, the A218, but this differed from its predecessor only through variations to the water circulation leaving its power output and general performance the same as before.

Amersham's route 336 called for the use of five RLHs on a daily basis, and it soon became unofficial local practice to use the sixth vehicle, when available, on route 305 in place of one of its scheduled STLs. This pre-empted the regular allocation of RLHs to the 305 from November 1952 onwards. RLH 6, photographed at Gerrards Cross in October 1951, also shows that Amersham's inside staff were ahead of the game by repositioning the front registration plate on the radiator instead of below it, a modification subsequently adopted as official policy in the latter part of 1953. *Michael Wickham collection*

At a quick glance the second RLH batch looked almost identical to the first and it was only on closer inspection that the various differences became apparent. Addestone's RLH 24 swings round on to the stand at Staines West station within a few days of entering service on 9th October 1952. *Alan B Cross*

The Weymann bodies followed exactly the same shape and dimensions as before and to a casual observer the two RLH batches could appear identical. However there were differences, some more visible than others which resulted in RLH 21-76 having the revised classification 2RLH1/1 Distinguishing features detectable on any vehicle of the new batch as it approached a stop would have been the polished aluminium radiator shell in place of the chromium plated metal type used previously, and the absence of a push-out ventilator in the driver's cab front dash panel. At the rear of the bus, the then-current RT type combined stop and direction indicator with its left and right arrows was now mounted above the registration plate assembly, while the used ticket box adjacent to the platform was now a standard RT attachment instead of the more complex earlier arrangement of a built-in box with cleaner's trap door below. The 'Ashanco' ventilators along each side of the roof were omitted, and within the saloons the seat tops and grab rails were of aluminium alloy instead of stainless steel although their shape remained the same. Further changes to be bodywork specification included a completely revised specification for the lower saloon floor, including floor traps, slats, tread plates and flywheel assembly, and there was revised instrumentation within the driver's cab. A cab heater and demister was specified which, though not fitted to the earlier batch at the time the specification for RLH 21-76 was drawn up, was added to them from May 1952 onwards following a trial with a pilot vehicle two months earlier. If the official figure is to be believed, the unladen weight of the second batch vehicles was exactly the same as the first at 7tons 10cwt.

It was arranged with Weymann that 32 of the new vehicles would be painted in country area green livery (RLH 21-52) with the remaining 24 in red (RLH 53-76). Chassis numbers for the batch spanned between 9613E6948 and 7003 although, once again, these were by no means in sequence with the vehicles' bonnet numbers. Body numbers once again ran in numerical order as 8032-8087 and the booked registrations MXX 221-276 again matched the fleet numbers. Considering all the pressures on manufacturing industries at the time in regard to material and staffing availability, the second RLH batch was built very promptly with the first delivery (RLHs 21 and 22) arriving at Chiswick from Weymann's on 8th October and the last (RLH 76) on 22nd December, fulfilling London Transport's plan to have them all in stock by the end of 1952.

RLH 21 and 22 were destined for Godstone garage and were officially recorded (perhaps erroneously) as being sent there on 8th October 1952, the same day on which they were received from Weymann's. It was not planned to complete the conversion of route 410 just yet as the 436 group of routes from Addlestone and Guildford garages was seen as having top priority based on vehicle age, but two of Godstone's STL19s were needed urgently to replace, albeit only temporarily until RLHs became available, a pair of STs then working on route 230 at Harrow Weald. The influx into Addlestone, which finally consisted of RLH 23-28, 30, commenced on 9th October followed by Guildford which received its very first RLHs from the 13th. A pair of STs latterly at Addlestone were withdrawn immediately the first RLHs arrived, and all the 'Godstone' STLs had departed from the area by 1st November. On the same date Godstone garage was the recipient of RLH 36-41 which saw the departure of the last of its more modern lowbridge STLs.

Renewal of the country lowbridge fleet was now complete but eleven new green RLHs still needed to be found homes. Some of these had been obtained to act as replacements when others of the class were away for overhaul once the first cycle got under way in 1953 and the remainder were held against possible new developments requiring lowbridge double deckers. Meanwhile work had to be found for them and between 1st and 3rd November RLH 42-45 were licensed at East Grinstead to work on routes 424 (East Grinstead–Reigate) normally scheduled for 4Q4 single deckers, and 428 (East Grinstead–Dormansland) instead of its regular RT. To relieve overcrowding, certain journeys on the 424 had, in fact, already been worked for several months by a lowbridge double decker in the form of an ST which was the very last of its class in service with London Transport when it was taken out of use just five days before the arrival of the first RLHs. RLH 46-50 enlarged the lowbridge fleet at Amersham between 1st and 12th November, becoming regular visitors in place of RTs on route 305 (Gerrards Cross–Beaconsfield), 305A (Gerards Cross–Chalfont Common) and 353 (Berkhamsted–Windsor) as well as providing a useful back-up to the regular RLH fleet on the 336. Last of all, RLH 51,52 entered service on 13th and 19th November respectively at Guildford on RT route 415 (Guildford–Ripley). These extracurricular operations at Amersham and Guildford mostly ceased in the later nineteen-fifties when the surplus RLHs were called away to work elsewhere.

Appearances by RLHs on Green Line reliefs were rare but not completely unknown. On this occasion Guildford's RLH 34 passes Baker Street station on route 715. The slipboard in the bulkhead window reads "GOD SAVE THE QUEEN – TO AND FROM CORONATION TERMINAL" indicating that the occasion is Coronation Day, 2nd June 1953. *London Trolleybus Preservation Society*

The influx of new RLHs on Harrow Weald's route 230 in November 1952 and the novelty of seeing them in red livery caused great excitement at the time. RLH 65 was one of fourteen received at Harrow Weald and it stayed there until displaced in August 1958 by ex-Merton RLHs as explained in the text. Subsequently brought back into use in May 1959, it served for a further decade at Dalston and Hornchurch before ending its life in Atlanta, Georgia. *Peter Mitchell*

Delivery of red RLHs followed immediately on from the green ones without a break, the first to arrive being the lowest numbered, RLH 53, on 14th November 1952. At first it was a great novelty to see RLHs in red, and the standard Central Bus practice of picking out mudguards, lamps and safety rails in black seemed to further enhance their appearance. Only two Central Bus garages ran low height double deckers, Harrow Weald and Merton, and the former was selected to receive the new buses first.

The busier and more heavily bussed of the two Central Bus lowbridge services was Harrow Weald based 230 which required a maximum of 14 vehicles to cover its 22 to 26 minute run (according to direction and time of day) between Raynes Park and Northwick Park. Latterly worked by a mixture of red and green STL19s, it received RLH 53-58/60-67 between 19th November and 8th December 1952, on which date the final STL departed. This left just Merton and its 'utility' Daimlers to be dealt with. RLH 59 was an early arrival, presumably for type training, on 1st December and the remainder, RLH 68-76, followed between the 10th and 22nd of the month. Route 127, which took a circuitous route between South Wimbledon and Morden, a 38-minute run that the direct 93 between the two points could accomplish in 5 minutes, only ran on Mondays to Saturdays. At the time a Metropolitan Police embargo still existed confining low height double deckers operating in the central area to routes 127 and 230, a restriction which London Transport continued to go along with despite the sheer illogicality that 146 low height Bristols on hire from Tilling had successfully operated on a wide variety of services, many of them serving the very heart of central London, from December 1948 to June 1950. However, to achieve better utilisation of Merton's low loaders, an arrangement existed whereby they could also work on route 152 (Mitcham–Feltham) and on special services such as Epsom races and Wimbledon tennis, which they did from time to time.

An upper saloon study of one of the second batch shows the same high-pitched seats as the originals. It also shows the single skinned ceiling which is devoid of ventilators although, as on the first batch, a series of small and not very effective air intake slots is provided above the front windows Because of the deeper rainshield at the front, forward visibility for seated passengers is even more restricted than through the side windows.
John C Gillham © Tony Peters

Merton's RLHs had official permission to operate if necessary on route 152, a useful concession especially on Sundays when their own service 127 did not run. On this occasion two 152s have drawn up together, with RLH 68 at the front, to disgorge passengers at Wimbledon stadium. *Alan B Cross*

The principle of using green RLHs on Central Bus services to cover short term deficiencies became well established in 1955 and was not confined solely to vehicles from the second batch. RLH 6 ran from Merton garage between June and December 1956 and is seen at the South Wimbledon terminus of route 127 in Milner Road. RLH 6 was later repainted red.
Alan B Cross

The new batch of RLHs had not been in service very long before complaints began to arrive about serious condensation in the upper saloons. The matter was investigated, and as early as December 1952 it was agreed that the problem was bad enough to warrant urgent action to overcome it. No similar trouble had arisen on RLH 1-20 due to the presence of their six roof ventilators which, even if they created draughts, at least managed to keep the air circulating and condensation at a low level. Advice was sought from the Chiswick laboratory as to whether matters might be improved if the single skinned ceiling panels were to be covered with rexine, but it was concluded that this was unlikely to provide a cure. The possibility of adding a second skin of roofing was examined but this was ruled out because headroom above the seats, which was already tight, would become inadequate. The simple expedient of adding ventilators similar to those on the first batch was rejected on the grounds of their susceptibility to damage from roof-washing machines. After almost two years of examination nothing was done to tackle the problem, the number of complaints was found to be diminishing, and the matter was closed.

By January 1953 the time had arrived for the initial RLH intake to go through its first overhaul cycle, which began on 5th January when RLH 1 was sent into works to begin the process, the first of three overhauls that most RLHs were destined to undergo during their service with London Transport. The time taken on each vehicle varied but was generally between six and seven weeks and no RLHs ever exchanged body or chassis identity. So leisurely was the process that the last of the 20 was not sent for overhauling until 18th May 1954, returning to service on 26th July. During this first overhaul a few alterations were carried out to bring RLH 1-20 more closely into line with the second batch. These were mostly related to the electrical wiring and therefore out of sight of the casual observer, although there was one visible amendment by which the offside lower saloon rear corner panel was split into two halves to facilitate replacement and also to bring standardisation with the later batch.

A couple of minor physical changes began to take place on the RLHs in 1953. In March the management at Chiswick recorded that odd cases had been noted of RLHs running in service with real wheel discs fitted, a feature which had been deliberately omitted from both batches when they were purchased on grounds of cost. How had this come about, they asked, and on whose authority? Enquiries were made, and it transpired that these dress guards (as they were then officially termed) were unofficial and unauthorised local garage initiatives to improve the appearance of the vehicles. The rear axle of the RLH being the same as that of the RT, fitment was a simple matter as the

The official adoption in 1953 of decorative rear wheel trims for RLHs, and also 15T13s, certainly helped to further enhance their appearance, although much of this gain was lost with the subsequent decision in February 1956 to paint over all the polished wheel parts on economy grounds. Vehicles of each type, Amersham's RLH 6 and Hemel Hempstead's T 775, both display their new wheel trims at Berkhamsted station but the T still awaits the repositioning of its front registration plate. *Buses of Yesteryear*

It was by no means unusual to find Country Area RLHs straying away from their scheduled haunts, and this practice seemed to occur more frequently at Amersham garage than anywhere else. On this occasion RLH 42 picks up passengers at Kingsbury Square, Aylesbury, which was one of the most far-flung points on the London Transport network. On the day in question this bus was London Transport's contribution to route 359 which, very unusually, was jointly worked with another operator, in this case United Counties. RLH 42 arrived at Amersham garage in November 1956, after a brief four month spell running alongside red RLHs at Harrow Weald, and stayed there until its demise on 9th November 1964.

necessary brackets and discs were readily available. In June it was decided to leave in place any discs that may have been fitted and not to remove them on overhaul, and from July 1953 onwards an abrupt change of policy saw them adopted as a standard feature which was then fitted to all RLHs as they passed through overhaul. The same also applied to the very similar Regal III chassis of the 15T13 class (T 769-798) as did a second amendment of 1953. This was an alteration authorised by the Main Technical Committee requiring that the front registration plate, which was suspended from the bottom of the radiator, should be repositioned so that it was fitted on the radiator itself with the bottom of the registration plate coinciding with the base of the radiator. The reason for this was stated to be to prevent injury to staff emerging from the pits. Both modifications took place over a period of time and it is probably correct to assume that every RLH had been dealt with by the time the first overhaul cycle for RLH 21-76 was completed in December 1956.

Two additional garages received an RLH allocation in 1954/55. First was Reigate where a single vehicle was supplied to cover short workings in place of the usual RF on route 447 between Redhill and the new London County Council housing estate at South Merstham. RLH 44 was transferred in for this purpose from East Grinstead on 7th July 1954 and thereafter Reigate retained a solitary RLH, occasionally rising temporarily to two, for this purpose for the next 13 years with a short break between May 1962 and February 1963 when no vehicle was available. Reigate became unique in being the only Country Bus garage ever to be officially allocated red RLHs with RLH 57 serving there for five months in 1960 followed by RLH 52 between February 1963 and April 1964.

The next garage to receive RLHs was Hornchurch where route 248 (Upminster–Cranham), which required three buses on its short 11-minute run, was converted from TD to double deck operation on 16th February 1955. Four buses were required, including an engineering spare, but only one red vehicle (RLH 76) was available. The others were green (RLH 21-23), which meant that, for the very first time, green RLHs could be found operating on Central Bus service. From this tentative start the use of green RLHs on Central Buses became firmly established, so much so that there were very few years between 1959 and 1969 when this did not happen. One of Hornchurch's early green contingent, RLH 22, was repainted red in September 1955. This was the first of eight to be dealt with in this way, the others being RLH 23 (November 1955), RLH 1 (November 1956), RLH 9 (September 1957) and RLH 7, 29, 49, 52 (all in April 1959). The removal of eight vehicles from the country fleet inevitably meant that RLH operations there had to be scaled down, and this resulted in the last of East Grinstead's allocation being removed on 1st October 1957.

At Hornchurch the spare RLH, if not required by the engineers, was permitted to run on route 249 (Upminster Park Estate–Corbets Tey) in place of its RT, and when the 249 was withdrawn in August 1958 Romford local service 252 was officially substituted although no cases were ever recorded of RLHs actually appearing on it. From its introduction on 6th April 1959, RLHs could also be used in place of an RT on the short Monday to Friday peak hour 248A (Upminster–Corbets Tey).

Britain's disastrous involvement in the Suez crisis of November 1956 when it invaded Egypt resulted in fuel rationing being imposed in December 1956, with a requirement on London Transport to cut consumption by 5%. Fuel economy rose high on the agenda, and even though rationing ceased on 1st April 1957 elements within London Transport, and the Country Bus & Coach department in particular, became more keen than ever to explore the use of more economical vehicles, with particular interest focussed on the highly-acclaimed Bristol Lodekka. It also wanted to assess what savings might be achieved by fitting conventional manual gearboxes and friction clutches to a number of RLHs. The proposal was looked at in depth, and a drawback was seen to be that such an alteration could involve a complete change to the braking system as the compressor could not then be accommodated on the 9.6 litre engine. Discussions went on until September when it was revealed that a two-week programme of comparative consumption tests was to be carried out at the Chobham proving ground starting on 7th October 1957 which would include two 3RTs, a Lodekka, a Routemaster prototype and an AEC Regent with manual gearbox. From this point onwards nothing more is known about the plan for modifying RLHs which, it is presumed, proved impracticable on cost grounds resulting in the idea being quietly dropped.

RLHs made their way into suburban Essex with the conversion of Hornchurch's route 248 on 16th February 1955 and RLH 22 was still in green livery at the time. It was the first of the class to be repainted from green to red and was photographed just after receiving its new colours in September 1955. Peter Mitchell

London Transport was particularly hard hit by the long busmen's strike of 1958 which lasted from 5th May to 20th June inclusive. The aftermath resulted in extensive service cuts which were implemented in stages and included the complete withdrawal of nineteen Central Bus services. The very first stage, on 20th August 1958, included the total demise of Merton's route 127. This had, in any case, been on a downward spiral, and despite a Monday to Friday extension beyond South Wimbledon to St Helier Avenue in October 1956, was reduced on 30th April 1958 to a Monday to Friday-only operation, with its RLHs uneconomically lying idle all weekend.

Merton's RLHs were not, however, delicensed with the loss of route 127. Totalling ten at the end, nine of them were immediately transferred to Harrow Weald to enable them to remain operational, with nine of Harrow Weald's own vehicles being delicensed instead and put into storage. The nine ex-Merton vehicles had been the subject of an important experiment that it was imperative should continue. Back in December 1953 it was decided that a prototype alternator and rectifier capable of providing a high output at very low vehicle speeds should be tried out on an RLH in place of the usual DC system of dynamo and heavy duty battery, the sphere of operation to be a Central Bus service with a characteristic of difficulty in maintaining high battery charge. By April 1957 the experiment, which was crucial to future Routemaster design, had been expanded to embrace nine vehicles at Merton, all alternator equipped and fitted with 90 ampere/hour STL-type batteries with dummy electric lead inserted to simulate a lighting lead. The possibility was also examined of using alkaline batteries instead of lead acid ones, and although it is not known if this was done on the RLHs it was certainly subsequently tried out on some RMs. Nine RLHs emerging from overhaul between 24th August and 31st October 1957 were used for the experiment (RLH 61-64, 66-69, 71) and these were the vehicles despatched to Harrow Weald. A single 'ordinary' RLH at Merton was transferred to Hornchurch.

Route 127 and its RLHs had barely been

A well-established bastion of lowbridge bus operation in suburban south London was lost with the demise of route 127 as a direct aftermath of the 1958 bus strike. Shortly before its withdrawal on 20th August 1958 RLH 61 leaves the St Helier Avenue terminus for another circuitous trip to Morden. It was one of the Merton RLHs that moved north to Harrow Weald when the 127 ceased. *Peter Mitchell*

withdrawn for a fortnight when the Chief Mechanical Engineer, A A M Durrant, sought authority at a meeting on 3rd September to write-off and sell 28 RLHs. These comprised 14 already surplus (including the 10 from route 127) and a further 14 due to be displaced later in the year from route 410 following completion of bridge work at Oxted. Such was the certainty of the disposals taking place that state-owned Scottish Omnibuses was written to, asking if any of their companies would be interested in the vehicles which would comprise 18 built in 1950 and 10 built in 1952. No sale took place because J B Burnell, Operating Manager of Central Buses, intervened a couple of months later seeking to use 24 of the surplus RLHs in place of RFs on route 213 on which the headroom under Coombe Road railway bridge was due to be increased by the middle of 1960 sufficient to allow the use of double deckers, but where the headroom at Worcester Park Station bridge would still be too low to accommodate RTs. Eventually none of this came to pass. The expectation that the road at Oxted Station would be lowered proved premature (route 410 retained its RLHs for another five years), meaning that sufficient RLHs for the 213 never became available. Instead most of the surplus RLH fleet found a new niche at Dalston garage in May 1959.

This last major new sphere of RLH operation, and the closest to central London that there had ever been, came on 13th May 1959 when the formerly RF-worked Monday-Saturday route 208A between Clapton Pond and Stratford (Maryland Station) was replaced by RLHs. To achieve this, a re-routeing was necessary in the Hackney Wick area and the new operation was renumbered 178. The full Monday to Friday service required 13 vehicles and Dalston garage received exactly this number for the start of operation. All were relicensed out of storage and included four newly repainted red buses (RLH 7, 29, 49, 52). This ensured that the whole of the starting fleet at Dalston was in the correct colour, but it soon became clear that spares were needed and before the year was out both RLH 10 and RLH 48 had worked for short periods in green livery on route 178.

The introduction of route 178 on 13th May 1959 brought RLHs to areas of truly urban operation for the first time. Dalston's RLH 59 looks positively diminutive when squeezed between a pair of Bow depot's N1 class trolleybuses in a traffic queue at Stratford Broadway. The two types ran together for only three months, Bow's trolleybuses being replaced by RTLs on 18th August. *Ken Blacker*

The nineteen-sixties marked a decade of contraction for the RLHs although it began with all of them being equipped with flashing trafficators, a process which began in 1959 and was completed by the end of 1960. Identical projecting 'ears' were used at the front to those on the RT classes, while at the rear the majority of RLHs needed only the blanking plates to be removed from the two-way arrows on the registration plate assembly, and for holders and bulbs to be installed. RLH 1-20 differed in having no two-way arrows and in common with 563 RT3 bodies still in stock, and a few T-type single deckers, it was necessary to modify the rear body framework on these to enable RM-style flasher units to be fitted each side of the advertisement panel.

All 76 RLHs were equipped with London Transport's distinctive style flashing trafficators during 1959/60 as demonstrated by RLH 61 which spent two spells at Dalston from January 1964 onwards and ultimately gained the honour of running the final RLH journey for London Transport in April 1971. It is seen in gloomy surroundings at Hackney Wick having just passed under the low railway bridge in Chapman Road. *Mick Webber*

The last new operation for RLHs was on Harrow Weald's 230A which they sometimes worked, on an unofficial basis as RT replacements, between October 1962 and October 1966. Covering it on this occasion is RLH 71, demonstrating that the era of lower case lettering on via displays has now well and truly arrived. *Peter Mitchell*

On 4th November 1964 Godstone's route 410 was at last converted to RT operation, a move made possible by adopting a diversionary route in Oxted to avoid the still-unmodified low bridge, and on 3rd October 1965 Amersham's route 336 succumbed to one-man operation using RFs. Reigate's single RLH, which had continued its Monday to Friday peak hour operation on route 447 even after the main service was converted to RF omo in December 1966, was delicensed on 1st December 1967 and officially replaced by an RF on the following day, while RLH operation at Harrow Weald concluded on 14th June 1969 when the 230 was replaced by flat-fare route H1 using new MBS single deckers. Prior to this, from 10th October 1962, Harrow Weald's RLHs had also made occasional appearances on new RT-worked route 230A (Harrow Weald Garage to Northwick Park) but this had ceased operation on 23rd October 1966. One of the final RLHs at Harrow Weald was RLH 27 which had the honour of being the last green-liveried member of the class to be used on a Central Bus operation.

Route 447 had latterly been a strange mix of one-man operated RFs plus a single crew-worked RLH on its Redhill to Merstham section. This arrangement ceased on 1st December 1967 when RLH 27 was taken out of service and the 447 became fully omo. It was not quite the end of the road for RLH 27 which was returned to service, still in green livery, at Harrow Weald between July 1968 and June 1969. *Gerald Mead*

Within only a few years of the RLHs entering service, the conventional lowbridge double decker with upstairs bench seats was rendered obsolete when full-scale production of the excellent Bristol Lodekka began in 1954. In stark contrast to RLH 11, Thames Valley's no. 766, a 1956-built LD5G, illustrates its low chassis line which eliminated the need for a special seating arrangement on the upper deck. Temporarily carrying Windsor (WR) garage plates, RLH 11 has been borrowed from Guildford to provide rolling stock for a railway replacement service. It was photographed in the covered forecourt of Windsor & Eton station which was not a location normally visited by London Transport vehicles.

75

The selling-off of surplus RLHs began in earnest in 1965 following a tentative start with the departure of RLHs 1 and 4 in December 1964. A few sales took place every year between 1965 and 1969, and they were related not just to the various service withdrawals but also to the ending of the RLH overhaul programme in 1965. Up to that date the policy had been to put all vehicles through their third overhaul cycle, but the abrupt cancellation of this left eleven vehicles that were not dealt with. The last one to emerge from overhaul was RLH 72 on 28th January 1966, after which there was no need to keep five or six vehicles in stock simply to replace others away for overhaul, so these were also sold. By the end of 1969 41 RLHs had been disposed of, leaving just under half the original fleet to enter the new decade of which all but two (RLH 13, 14) were of the second batch.

January 1st 1970 was a momentous date for London's passenger transport. Implementation of the Transport (London) Act 1969 transferred the Central Bus department into municipal control under the aegis of the Greater London Council. The London Transport Board, which had replaced the former London Transport Executive exactly seven years earlier under the Transport Act 1962, now ceased to exist and was replaced by another London Transport Executive. Country Buses, being outside the scope of the GLC's powers, remained within the nationalised sector and its assets were transferred to a new company, London Country Bus Services Ltd. Eighteen RLHs remained with London Transport: RLH 29, 49, 52-55, 57, 58, 61, 64-69, 71-73 (of which RLH 65 was out of use), while London Country inherited seventeen: RLH 13, 14, 21, 24-26, 31-36, 44-47, 50.

London Country's early travails have been widely documented, notably the unfortunate composition of its acquired fleet much of which, when not obsolete and time expired, was unsuited to country operation and ill-equipped to meet current trends within the industry including its inexorable surge towards one-man operation. Apart from new fleet names and legal ownership inscriptions, the eleven RLHs at Addlestone and six at Guildford continued in operation virtually unaltered, but not for long. All had exceeded the 15-year life originally expected of them and would have been of little book value. The end came abruptly on 1st August 1970 when all were delicensed and replaced by one-man operated SM class single deckers. It is believed that RLH 44 was the last one in London Country service on 31st July, their final day of operation. This vehicle was then retained at Addlestone for conversion into a mobile uniform store while the others all went to Garston garage for storage and eventual sale.

Still performing well under new ownership during their final few months of service, vehicles of each batch stand side by side at Staines West station. RLHs 31 and 14 are still in London Transport green but carry the LONDON COUNTRY fleet name of their new owner. Interestingly both display advertisements for seven shilling Green Rovers, the original version complete with London Transport bullseye on RLH 31 and the London Country version, with 'flying polo' symbol, on RLH 14. *Denis Battams*

The end of an era. Route 178 ran for the last time on 16th April 1971, and with its demise the RLH class departed from the London scene. RLH 61 worked the last journey of all at 8.34pm from Maryland Station, suitably adorned with commemorative notices and with its mudguards newly repainted black for the occasion. *Tom Maddocks*

Not long after this, on 19th September 1970, RLH operation ceased at Hornchurch garage when route 248 was revised and, in a much-extended form, taken over by SMS single deckers. The 248A, on which RLHs had also frequently operated, was converted at the same time. This left only the Monday to Saturday 178 operation at Dalston with its maximum requirement of 13 RLHs. These lasted into 1971, but their days were also numbered and arrangements were made for new flat-fare single deck route S3 to replace the 178, although only on its Hackney Wick to Stratford section.

The final day of operation for the RLHs was Friday 16th April 1971 when RLH 61 performed the very last journey. Next day the same vehicle ran a private hire for enthusiasts covering former RLH territory in both central and country areas, bringing the story of the RLH on London Transport to an end after almost 21 years.

All that remained was to dispose of the now-redundant RLHs. With one exception, which went to a scout group in Reigate in December 1970, London Country's were all sold to dealer PVS at Silver End, Essex, in March 1971. The last six on London Transport's books all went for scrap to Wombwell Diesels on 8th September 1972 and, remarkably, these were the only six out of the whole class of 76 that were not put to further use in one form or another after their London careers had ended. As early as 1965 a few had begun to appear with other stage carriage operators, notably RLH 2, 4, 6, 8 which joined the well-known Samuel Ledgard fleet based at Armley, Leeds, RLH 37, 38, 48 with Whippet Coaches who were in those days based at Hilton in Huntingdonshire and, much closer to home, RLH 3, 15, 41 with Super Coaches at Upminster. Some found new lives transporting factory workers with manufacturers such as Elkes Biscuits of Uttoxeter, Trebor-Sharps at Woodford Green and 'Matchbox' toy maker Lesney Products at Hackney.

The most surprising part of the story, however, is the sheer number of RLHs that found a new life overseas where their low height, coupled with their novelty value as London double deckers, found them snapped up for use as tour buses, promotional vehicles, and for various other purposes. Incredibly, no fewer than 53 were exported. Buyers were found in Belgium, Canada, Holland, Italy, New Zealand and Switzerland, but by far and away the most important foreign destination was the USA where 43 RLHs were well distributed amongst a variety of new owners in 13 different states, often repainted in full London Transport red livery to recreate the 'real' London bus experience.

The American connection had begun by pure chance when an enquiry from the Associated Chartered Bus Company of Van Nuys near Burnbank, California resulted in the direct sale to them of RLH 39 in January 1965. This led to a growing number of enquiries from the USA which London Transport was pleased to receive as a better price could be obtained than by selling on the home market. The American demand built up to the extent that every RLH disposed of in 1969 was shipped to the USA. Meanwhile some vehicles that had initially been re-used in this country, such as those with Ledgard and Super Coaches, also found their way across the Atlantic in the late nineteen-sixties. A few more were exported through dealers in the early years of the next decade, and the final sales to American owners were made in 1973. Interestingly, eight out of the ten Midland General 'RLHs' in the batch ONU 630-639 also ended their days in the USA.

Fortunately, a number of preservation projects have taken place over the years, both overseas and in the UK, so the memory of the RLH is far from dead. RLHs 23, 32, 48 and 61 have all appeared on the British rally scene (RLH 32 is currently in Ledgard livery), and so has the former London Country mobile uniform store RLH 44 which was saved for preservation following its withdrawal in April 1982. Deserving special mention is the joint operation by Roger Wright's London Bus Company and the London Bus Preservation Trust to repatriate three RLHs from the USA for preservation in 2012. RLHs 53, 69 and 71 had all been at Dalston on the final day of RLH operation, and had stayed together under various ownerships during their 40 years sojourn in the USA, ending up in Oregon and looking for a new owner. They docked together at Liverpool on 10th April 2012. A remarkable story, and these three met up again on 18th April 2021 at a recreation of their old route 178 fifty years after the last RLHs ran in the central area.

RLHs were no stranger to Upminster before being purchased by Super Coaches (Upminster) Ltd. Looking a little battered, RLH 3 is seen in Romford in May 1967 carrying the 'Upminster & District Motor Services' brand name and it remained in the same ownership until about January 1968. Like RLH 2 (on next page) it ended its working life in the USA. This photograph shows the trafficator repeater lights fitted by London Transport to the rear of RLH 1-20. *David Christie © Chris Stanley*

Opposite top RLH 2 joined the Samuel Ledgard fleet in Yorkshire in February 1965 and is seen at Otley bus station in the following September looking attractive in the blue and grey Ledgard livery. It was bought specifically for the Otley–Horsforth service which required low height double deckers and remained in service until the Ledgard operation was sold to the West Yorkshire Road Car Company in October 1967. In the background are various Ledgard and West Yorkshire double deckers with Ledgard's Otley garage visible in the distance. *Ken Blacker*

RLH 44, the last to operate for London Country, was retained by the Company when all its others were sold and was converted into a mobile uniform store equipped for clothing distribution to staff at garages throughout its widespread operating area. Renumbered 581J it is seen heading south through Brixton in July 1971. It served in this form until April 1982 and has been in preservation since the following January.

The farthest travelled to overseas locations in post-London days were two RLHs which found their way to New Zealand. One of these, RLH 45, still survives. It has been owned by Robbie Murdoch of Auckland, North Island since 1994 and is called 'Daisy'. Although never actually red when in London, RLH 45 has appeared in this form for many years and, when photographed, was undertaking its regular summer (September to May) stint running vineyard tours on Waiheke Island. *Dave Brundrit*

In April 2012 three RLHs were unloaded at Liverpool docks on their way back home after many years in the USA, destined for preservation here. RLH 69 and RLH 71 (along with RLH 53 not shown here) had all latterly been with the proprietors of the Urban Minx fashion firm in Oregon where RLHs 69 and 71 had been restored to running order and virtually full London condition (except for the light-coloured roofs for heat reflection). All three had been present at Dalston on the final day of operation 41 years earlier and, quite extraordinarily, had been together through various ownerships while in the USA. *David Thrower*

LUXURY COACHES – THE RFW CLASS

The clock in the roof records the time as a quarter to twelve in ECW's body shop at Lowestoft. New RFWs are very much in evidence there in the spring of 1951 with the London Transport and Tilling batches both on the same production line. The front panel of the centre vehicle, with plain circular cut for the filler cap, denotes that it is destined for Tilling; the two on either side have provision for the bullseye motif and will be for London Transport.

The unusual and unpremeditated way that the RFW class was brought into existence acted as the first tangible proof that London Transport was no longer master of its own destiny. Nationalisation on 1st January 1948 had brought it under the wing of the British Transport Commission which set up the Road Passenger Executive to handle its bus and coach operations and to which London Transport now reported. It probably came as a surprise to London Transport to receive notice from the BTC on 23rd May 1950 that it could henceforth operate contract carriages well outside its statutorily defined territory known as the London Transport Area, within which all its operations had previously been confined with the exception of a few specified outward runnings to points such as Aylesbury, Tilbury and Tunbridge Wells. The BTC "requested", and London Transport was in no position to disagree, that the latter should now be the BTC's 'agent' for contract carriages to points within 100 miles of 55 Broadway.

London Transport's problem with this arrangement was twofold: it did not have suitable vehicles for this extended operation and nor did it have sufficient staff to take on a big expansion of private hire work. With regard to vehicles, it had settled on a post-war fleet of 25 (24 LTC and one TF) as being adequate to manage its tours programme plus a certain amount of private hire, with hires above this level being fulfilled using ordinary service buses. A new fleet of 25 RFs had just been ordered to replace the pre-war vehicles on a one-for-one basis, and while these were designed to be ideal for urban sightseeing and short distance hires, they lacked the seating comfort and luggage-carrying ability necessary for longer distance work and would be at a disadvantage when compared to modern coaches provided by the multitude of independent operators with whom London Transport could expect to be in competition.

The Commission indicated that it would be prepared to allow London Transport to order up to 20 new coaches beyond its normal vehicle replacement programme and arranged for a new Bristol LWL with Eastern Coach Works body to be made available for inspection. The Commission was particularly keen that the new bodies should be ordered from ECW, which it also controlled. ECW's standard coach body of the time was a full-fronted design built on a hardwood frame using a teak substitute, with curved waist rail and sloping pillars. London Transport rejected it outright, noting that the Bristol chassis was of front-engined layout whereas the market was now moving on to underfloor-engined vehicles, and objecting to its crash gearbox transmission which it claimed would be unacceptable to drivers now used to preselectors and fluid flywheels.

Things moved quickly, and in July 1950 the Commission came back with a compromise proposal. One of the Tilling companies (it did not reveal which one at the time) had ordered a batch of underfloor-engined AEC Regal Mark IV chassis with ECW bodies to full coach specification, and the company concerned would be prepared to release five of these and take Bristols instead. The vehicles would be of the 30ft long layout on two axles which had been permissible since June 1950, 8ft wide, and to a fully luxurious specification capable of carrying 39 passengers.

The Tilling company concerned turned out to be Tillings Transport (BTC) Ltd, the Commission's London-based private hire and touring company which was the last remaining remnant of the once-large London-based Tilling organisation still running vehicles. Its fleet at the time consisted solely of AEC and Bedford coaches and, unusually for a Tilling fleet, it had never run Bristols, presumably on the grounds that these would have been regarded as too coarse and basic for the type of work that it carried out. It had recently ordered ten new 30ft-long 16ft 4ins-wheelbase Regal IVs with a view to making them the flagship of its fleet, as fully luxurious as those of its competitors and well suited to undertake continental work when required as well as home bookings. A brand new style of aluminium alloy framed bodywork to meet the Company's specific requirements was currently being designed at ECW's works in Lowestoft.

It was with trips to mainland Europe in mind that a centrally situated and conveniently wide offside emergency door had been specified with discreet fold-away steps enabling the door to be used as the main access point at continental locations. Tilling's specification also included an outward-opening hinged door on the nearside and full-drop windows, both of which, incidentally, were features that London Transport had discarded as undesirable on its own coaching fleet as long ago as the mid-nineteen thirties. The specification also called for deep comfortable seats with ash trays, corner roof lights, two sliding roof panels, internal heating, public address equipment, interior luggage racks and spacious under-floor locker space for the stowage of suitcases and other large items of luggage. The BTC let it be known that, in accepting five of these vehicles, London Transport should adhere to the Tilling specification so that they could be hired to the latter company if necessary, although there is no subsequent record of this ever having actually taken place or of the London Transport vehicles ever venturing abroad.

London Transport discussed the practicalities of switching part of the contract with representatives of both AEC and ECW, and in the case of the latter inspected the now almost complete body drawings. Both manufacturers promised that delivery could be completed by Easter 1951 just in time for the expected huge influx of incoming tourist traffic for the forthcoming Festival of Britain. In addition, London Transport enquired about the provision of fifteen extra, identical vehicles to form a fleet of twenty coaches suitable for longer distance private hire work which, even if limited in the first instance by staff shortage, could hopefully pick up in future. After negotiating over price, AEC agreed to provide the chassis at the same preferential rate as the new RFs then on order, subject only to any extra costs involved in building to an 8ft width, while ECW was happy to build additional bodies on the same costing basis that applied with all its other nationalised customers: cost price plus 5% for profit.

The decision to go ahead was taken by the London Transport Executive in August, but only for a total of 15 vehicles including the five diverted from Tilling, and approval to place the necessary contracts

Above and facing page Aspects of the rather boxy ECW body are seen in these photographs of RFW 4 and RFW 11. The six glass cove panels on each side throw plenty of light into the interior of the vehicle and, viewed from outside, the seats look comfortable and welcoming. No provision is made for carrying garage recognition plates, but in fact these two coaches both entered service at Chelverton Road garage, RFW 4 on 4th May 1951 and RFW 11 on 1st June. *London Transport Museum*

was received from the BTC on 5th September. A Special Expenditure Requisition was duly issued authorising a total expenditure of £62,935. At an unknown date it was decided that the new coaches would be classified 3RF3 (following on from the 25 1RF1 private hire coaches and 200 2RF2 Green Line vehicles then on order) and they were to be known as the RFW class, the letter W denoting 8ft width in the same manner that had already been adopted in the double deck fleet for the RTWs. In due course body numbers 7404-7418 and registrations LUC 376-390 were allocated to them.

The first RFW chassis was delivered to ECW on 22nd January 1951 and all 15 had reached the Lowestoft factory by 13th March. AEC records show RFW 1-15 as carrying chassis numbers 9821E318-32 in numerical order, but on London Transport records they appear as 9821LT318 etc in line with the special LT classification given to the RF class. They were powered by AEC's standard A219 9.6 litre 120mm x 142mm 125 bhp engine, which was basically the equivalent of the A218 used in double deckers but laid on its side and with modified lubrication and cooling systems to suit, while to achieve quieter running they were equipped with a special Swedish-designed injection system known as Atlas pilot injection. An air pressure system was used for both brake and gearbox operation; steering was of the worm and nut type and a rear axle ratio of $5\frac{1}{6}$:1 was adopted.

The first completed vehicle, RFW 1, made its appearance at Chiswick on 27th April 1951, just three weeks after the first RF had arrived on the scene. Both new batches of hire coaches were completed concurrently with the final RF delivery (RF 25) being on the 18th May followed by the last of the RFWs (RFW 13, 14) on the 29th of the same month. Though very different in appearance from each other, both carried the same attractive new livery of Lincoln green on the lower half of the bodywork with flake grey above. External lettering was in red. A feature common to both was a prominent raised bullseye motif at the front on which the top half of the circular section was hinged to open up and reveal the filler cap. This huge influx of new coaches came just in time to play a full and busy role throughout the summer-long Festival of Britain which opened to the public on 4th May 1951. In fact, demand throughout that glorious and hectic season was such that the 25 pre-war coaches, which were now theoretically redundant, continued in service alongside the new RFs and RFWs until the Festival finally drew to a close.

Beauty lies, of course, in the eye of the beholder, and though the angular RFW body had some advocates there is no doubt that, to the majority who compared it unfavourably with some of the classic coach bodies of the time such as the Burlingham Seagull and the Weymann Fanfare, it looked positively mundane and even ungainly. Such contemporary features as the body styling possessed, for instance, the double width side windows divided by a slender stainless steel strip and the side and head lamps projecting in modernistic half-cone form from the corner curvature of the front body panels were lost in the general squareness of the overall design. Had it not been for the corner glasses at front and back the vehicle would have looked very boxy indeed, and the lack of any destination equipment and the plainness of the front dome left the front looking unusually barren. Particularly surprising was the presence of glass louvres over each of the six opening windows per side, a styling feature from days gone by that had not been used on any new London Transport vehicles since the 'Godstone' STLs of 1934. On the plus side, semaphore-type trafficators were located just ahead of the front corner pillars while there were no fewer than four lights at the rear, including two marker lights on the dome and a lamp on each side at the bottom adjacent to the luggage boot doors.

Even if the exterior of the RFW did not score too highly for its looks, the interior was bright and well thought-out, and though it lacked the decorative adornments of many of its contemporaries it projected an air of comfort and offered a pleasant and comfortable environment to travel in. The wide side windows were all fitted with PYP full-drop mechanisms worked by handles positioned just below the waist rail, and the twelve roof corner lights were all fitted with blinds which could be pulled down when needed to prevent sun glare. The driver was situated within the main saloon with no partition behind him, and the internal heating system served both him and the passengers while the deep windscreens and front side windows gave the driver excellent all-round vision. The luggage racks were positioned so as not to reduce vision through the glass roof panels, and individually worked lights were positioned under them with further lights along the centre of the ceiling, all covered with decorative shades. There were two bell pushes, one on the front panel and the other on the rear dome above the loudspeaker outlet. Seating was all forward-facing with eight pairs on the offside and nine on the nearside plus a bench seat for five at the back, bringing the total to 39. The seats were all made by ECW themselves on hardwood frames with Dunlopillo filling, covered mainly on the front with identical Green Line style moquette as used on RF 1-25 but with extensive use of hide on the headroll, sides and back, including a sunburst design on the latter incorporating the ash tray. Sliding roof sections were built into the first and fifth bays.

Opposite: With the offside door in the open position, the fold-away steps specified by Tilling with continental touring in mind are revealed. It can be safely assumed that the seat blocking the doorway was intended to be removed whenever an overseas trip was to be undertaken, but there is no evidence that the RFWs ever travelled abroad under London Transport ownership. *London Transport Museum*

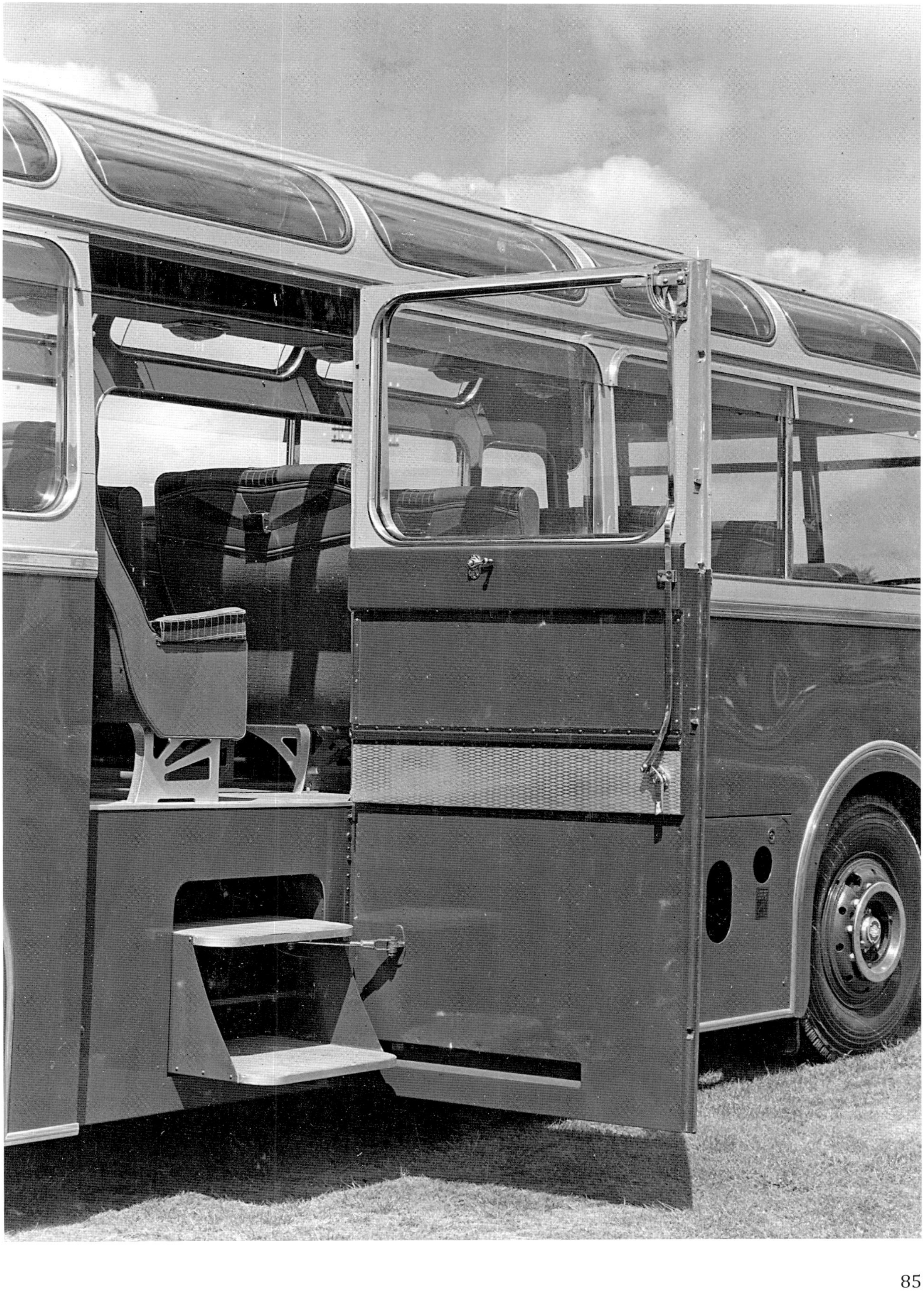

The RFW body lacked the ornate wooden panelwork, fancy floor covering and other 'luxury' features often encountered in touring coach bodies of the time, but the headrolls and 'sunburst' features on the seats helped to establish a semi-sumptuous air and the roof cove lights were a bonus. The overhead luggage racks were designed to keep obstruction of the views through the roof lights to a minimum. The cord hanging from the centre box on the front bulkhead is part of the on-coach communication equipment. *London Transport Museum*

The RFWs were the first 8ft wide and 30ft long vehicles in the bus and coach fleet, and the fact that they were very substantially built was signified by their high unladen weight of 8tons 5cwt. Their heaviness meant that a smooth ride was ensured but without any notable turns of speed being accomplished. They also turned out to be very expensive vehicles to buy, costing £4,765 each as against the £4,196 originally authorised. The main cost over-run was on the bodies where ECW's initial estimate of £2,230 per body ended up in a charge of £2,777.16s.0d each, a substantial over-run of more than 20%. ECW explained that a number of factors contributed to the high price including the need to work large amounts of overtime to meet London Transport's request for delivery in time for the Festival of Britain, while the relatively small number of bodies in the batch did not justify expenditure on what would normally be regarded as an adequate scale of tooling resulting in many items being hand made. Clearly embarrassed by the high charge, ECW waived its normal 5% charge for profit which meant that the bodies were supplied purely at cost.

The 15 RFW bodies and the five almost identical ones for Tilling were built as a single batch, ECW's order book showing them with body numbers 5465-5479 for the RFWs and 5480-5484 for the Tillings (none of which were matched to the chassis in strict numerical sequence). The Tilling vehicles, registered LYM 728-732, were painted in the group's then-standard coach livery of cream with black mudguards, the plainness of which made them look even more austere and uncoachlike than the RFWs. The polished moulding separating the green from the grey on the RFWs was missing from the Tilling batch, and a narrower moulding, placed lower down on the sides only did nothing to alleviate the slab-sided appearance of these vehicles. At the front, the raised bullseye motif covering the filler cap aperture on the RFWs was replaced by a circular device with the word TILLING embossed on it.

To complete the Tilling part of the story, it should be recorded that their five 'RFWs' lasted only until 1960 when the bodies were removed and sold to a dealer. LYM 728-732 were then fitted with new MW-style ECW coach bodies and ran in this form until they were sold out of service in 1964.

The plain cream livery for coaching stock imposed from Tilling group headquarters on its operating companies emphasised the RFWs' somewhat boxy lines even more than their London Transport counterparts. LYM 732 was photographed in Leeds in August 1958 during its penultimate season carrying its original body. It illustrates that Tilling did not try to embellish the vehicles by fitting decorative rear wheel discs as London Transport had done, and it also shows the additional small grille on the bottom front panel subsequently fitted to all five, perhaps for brake cooling purposes. LYM 729 was little more than a year old when seen during a stopover at Keswick in July 1952. The Tilling vehicles carried a glass-fronted name panel at the back capable of being illuminated after dark, which London Transport omitted when drawing up the specification for its own RFW bodies. *John Cockshott*

Seven of the new RFW coaches were licensed for service between 3rd and 9th May 1951 with the remainder following later in the month and in June as the summer tourist trade picked up. It had been decided beforehand that, although the majority would be based at Central Bus garages, roughly a third would go to the country area where it was thought a pent-up demand for them existed. As had been the case in pre-war days, no garage plates were carried on the luxury coach fleet so it was not possible to determine by sight which garage any individual vehicle was running from. The initial allocation was, in fact, as follows:

Central Buses
Chelverton Road (AF)	RFW 4, 11, 15
Dalston (D)	RFW 1, 8, 9
Old Kent Road (P)	RFW 2, 7, 13

Country Buses
Leavesden Road (WT)	RFW 5
Northfleet (NF)	RFW 10
Reigate (RG)	RFW 3
Romford (RE)	RFW 6, 14
Windsor (WR)	RFW 12

Barely had they entered service when a few bodywork modifications had to be made. The wings had to be replaced using new fitments supplied by ECW to facilitate wheel removal, the loudspeaker system needed rewiring to avoid interference noises, stronger locks were required on the luggage compartment doors, and a revised type of towing bracket had to be installed. Thereafter, apart from the subsequent removal of the pilot injection system in line with vehicles in the RF class, the RFWs performed steadily and reliably on a pattern requiring the whole fleet to be in service during the summer months, reducing to between 8 and 11 active each winter according to passenger demand. The winter of 1953/54 was the only one in their whole career when all fifteen remained in use.

With the passage of time the schedule of garages to which the RFWs were allocated fluctuated. From as early as October 1951 Riverside was added to the list of Central Bus locations holding an RFW allocation, and in June 1952 Garston took over from Leavesden Road when the latter closed. In March 1954 Dalston's four RFWs were transferred to Athol Street, and when the latter closed on 10th May 1961 its RFWs moved to the former trolleybus

Windsor was a destination regularly included on the itinerary for the RFWs as part of the very popular half day tour on which they frequently participated. RFW 1 is seen parked up on the distinctive cobbled surface of Thames Street with the castle wall close by. *Frank Mussett*

depot at Poplar. After Old Kent Road's closure on 26th November 1958 responsibility for its RFWs was split between New Cross and Camberwell. More significantly, the stabling of RFWs at Country Bus garages had not been a great commercial success and it ceased completely after the 1954 summer season with the exception of Romford, and the vehicles concerned were transferred into the central area where an additional RFW base was set up at Victoria garage.

The end came in rather a sad way and was linked to London Transport's gradual decline brought about by its ever-worsening staff shortage. By the early nineteen-sixties the operation of commercial private hire work had become increasingly difficult to arrange and hard to justify at a time when the coverage of scheduled daily services was proving ever more problematic, and the summer seasons of 1962 and 1963 both saw only 14 out of the 15 RFWs licensed for service. A dispute with staff over the continuation of private hire work led to all RFWs being withdrawn from Central Bus service on 1st October 1963 never to return, and from the summer season of 1964 onwards all of the department's touring and private hire work was contracted out to private operators. The Country Bus department continued in the hiring market for a little longer. Romford was still the only operational base and a single RFW was allocated there throughout the winter of 1963/64. The summer season of 1964 found four RFWs (RFW 1, 6, 11, 14) at Romford, but when these were delicensed at the end of the summer season, on 1st October 1964, their demise brought operation of the class by London Transport to a permanent halt.

RFW 8 was probably on a private hire job from Dalston garage when it was photographed on a sunny day cruising along Victoria Embankment. The new surface on this section of roadway is a recently-installed replacement for the tram tracks that once carried such an intensive service along here. Now RFW 8 is the only public transport vehicle in sight. This was one of ten RFWs taken out of service at the end of the 1963 summer season and subsequently sold to the Ceylon Transport Board. *London Transport Museum*

Almost at the end of its London career, RFW 6 is seen crossing Lambeth Bridge with a full load on board. At thirteen years old, it had barely altered in appearance from when it was new in 1951. The only visible change is that green paint now covers the once bright wheel embellishments and the decorative strip around the bottom of the bodywork. RFW 6 was one of four still running in service until 1964 from Romford Green Line garage. *London Transport Museum*

In the knowledge that no further use was likely to be found for them the RFWs were put up for sale and departed from the London Transport fleet between September 1964 and January 1965, the last of all to leave being RFW 6 on 8th January. All of them would have been in good condition having undergone two full overhauls during their time with London Transport whilst accumulating relatively low operated mileages. Ten found a ready buyer in the Ceylon Transport Board which took over ownership of them on 30th December 1964. Although none found renewed commercial use for any length of time within the UK, one (RFW 11) operated in the Keneally Bus Service fleet at Waterford in the Irish Republic from about April 1966 for some seven years. However, the best remembered, and probably most photographed, were RFWs 1, 6 and 14 which could often be seen out and about on London streets until 1970 working as staff transport for St Thomas's Hospital. One of these, RFW 14, has since been an active participant in the preservation scene for many years, ensuring that the class is not forgotten, and RFW 6 has also been the subject of a preservation project.

The 'RFW' bodies were far from worn out when discarded by Tilling and quickly found new buyers. In this instance one of the bodies is on a Regal IV chassis formerly in the Western SMT fleet and now owned by A & G Taylor of Glasgow. It now has the benefit of an additional front grille, a lower glass panel in the door, and flashing trafficators, but the distinctive outline of the RFW body remains unmistakable. *R H G Simpson*

RFW 1 was one of only four that pursued a post-London Transport career in England, three of which retained quite a high profile working a staff contract on behalf of St Thomas's Hospital in London until 1970. Largely unaltered from its original condition apart from the fitment of modern trafficators, and displaying a few small knocks, RFW 1 is the only one of the three that has failed to survive to the present day.
Michael Dryhurst

The ten RFWs sold in December 1964 to the Ceylon Transport Board were well maintained by its Special Tours Division and gave good service there, the body from RFW 7 being subsequently transferred to a newer, Leyland Tiger Cub Chassis. Ceylon was renamed Sri Lanka when it became an independent republic in June 1972 but the CTB initials were retained, and the former RFW 5 is seen still in its service at Trincomalee in August 1980. It was then 29 years old and still looking quite sprightly.
Ken Blacker

Following its post-London Transport career conveying staff to and from St Thomas's Hospital, RFW 14 has been in preservation for very many years looking just as it did in London Transport days. It was photographed at Gisleham Middle School in Suffolk during an Eastern Coach Works commemorative event organised in 1997 by the East Anglia Transport Museum. *Tim Major*

ONE-MAN GUYS – THE GS CLASS

Sparkling new, and showing barely any road dust even on its newly blackened tyres, GS 2 was the first completed vehicle to reach London Transport a week ahead of any others. Still with its Eastern Coach Works delivery labels in the windows, it already carries blinds for Hitchin garage to which it was allocated on 8th October 1953.

The GS class will always rank as one of the most aesthetically pleasing single deck designs ever produced by London Transport. In addition to its good looks it succeeded in fulfilling reliably and reasonably economically the duties expected of it while gaining the respect of staff and passengers alike. The sadness is that it came upon the scene just as circumstances were changing radically, both within the passenger transport industry and on a wider social scale. Because of this the full class of 84 vehicles never came anywhere near to achieving its full potential and many GSs fell well short of reaching their anticipated 12-year working lifespan with London Transport.

In the years immediately following the end of the Second World War, London Transport had been faced with horrendous problems over fleet maintenance and replacement, and it was not until the latter part of 1950 that the Executive was able to focus its attention on finding replacements for its comparatively small fleet of C and CR class one-man operated single deckers (which were nearly always referred to internally under the generic term of 'Cubs' irrespective of class). The relative modernity of these vehicles, coupled with the low mileage operated by many of them, had initially placed them well down the priority list for replacement, but increasing age and spiralling difficulties in sourcing spare parts, especially for the CRs, meant that something now had to be done.

The question of what sort of vehicle to seek for the future was clouded because of internal uncertainty over whether to opt for 20-seaters or slightly larger vehicles seating 26, or a mixture of both. Construction & Use Regulations still basically restricted one-man operated stage carriage operations to 20-seaters although a modification of 1941 permitted vehicles with up to 26 seats to be used on specified routes provided that authority was received to do so. London Transport's Cub routes were all heavily loss-making with pence-per-mile receipts ranging from a mere 8.2d on Swanley's route 479 to 11.7d on the 333 at Hertford and 485 at Chelsham, with just one notable exception, the recently acquired ex-independent Loudwater estate bus 336A being the only Cub route to take more than a shilling per mile at 13.1d. The problem was that, despite these pathetically low takings, some peak-hour and Saturday afternoon journeys were over-subscribed meaning that duplicates had to be run, thereby making the operation even more loss making. The availability of 26-seaters would rule out the need for duplicates, and the Country Bus & Coach department was keen to investigate getting some of these. Fortunately, at some time in 1951, the Metropolitan Traffic Commissioner issued a 'blanket' approval for the use of 26-seaters on all of London Transport's one-man services. This settled the matter, but not before enquiries had already been made with a variety of manufacturers about the provision of both 20 and 26-seaters.

Only two manufacturers responded positively to London Transport's request for the supply of normal control 20 and 26-seaters, Ford and Guy. Ford offered its 13ft 1in wheelbase Fordson Thames model as a 20-seater which it was prepared to extend to 14ft 9ins to accommodate 26 seats. This was principally a goods chassis although a few had been sold for psv use and appeared to be operating satisfactorily. The Thames was a well-known model distinguished by its modern and curvaceous front end incorporating scuttle, bonnet and front wings supplied to Ford's by Briggs Motor Bodies of Dagenham who were also its main supplier of car bodies, and it could be offered in diesel powered form with a Perkins P6 Mark IV lightweight 4.73 litre indirect injection engine, rated 86bph at 2,600rpm. Guy offered its Wolf model with 13ft 0ins wheelbase as a 20-seater and its Vixen 14ft 9ins 26-seater as an alternative. Both of these Guy models were, effectively, goods or passenger chassis and the Vixen was often built in forward-control form, although it was the normal-control version that interested London Transport. In their diesel-engined form both would normally have been powered by the 4-cylinder Perkins P4, but in the knowledge that London Transport required more power than this the Perkins P6 was offered for the Vixen with the option of a Gardner 4LW as an alternative. In fact, although it was of compact design, the P6 could not be fitted into the Vixen chassis frame in its standard form and Guy's intention was to use a modified version of its heavier Otter chassis to help it gain this prestigious contract, although the vehicles in question were always referred to by Guy, both in correspondence and for publicity purposes, as Vixens.

Meanwhile, London Transport turned to the question of obtaining bodies for the new chassis and was directed by the British Transport Commission to approach Eastern Coach Works at Lowestoft. The Commission was anxious to find work for ECW which, like chassis manufacturer Bristol, had been prohibited under the terms of the Transport Act 1947 from accepting orders from outside the Commission for manufactured goods since its sale to them on 5th November 1948. As a result ECW was now short of orders to fill its 1952 work programme and was only too pleased to accept a contract from London Transport, even though the proposed bodies were well outside its normal production range which had not included any bonneted chassis since 1940.

At about the same time, during the early months of 1951, London Transport decided that, if 26-seaters were ordered, the exact number of new vehicles would be 84, made up as follows:

Current operational requirements for 20-seaters (less 2 saved on conversion)	53
Future augmentations of existing routes	3
Substitution of 26-seaters for larger vehicles	14
Engineers' spares and overhaul float (at 20%)	14
Total	84

Behind the scenes, development work was sufficiently advanced for detailed body drawings to be produced in April 1951 covering both 20 and 26-seat variants of the proposed new bus on both Ford and Guy chassis. The body, which was designed in the drawing office at Chiswick, bore many of the same characteristics for both lengths of vehicle, the only notable external difference being that the 26-seater had four equal-sized side window bays whereas the 20-seater would have employed only three full-length bays with a shorter one at the back. As far as the seating arrangement was concerned

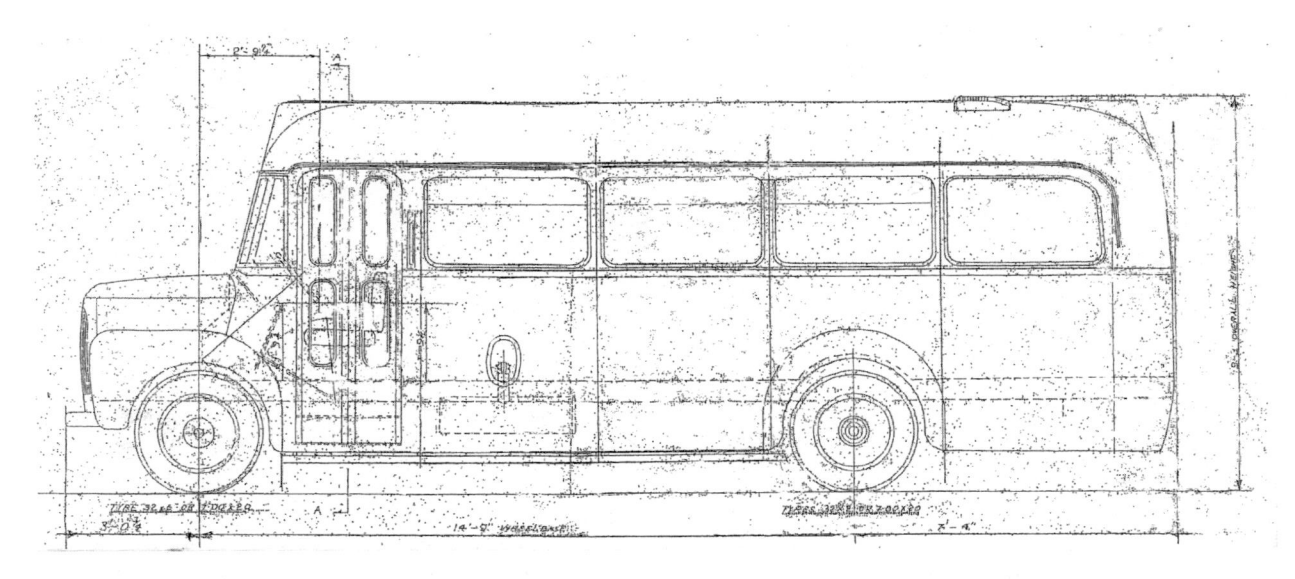

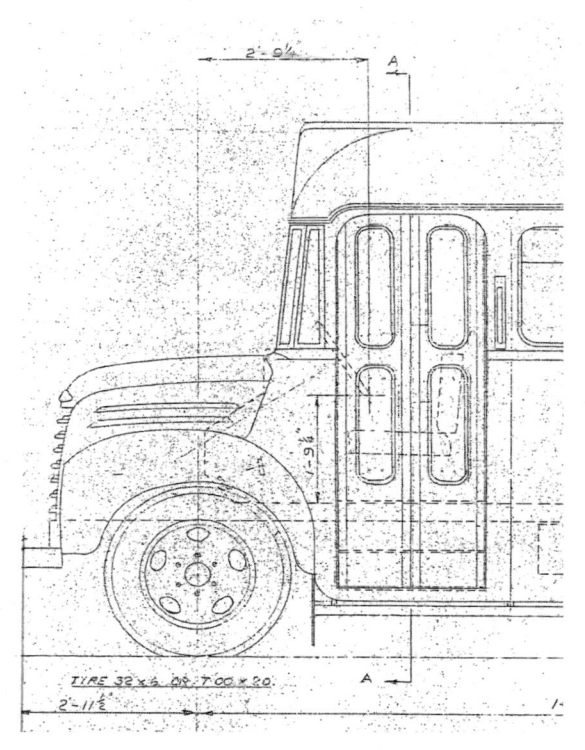

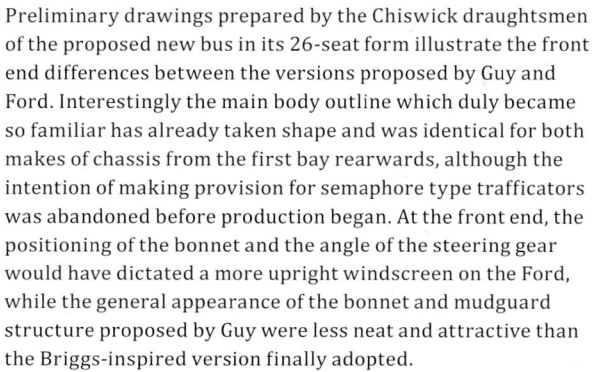

Preliminary drawings prepared by the Chiswick draughtsmen of the proposed new bus in its 26-seat form illustrate the front end differences between the versions proposed by Guy and Ford. Interestingly the main body outline which duly became so familiar has already taken shape and was identical for both makes of chassis from the first bay rearwards, although the intention of making provision for semaphore type trafficators was abandoned before production began. At the front end, the positioning of the bonnet and the angle of the steering gear would have dictated a more upright windscreen on the Ford, while the general appearance of the bonnet and mudguard structure proposed by Guy were less neat and attractive than the Briggs-inspired version finally adopted.

The front-end body mock-up produced in the Chiswick experimental shop in 1952 on a chassis section provided by Guy was fully painted in Country Bus livery carrying fleet number GS 1. A particularly nice touch was the painted Guy 'Feathers in Our Cap' emblem on the bonnet top mounted above the enamelled LONDON TRANSPORT emblem. Apart from a modified ventilation arrangement on the bonnet sides, the insertion of air intakes in the front dash and the addition of ribbed plates on top of the mudguards, this represented the GS design in its final form.

both had three rows of double forward-facing seats at the front, the difference lying beyond this where the 20-seater had inward-facing sets for two over each wheel arch followed by one more forward-facing pair whereas the 26-seater accommodated three seats over each wheel arch with two forward-facing rows beyond.

Both chassis manufacturers submitted their quotations in May 1951 with Guy's coming in at £170 more per vehicle than the Ford for the 26-seater. It appears to have been about this time that London Transport finally abandoned the idea of obtaining any more 20-seaters and all future development work was based on the larger vehicle. With both manufacturers offering simple, straight-framed chassis powered by the Perkins P6 engine and with crash gearbox transmission, other factors had to be taken into account when deciding which to purchase. The ultimate decision to go for the Guy Vixen despite its higher initial cost was influenced principally by its more substantial construction guaranteed to give a life span of 12 years as against only 8 for the Ford, arising from which annual depreciation costs would be lower for the Guy at £66 per vehicle as against £89 for the Ford. Ford proposed to take a standard chassis and extend it to achieve the required wheelbase, which was seen by London Transport as disadvantageous in that it would involve extra weight without adding anything to the overall robustness, and a further factor in favour of the Guy was that it had a smaller turning circle, which London Transport considered beneficial.

A feature which London Transport wished to retain from the Ford Thames specification was its Briggs front end which was both neater and more compact than the one proposed by Guy as well as being visually more attractive. This was Briggs' own design and similar but individually different versions of it had also been manufactured for Dodge trucks built at Kew and for the Leyland Comet bus and truck range. Guy approached Briggs who agreed to supply the required number of bonnet assemblies suitably modified and re-styled during the production process to suit the Guy chassis. The most visible modification from the design mass-produced for Ford was an amended radiator grille which neatly incorporated Guy's well-known Red Indian emblem above the Company's "Feathers in Our Cap" slogan mounted on a hinged flap covering the radiator filler cap, and the LONDON TRANSPORT bullseye monogram incorporated in a rectangle at the top of the front grille. The grille itself, which had a polished outline to resemble a conventional radiator, was partly attached to the bonnet top and could be lifted, with the lower half on the fixed panel below between the wings.

Although Guy referred to the 84 London chassis as being Vixens, London Transport always referred to them as 'Guy Specials' from which the GS class designation was derived. This was the second occasion on which it was used, the earlier GSs having been a very different type of Guy, the large FCX type six-wheeled double decker that had died out from the London fleet in 1935.

The procurement process for the new GSs, which was already well advanced, moved towards a conclusion on 10th December 1951 when a detailed joint report from the Chief Mechanical Engineer and the Operating Manager (Country Buses & Coaches) recommending the purchase was accepted by the Executive, following which approval was sought from the British Transport Commission on 3rd January 1952 to officially proceed. Approval was rapidly given, just five days later, with the Commission commenting that it was pleased to note that the body contract was going to ECW. Formal approval from the London Transport Executive then followed on 17th January at a cost of £116,130 for the bodies and £83,975 for the chassis, or just over £2,382 per complete vehicle. At the time it was anticipated that chassis construction would begin in mid-1952 and that the whole batch would be completed by the end of the year, but events were to prove that this expectation was somewhat over-optimistic.

Both manufacturers appear to have been unprepared for the deep level of involvement and scrutiny that London Transport would take in the design and manufacturing process. Guy, in particular, seem to have underestimated the amount of design work that would be required to comply with London Transport's requirements, coupled to which external pressure was being placed on

The GS was arguably one of the most aesthetically pleasing normal control bus designs ever produced. Although its London Transport ancestry was immediately evident, especially through its livery similarity to the RF, the ECW influence was also visible thanks to the distinctive window pans and the type of sliding window used in them. GS 17 arrived at Leatherhead garage as a CR replacement and went on to perform a fulfilling 17 year operational career with London Transport and London Country. *G A Rixon*

its resources through the growing demands of the nation's re-armament response to developments behind the Iron Curtain. London Transport's evolving requirements included a lengthening of the wheelbase from the originally planned 14ft 9ins to 15ft 0ins with a consequent shortening of the rear overhang, a move believed to have been related to re-siting the battery cages from the front of the chassis beneath the driver's seat to the very rear, requiring a major weight redistribution at the back end.

London Transport set up a series of so-called Technical Liaison meetings, usually held at Wolverhampton or Lowestoft, to review progress and to deal with any problems or difficulties that may have arisen. Very little of substance appears to have happened for much of 1952 although a front end chassis 'mock-up', complete with bonnet and wings, was constructed by Guy and sent to the experimental shop at Chiswick where a section of body structure was added to it to demonstrate the finalised design for the driver's position and entrance step arrangement. Constructed on a wooden framework and fully painted in country area green and cream, it was lettered GS 1 and showed the styling and livery that London Transport required in the finished product. This mock-up was subsequently sent to ECW at Lowestoft, and when Guy wanted its chassis unit back in April 1953 the body section was removed from it and remained at the coachworks mounted on stilts.

At some time during the closing months of 1952 Guy arranged for the first two chassis to be completed as prototypes for the forthcoming fleet. Chassis NLLVP44208P, which was intended for GS 1, was completed and extensively tested by Guy before being delivered to London Transport at Chiswick where it underwent further testing. The date of its arrival at Chiswick is uncertain, but it is known to have passed from there to Eastern Coach Works for examination early in January 1953, and certainly by the 15th at the latest. After a brief return to Wolverhampton for general servicing it returned to Chiswick on 2nd February 1953 on which date it was officially taken on to London Transport's books. GS 2's chassis had now been assembled and tested, and after examination at Chiswick arrived at ECW's works on 8th April 1953, although several months were yet to elapse before a start was made on building a body for it.

ECW had the problem that the GS bodies had missed their allotted production slot in 1952 and now had to somehow be fitted into the 1953 programme. Meanwhile, the production run of new GS chassis had now got under way, albeit somewhat spasmodically at first, with the delivery of GS 3-6 direct to Lowestoft on 30th April. Disquiet about the steering arrangements on them led to the chassis of GS 6 being sent to Aldenham towards the end of May and then back to Guy to receive a revised steering drop arm and drag link, features which were then incorporated into all chassis built subsequently and retrofitted by ECW into the five that had already been delivered. Series production of the new chassis began at Wolverhampton in May with a steady flow arriving at Lowestoft from the 21st onwards. Although ECW was still not yet ready to start construction work on the bodies, its mechanical inspectors examined each new chassis upon arrival and reported various defects and inconsistencies that had occurred during assembly and needed to be put right. London Transport took these observations seriously and arranged for the new chassis of GS 34 to be sent direct from Wolverhampton to its Aldenham Works on 24th July and thence to Chiswick for close examination by the Rolling Stock department. A Technical Meeting was subsequently convened at which it was arranged for a party of fitters from Guy to be sent to ECW on 24th August to make alterations and correct defects on items such as exhaust pipes, battery cradles, front cross beams, and the front dash and floor plate structures on chassis that had already been delivered. Meanwhile, GS 34's chassis remained with London Transport for a while and did not finally arrive at ECW until 29th September.

With a regular inflow of new chassis now established, Technical Liaison Meeting no. 39 held at Lowestoft on 18th and 19th August 1953 was able to record that progress was at last being made on construction of the first body. The completion date for this had originally been pencilled in for June but this deadline had been missed. Even at this late stage London Transport could not resist specifying amendments to the design, one of which was to eliminate the fitment of a reversing light at the rear of the body. Unfortunately these lights had already been purchased, and London Transport was obliged to buy the fittings from ECW with a suggestion in June 1954 that they might come in handy in the future as step lamp assemblies. The first completed vehicle, GS 2, was delivered to Aldenham on 2nd October 1953 followed by GSs 1 and 3 on the 8th. Thereafter a steady flow of the type was achieved with the last delivery of all, GS 84, arriving on 21st January 1954.

At the rear the GS bore a superficial similarity to the RF although its proportions were, if anything, neater. GS 32 entered service at Dunton Green in November 1953 and was photographed later in the same month by which time advertising material had been pasted on the back panels. A reversing light and rear reflectors had still to be applied at this stage.
London Transport Museum

The GS was quite a novelty when it was first introduced, not least because it appeared so much more sleek and modern than the now-outdated Cubs that it was replacing, as well as being more impressively large and robust. With an overall length of 25ft 0½ins, it was demonstrably longer than the Cub, and taller too, with its unladen height of 9ft 6¼ins exceeding that of the Cub by more than 1ft. It was similar only in its width, 7ft 5½ins. The Perkins P6 engine was of a well-proven design (it dated from 1937) and gave all the performance that was required of it even though London Transport de-rated it for economy reasons down to 65bhp at 2,200rpm. Thanks, presumably, to the provision of superior noise insulation, it sounded much less raucous and far more refined than it did when mounted as a conversion kit in chassis such as the Bedford OB or Commer Commando. The fact that the GS was fitted with a 4-speed constant mesh gearbox and conventional clutch instead of London Transport's preferred preselector and fluid flywheel did nothing to detract from its acceptance by staff who had been well used to handling crash gearboxes anyway. In typical Guy fashion the gear change gate was reversed from the customary arrangement, with first and second gear on the right of the gate instead of the normal left, while the gear lever stick was sited on the left of the steering column instead of to the right of it as on the Cubs. The drive from the gearbox led into a spiral bevel rear axle with a ratio of 5.7:1, and a Lockheed hydraulic braking system proved effective and gave confidence in the vehicles' stopping ability. The little Guy Specials ran reasonably economically at about 15.25mpg and proved much more versatile, especially at hill climbing, than the Cubs had been. Their only real drawback seems to have been that the P6 engine was a comparatively heavy user of oil which tended to sludge, resulting in complete oil changes being required more frequently than on most other engines.

In constructing the bodywork, Eastern Coach Works adapted London Transport's detailed drawings – which specified the contours, styling and dimensions – to suit its own standard method of construction. ECW was one of the few manufacturers at the time to standardise on aluminium alloy for its body framework which combined hollow section flanged pillars and roof sticks with extruded section continuous waist and cant rails, all solid riveted or bolted together as required and with 'Chobert' rivets holding mouldings and finishers in place rather than screws. All interior lining and stress panels were also in aluminium. Timber was only used structurally for the floor cross bearers and these were reinforced on each side by aluminium alloy plates. The window pans and aluminium-framed sliding windows were all very obviously standard ECW fitments.

Despite the presence of many standard London Transport fittings such as seats, wooden floor slats, fareboard holder and ticket box, bell cord etc, there was no disguising the ECW influence on the interior of the GS body. This was particularly noticeable in the completely flat side panelling which gave a small but useful gain in internal body width compared with other makes, and was covered in brown leathercloth up to the window line and green above. Above the windows, a standard LT section cream cantrail moulding with insert red line was a reminder of RT decor. Partitions were installed at the rear of the entrance door and behind the driver, and an unusual feature was that the nearside windscreen window was designed as an escape hatch which could be easily pushed out in an emergency. Electrically-operated jack-knife doors with finger pull to permit manual opening if necessary were fitted at the main entrance and the usual hinged emergency door was installed at the centre rear.

With an unladen weight of exactly 4 tons the GS was only one hundredweight heavier than the Leyland Cub, a remarkable achievement to which the use of so much aluminium in its structure no doubt contributed, with a seat-to-weight ratio approximately 12% better than on the Cub. Classified as 1GS1, the vehicles received London Transport body numbers 8166-8249 and had matching registration numbers MXX 301-384. Their chassis numbers, which spanned between NLLVP44208P and 45066, were intermixed with other Guy vehicle production and were probably a good guide as to how busy fulfilling orders the Company was at that time.

Plenty of standard London Transport fixtures were immediately apparent within the neat interior of the GS body including the seats and their upholstery, the bell cord, hand rails, all the signage, and even the floor with its prominent stained wooden slats. There was also no mistaking the ECW influence in the neat, flat-profiled pillars and the sliding windows. *London Transport Museum*

The final cost of the whole GS project worked out at £233,310 (or £2,777.10s.0d per bus), a significant 16.6% overrun on the amount originally budgeted, and this was after London Transport had disputed ECW's charges and obtained a rebate of £30 per body. An audit inspection found that, whilst unavoidable rises in the price of materials and labour had occurred, higher costs than anticipated for inspection and finishing had arisen and the cost of the mock-up had also to be taken into account.

Long before the first GS was ready for service a list of future allocations was drawn up by the management/union Bus Allocation Advisory Sub-Committee showing the order of priority by garages which was as follows:

Priority	Garage	Routes		Requirement	Spare	Total
1	Hitchin (HN)	383	Hitchin–Weston	1	1	2
2	Chelsham (CM)	464	Holland–Westerham			
		465	Holland–Edenbridge	7	1	8
		485	Westerham–Edenbridge			
			Duplication	1	1	2
3	Hertford (HG)	333/B	Hertford–Chapmore End	4	1	5
		329/A	Datchworth–Hitchin/Hertford	1	–	1
		388	Hertford–Mardley Hill	1	-	1
4	Leatherhead (LH)	481	Epsom–Wells Estate	1	-	1
			Duplication	1	-	1
4A	Swanley (SJ)	478	Swanley–Wrotham	1	-	1
		479	Swanley–Dartford	1	-	1
5	Dunton Green (DG)	471	Orpington Circular	5	1	6
6	Guildford (GF)	448/A	Guildford–Ewhurst/Pewley Way	4	1	5
7	Dorking (DS)	449	Dorking–Ewhurst	2	1	3
		433	Coldharbour–Ranmore	1	-	1
8	Epping (EP)	393	Harlow–Hoddesdon	2	1	3
		381	Epping–Toothill	1	-	1
9	Northfleet (NF)	450	Dartford–Gravesend	2	-	2
		490/A	Gravesend–Hartley Court	5	1	6
			Duplication	1	-	1
10	East Grinstead (EG)	494	East Grinstead–Oxted	1	-	1
			Duplication	1	-	1
11	Amersham (MA)	384/397	Chesham–St Leonards/Tring	5	1	6
		373/398	Beaconsfield–Penn/Amersham	4	-	4
			Duplication	1	-	1
12	Garston (GR)	336A	Rickmansworth–Loudwater	1	-	1
13	Tring (TG)	387	Tring–Aldbury	1	1	2
			Totals	56	11	67

At many of the fourteen garages with one-man operations, journeys scheduled for positioning purposes, factories and schools would have found GSs appearing from time to time carrying a whole variety of route numbers additional to those listed above, such was the complexity of scheduling within the Country Bus & Coach department. *(Full details of all the services that GSs operated and of the various changes to them while with London Transport are not given in this chapter but can be found in 'GS – The London Guy Special' by Peter Aves and Alan Charman – Capital Transport, 2019).*

For a few days in October 1953 it was possible to find Cubs and GSs working actively together until driver training was fully completed and the Cubs could be removed. The difference in height and stature between the old and new types is illustrated in Chelsham garage yard where GS 1 and GS 9 stand either side of C 59. *Michael Dryhurst*

The Cub replacement programme proceeded exactly as planned with the garage sequence remaining unchanged from the published schedule except that, because of the special circumstances described in the Pre-War volume, Garston's route 336A could not be dealt with and the Cub continued running it well into 1954. With this one exception, the GS reigned supreme on one-man operation from 1st January 1954 onwards.

At the start of the introduction programme a system was adopted of allocating a licensed GS ahead of the main allocation specifically for staff training purposes. Thus Hitchin garage received the very first one to be licensed, GS 2, on 8th October 1953, followed by Chelsham (GS 3), Hertford (GS 4) and Leatherhead (GS 5) on the 13th. Chelsham, with its larger training requirement than other garages, also received GS 1 on the 14th. It can never be known for certain when the actual first day of GS operation in service occurred as this would have been dependent upon when training was completed. At all the garages mentioned above, Cubs were retained for a few days after the full GS allocation was in place, partly as a back-stop in case early mechanical problems arose on the GSs and also to cater for staff who might have been sick or on holiday when initial training took place and had to continue working with a Cub until an instructor became available to deal with them. Thus Hitchin, Chelsham and Leatherhead had both types of vehicle licensed up to an including 31st October and Hertford until 8th November. Swanley and Dunton Green, which received their first GSs on 6th and 10th November respectively, similarly retained a Cub or two for a few days longer. It must be noted here that the old vehicles displaced were all traditional bonneted C class Cubs except at Leatherhead where two rear-engined CRs were replaced, the only members of their class ever to be directly ousted by the new GSs.

By the time that staff at the last few garages needed training on GSs there were enough available vehicles of this type around the fleet to permit inter-garage borrowing, so specific vehicles were no longer allocated in advance of the main allocation for this purpose. At Guildford, Dorking and Epping the Cubs all ceased running on 30th November and GSs took over the next day. Northfleet, East Grinstead and Amersham kept both types for a few days in December but all the Cubs at these locations, plus those at Tring, were delicensed on 1st January 1954 when, with the exception of the single bus at Garston, the Cub replacement programme was complete. Sixty-eight GSs had now been licensed for service, with work still having to be found for GS 67, 69, 71-84 stored unlicensed in Garston garage.

101

GS 40 was one of the four placed into service at Epping garage on 1st December 1953 on routes 381 and 393 and is seen on the former at the Toothill terminus four weeks later. Like most early GS deliveries, it remained at its original garage until it was delicensed prior to its first overhaul which, in this case, was on 1st September 1956.
Peter Mitchell

A mixture of old and new neatly lined up in Garston garage waiting either their first call to duty or for a dealer to come and collect them. The scrap vehicles on the right include C 56 and C 42, and instantly recognisable among the defunct STLs at the back is one of the former Blackwall Tunnel vehicles with its exaggeratedly domed roof. Behind the as-yet unused GSs are brand new RTLs for which no immediate work is available and which are destined to be mothballed here for up to 3½ years. The GSs (from left to right GS 82, 78, 69, 79, 74, 73) were all put into service between April and December 1954. *G A Rixon*

After being a storage centre for surplus GSs, Garston became an operator of them in May 1954, receiving two on 1st May to provide an operating vehicle plus a spare for route 336A and a further three on the 19th for the 309 and 361. Three of these are seen meeting up on the stand at Rickmansworth soon afterwards. GS 76 is on the 309, GS 67 has come in from its Loudwater outstation on the 336A, and the unidentifiable one in the foreground is presumably working the 361. *Alan Nightingale collection*

Gradually, during 1954, more of the GSs were put into service. On 14th April two were licensed at Hertford ready to replace crew-operated single deckers on the 21st: one of the last remaining 10T10s still in service and two RFs. The routes affected were 389 (Hertford-Sawbridgeworth) and the market day 386 along with positioning journeys on 386A. The 386 linked Buntingford with Bishops Stortford on Tuesdays and Hitchin on Thursdays with a through Bishops Stortford-Hitchin operation only at weekends. Next garage on the list was Garston where the Cub on 336A, which outstationed at Loudwater, was finally replaced on 1st May. Later in the same month, on the 19th, routes 309 (Rickmansworth-Harefield) and 361 (Rickmansworth-Chorleywood) changed over from post-war 15T13s to GSs, also worked from Garston. On 12th July GSs were introduced to Windsor garage on routes 442 (Slough-Farnham Royal) and 445 (Windsor-Datchet Common) in place of RTs.

The final GS introduction of 1954 was in a different category from the others and introduced the class to Crawley garage as a direct result of the financial failure of F H Kilner (Transport) Ltd. One of Basil Williams's sprawling range of Hants & Sussex operations, it was well-known by early 1954 to have been approaching insolvency and was placed in the hands of its bank's directors on 10th September. A receiving order against the Company on 9th December spurred the Traffic Commissioner to seek alternative operators for its network of services radiating from Horsham which included the 33 (Horsham-Three Bridges) and 34 (Horsham-Ewhurst). London Transport agreed to take these two over at short notice with the intention of running them from Crawley garage as a through Three Bridges-Crawley-Horsham-Ewhurst operation numbered 852, and the Traffic Commissioner duly issued a short term licence for this. Three new GSs were licensed at Crawley (two for service and one to act as a spare) in readiness on 13th December and they did not have to wait long. Hants & Sussex buses ran for the last time on Tuesday 21st December and the 852 sprang into action the next day. Although the GSs had a slightly lower seating capacity than the Bedford OBs that they replaced this was of no consequence as passenger demand was not heavy. With the subsequent issue of substantive road service licences A T Brady's Brown Bus Service of Forest Green was awarded the Horsham-Ewhurst section which he took over on 18th May 1955. Just one GS remained at Crawley thereafter to work what was left of the 852.

GS 80 was one of three retrieved from storage at Garston on 12th July 1954 to re-introduce one-man operation at Windsor on routes 442 and 445. A "Please Pay As You Enter" label is now carried on the nearside windscreen. Typical of so many GSs, this one was destined for a relatively leisurely career with London Transport, notching up only 7 years and 1 month of active service during its period of ownership which lasted just one month short of 10 years.

An animated bus scene at Chesham Broadway finds Amersham's GS 56 about to set off on a 397 journey to Tring. Behind it a Thurgood-bodied Bedford OB of Rover Bus works to Hemel Hempstead jointly with London Transport on route 316, and RT 1043 is at the rear. The GS now carries the polished metal grab handles on its front scuttle just below the windscreens which were a feature of the class for most of their lives. *Fred Ivey*

1954 ended with all except three of the 84 GSs licensed for service. The three vehicles out of use were GSs 11 and 45, which were both at Chiswick unlicensed and undergoing accident damage repair, and GS 84 which was now the only member of the class never to have entered service and had now been moved for storage at Reigate. For a short while from April 1955 the number in service rose to its maximum of 83, but this was the only time the GS class reached its full potential and the story thereafter was one of decline. The ravages of the post-war television boom coupled with a huge growth in private car ownership resulted in the now-familiar story of inexorable decline for bus usage, and once the employment of RFs on one-man operation became permissible the retention of a small non-standard class such as the GS became ever more uneconomic.

However back in 1953/54 the GS was viewed as the small bus of the future and it went into service with high hopes. Inevitably, as with any new class, teething troubles were encountered in the early days, but once the inside staff had become knowledgeable about when oil changes were due etc, and drivers had fully mastered the techniques of handling them, the GSs developed a reputation for being strong and reliable workhorses. After its accident repair at Chiswick was completed, GS 45 was tried out at various garages with variations to the standard 5.7:1 axle ratio to test performance particularly on hill-climbing, but nothing came of this and the GS class spent its whole career with its mechanical specification basically unchanged from start to finish.

The bodywork, however, was subjected to a number of modifications in the early days. As early as October 1953 staff were recording problems with the doors which tended to drop and then jam. Various corrective measures had to be devised including insertion of an additional door stop, the replacement of timber slats on the entrance step by thinner, metal tread plates to improve clearances, and the insertion of a 3 ohm resistance in the wiring circuit of the motor to slow the door operation, all of which were incorporated as built from about the 40th body onwards and retro-fitted to the remainder. A request from staff resulted in the fitting from May 1954 onwards of grab handles – identical to those used on RTs – on the front scuttle below the windscreens for the benefit of cleaners, while from August 1954 deflector plates were fitted to the front nearside saloon lamp to eliminate reflection on the windscreen at night time. In March 1955 a programme began to re-site the driver's cab light to make fare values on the ticket machine easier to see.

After about a year in service a major structural defect started to appear on the no 1 body bearer which was fracturing, a problem that by February 1956 had been found on some 57% of all GS bodies. Strengthening of this and the wing structure was easiest achieved by lifting the body from the chassis and this was carried out on overhaul in most cases. Also in 1956, and in response to drivers' complaints, a programme commenced in February, but took several months to complete, of installing a reversing light at the rear of each vehicle, a feature which the engineers had earlier deemed unnecessary after having initially included it within the original specification. The light was installed on the detachable rear panel below the emergency exit door behind which was the fold-out battery crate. It was on this panel that reflectors had been installed when they became required by law in 1954 and to which a bulls-eye transfer was later attached as a livery enhancement. Under each vehicle, an additional mud flap was installed to overcome complaints of mud splashes covering the batteries and rear windows in inclement weather.

The first GS overhaul programme was scheduled to commence at the start of 1956 and in preparation for this the last-remaining still-unused GS was licensed at Leatherhead on 1st January. The first vehicle to actually go into overhaul, on 2nd January, was GS 2 from Hertford, although GS 5 had been delicensed for this purpose on the 1st but did not actually go to the works until 29th February. The principle then generally applied was for vehicles due for overhaul to be delicensed at the start of the month that their overhaul was due, or sometimes even two months beforehand, and to remain unlicensed after the overhaul was completed until the 1st of the month in which they were actually needed for service again. With ample spare vehicles on hand, this was a tax-efficient way of organising things.

As with other small, non-standard classes overhauls were carried out at Chiswick rather than Aldenham. The usual process was for mechanical work to be carried out at the main works with bodywork dealt with in the overhaul shops at the old Chiswick tram depot. In every case the original combination of chassis and body was maintained.

The first cycle of overhauls at Chiswick turned out to be an extremely leisurely one with the last vehicle, GS 81, not going into the works until 4th March 1959, more than three years after the programme had commenced. The next cycle followed straight on from this, with GS 2 going for its second overhaul on 6th May 1959.

The GS class underwent a gentle and premature decline through the second half of the nineteen-fifties. From a high point in 1955 of 83 being licensed for service, the number gradually dropped as follows:

31st December 1956	-	78
31st December 1957	-	74
31st December 1958	-	65

With no hope of the full fleet ever being needed for service again, A A M Durrant proposed as early as October 1958 that some of the surplus vehicles should be sold while a good price could still be obtained for them. Ramsbottom Urban District Council had already shown an interest in buying one and others would surely follow. The proposal was rejected on the grounds that surplus GSs might be used to replace larger single deckers on uneconomic routes, but this was, in fact, contrary to the way that things were destined to go and it simply resulted in some vehicles remaining in store for between 2 and 3½ years before sales finally commenced in 1961.

When the brand new garage in the centre of Stevenage New Town opened on 29th April 1959 Hitchin garage closed and its fleet, including three GSs, moved to the new premises. Although the development of new towns was all the rage at that time, the general trend in bus usage was one of decline as a result of which two more garages were introduced to GS operation during this period, the first being Hemel Hempstead where route 316 (Hemel Hempstead–Chesham) was placed in the hands of a GS on 11th July 1956. A joint operation with J R G Dell's Rover Bus Service, the 316 had featured as an early trial run for the use of large capacity single deckers on one-man operation now that this had become permissible. A GS was now replacing the RF on the grounds that nothing larger was required.

The next garage to receive a first-time GS allocation was St Albans on 13th November 1959, where a single vehicle was used on schools and general duplication work, and also to cover journeys formerly worked by RFs on route 382 (St Albans–Codicote). On the minus side, Swanley garage lost its GS allocation from route 478 in favour of RT operation on 16th October 1956 while its final GS departed when the 479 ceased on 1st November 1958 as one of the service withdrawals that followed the bus strike. A second garage to lose its GS allocation was Epping on 10th June 1959 when its last GS route, 381, went over to RF omo operation, although in this instance the loss proved to be temporary and a GS was restored to the roster in May 1960.

An interesting episode for the GSs kicked off on 21st June 1958 when Ralph Bennett, the recently-appointed General Manager & Engineer of Great Yarmouth Corporation Transport, wrote to London Transport to enquire if it had any suitable vehicles available which he could buy or borrow for a trial of one-man operation that he had in mind. This was the same Ralph Bennett who, twenty years later, was to become Chairman of the London Transport Executive, a position which he held until the early termination of his contract in 1980. With surplus GSs on hand, London Transport was happy to oblige by providing some on loan, and arranged for a GS to be available at Victoria garage for inspection on Friday 4th July. Suitably impressed, Mr Bennett arranged to borrow five vehicles for a period of a year from 1st October at a hire rate of 25s 0d per vehicle per day plus a 2¾d mileage charge which would include the tyre contractor's costs. The five GSs selected (GS 61, 63, 68, 70, 72) were all taken directly out of service and not from the delicensed fleet, and had all been overhauled within the last nine months. They were collected from Victoria garage by Great Yarmouth staff at the rate of one per week, starting with GS 72 on Sunday 17th August and ending with GS 70 on 14th September.

Outside the distinctive frontage of the Great Yarmouth Corporation Transport depot in Caister Road are GSs 68, 63 and 61, with the first two standing on top of long-disused tram track. With blinds set for local routes 5 and 6, they display no attempt to disguise their London Transport ownership and carry prominent slip boards reading "On loan to Great Yarmouth Transport". Of these three, only GS 68 saw further service in London after their time in Norfolk came to an end.

GS 61 started work at Great Yarmouth on 28th September 1958, presumably initially on driver training until it was joined for service on 1st October by GSs 68 and 70. The other two were not immediately required because the Eastern Counties Omnibus Company had appealed against a Traffic Commissioner's licence decision, and London Transport offered to waive hire charges on these two until they were finally cleared to begin operation on 8th February 1959. So successful were the trials that the Corporation lost no time in arranging the purchase of its own vehicles to replace the GSs in the form of new Albion Nimbus 31-seaters. London Transport agreed to terminate the hire arrangement in less than the stipulated year, and as the new Nimbus vehicles became available for service the GSs were withdrawn; GS 68,70 on 12th July 1959, GS 61,63 on the 19th and, finally, GS 72 on the 26th. All five were returned to Victoria garage on 30th July. Great Yarmouth Corporation found the GSs to be reliable and largely trouble-free, but the same by no means applied with their new Albions which constantly suffered mechanical problems and had all been disposed of by 1966. Of the five GSs only GS 68 and GS 72 re-entered service with London Transport. The others remained in storage until sales of the class finally commenced in 1961.

The first year of the new decade saw the fitment of London Transport's standard style of front trafficator to the GS class from May 1960 onwards, but in a tacit admission that some vehicles were now permanently surplus and would inevitably be disposed of, ten currently unlicensed vehicles were not dealt with (GS 24, 32, 37, 40, 41, 43, 49, 61, 63, 70). In July 1960 the sale of surplus GSs was once again proposed, this time by Geoffrey Fernyhough, Operating Manager (Country Buses & Coaches) who suggested selling ten out of the nineteen then currently delicensed. This time the proposal was agreed, and on 15th August 1960 tenders went out to the Tilling, Scottish Bus and British Electric Traction groups offering ten vehicles for disposal, only to be met with speedy rejections from all three. An offer to the Ceylon Transport Board on 7th September had been declined by mid-October and this resulted in a general tender to all and sundry being issued on 21st of that month.

With the passage of time, it was probably inevitable that the bright areas at the front of many GSs would succumb to paintwork, the radiator surround in green and the bumper bar generally in black. Stevenage garage took over Hitchin's GSs when the latter garage closed on 29th April 1959, and their workings included route 807 which had linked the New Town with Letchworth since 17th October 1956. Unlike RF 628 standing next to it, black-bumpered GS 9 has yet to receive trafficator ears. *Alan B Cross*

An initial display of interest from the Spanish city of Bilbao fizzled out and the first successful sale was concluded on 5th January 1961 to West Bromwich Corporation following an enquiry received from them towards the end of 1960 for the purchase of two out of the ten vehicles on offer. As a result GSs 40 and 41 left the fleet on 16th January heading for West Bromwich where, a few weeks later, they became the first GSs ever to appear in a livery other than London Transport's. As initially purchased, one of the pair (GS 41) was destined to join the Council's bus fleet while the other was bought for use by its welfare department for carrying handicapped people, although by March 1963 both were in service there as buses. Between April and June 1961 the other eight also departed of which only GS 32 went initially to a dealer, Bird's at Stratford upon Avon. The rest were all direct sales to potential users including no less than five to the Corvedale Motor Company Ltd of Ludlow, Shropshire. One of the Corvedale batch, GS 43, departed holding the dubious honour of being the least-used GS of all whilst in London Transport ownership, having been licensed for service for a mere 3 years 5 months out of its 7½-year existence.

The year 1962 proved to be the turning point for the GS class, heralding the real start of what was to be a long drawn-out decline. Although its immediate nemesis was to be the larger and more acceptable RF, the underlying cause was the delivery of new Routemaster RMC coaches for Green Line service from August 1962 which made the RFs available. The single GS remaining at Tring was officially replaced on 23rd May 1962 and finally moved out on 1st July, but the biggest inroad into the sphere of GS operation came with the start of the winter programme on 24th October when GS operations at Amersham, Chelsham, Epping and Grays were all brought to a halt. The Grays operation, not previously mentioned, had been experimental route 372 within the new Belhus Estate, part of the huge London County Council overspill development at Aveley, which began on 18th June 1962 but failed to establish itself and was now permanently withdrawn. Whereas 1962 had started out with 66 GSs licensed for service it ended with only 42, which meant that exactly half the GS fleet was now either out of passenger service or had been sold.

Although the GSs had been equipped with a heater and demister for the driver from new,

One of the earliest disposals, ahead of the fitment of flashing trafficators, was GS 40 which was purchased by West Bromwich Corporation from whom in passed, in October 1969, to the newly-formed West Midlands Passenger Transport Executive. In preservation since 1974, it continues to carry West Bromwich's lined-out two-tone blue livery and is now kept at the Black Country Living Museum where it is seen with a former West Bromwich Daimler double decker visible behind it just inside the shed.
Ken Blacker

they were not fitted with saloon heaters. Modern expectations now demanded that the benefit of heating should be extended to passengers too and this resulted in just slightly more than half the class, 47 vehicles to be precise, being fitted with saloon heaters, the great majority in September and October 1962 starting with a trial run on GS 28 on 7th September. The vehicles selected had all either been overhauled from 1960 onwards or were actually in overhaul or delicensed in readiness at the time the heater fitment programme was in process. This was an economical way of doing things, but it meant that many of the lowest numbered vehicles (GS 1-9, 11) would now miss out on their third overhaul and would leave the fleet whilst, in a similar way, the highest numbered (GS 67-84) would not now receive their second overhaul and could also be disposed of. Various inter-garage allocations were made to ensure that heater-fitted GSs were in the right place after the 24th October withdrawals, and a target of getting all non-heated vehicles out of service by the end of that month was almost achieved. The only exceptions were that GS 74 remained in service at Hertford until 1st December, GS 84 at Crawley until 1st January 1963, GS 6 at Dorking until 1st February while, finally, non-heater GS 69 was relicensed at Garston on 25th January – presumably as emergency cover – to be withdrawn 13 days later on 7th February. It was the very last non-heater fitted GS in public service with London Transport.

Not so far mentioned is the employment of GSs as staff buses, a sideline which began with GS 26 at Harrow Weald in February 1960 and continued until the final one, GS 52, ran for the last time from Abbey Wood garage on 31st March 1974. During the intervening years no fewer than 20 individual GSs were used as staff buses at one time or another, always in green livery even when they were attached to Central Bus garages. With their engines sometimes tinkered around with to obtain a bit of extra speed, especially the pump settings, the vehicles were primarily used for transporting engineering and coachwork staff from their now-closed places of work at the Charlton and Reigate overhaul shops to their new employment at Chiswick and Aldenham, being based overnight at Abbey Wood, Plumstead and Reigate with everyday maintenance normally carried out at Chiswick. The Harrow Weald staff buses, which ran only from 1960 to 1963, ferried railway staff to various points along the Metropolitan Line during its upgrading and its conversion from steam north of Rickmansworth. New Cross and Tring garages also housed and maintained GS staff buses for short periods.

Two attempts were made to introduce new GS-worked services from Grays garage during the nineteen-sixties both of which proved spectacularly unsuccessful. GS 76 was used to inaugurate route 372 on 18th June 1962 but it was quickly replaced, on 1st July, by newly-overhauled GS 34 which remained until the demise of the 372 on 24th October of the same year. An early example in the country area of the use of lower case blind lettering, it stands completely empty on the Belhus Estate demonstrating the reversing light and rear bullseye motif that the GSs carried for most of their working lives. *Peter Mitchell*

Almost one GS in every four served as a staff bus at one time or another between 1961 and 1974. In this instance GS 35, based at Plumstead, makes the long journey from south east London to Chiswick and Aldenham, a task which it undertook between February 1966 and February 1967. It did not return to revenue service and was sold in January 1968 for use as a van in South Wales, finishing up with Southern Motorways at Emsworth as a source of spare parts. *Alan B Cross*

In 1963 and 1964 visitors to Guildford were treated to the novel sight of GSs running for two operators, London Transport itself and also Tillingbourne Valley Services to whom direct sales of surplus GSs commenced in March 1963. On this occasion GS 21, still in London Transport ownership, swings into Onslow Street bus station followed by RT 4773, while a GS in Tillingbourne's maroon livery prepares to depart. GS 21 survived the disposal of routes 448 and 448A to Tillingbourne Valley on 12th August 1964 and finished its working days at High Wycombe in February 1968. *Ken Blacker*

Although from 1964 onwards the GS story was one of decline, three occasions occurred where this pattern was temporarily reversed and they were used to explore new territory. The first was at Harlow garage where experimental route 389 began linking Potter Street with Harlow Town station on 6th May 1964. It survived for a mere eight months and, despite local objections and attempts to keep it going, ran for the last time on 12th January 1965. On 2nd June 1965 GSs were reintroduced at Grays for a new limited stop route 399 linking Grays in Essex with Dartford in Kent via the Dartford Tunnel. In this case the end did not come so swiftly, but on 12th May 1967 the service was finally withdrawn owing to lack of demand. High Wycombe's first and only introduction to GS operation came on 3rd October 1965 with shoppers' service 442 from the town to the Hicks Farm Estate. This was the longest lived of the three new ventures and prospered well enough to be converted to RFs on 17th February 1968. In addition to these three new operations, St Albans garage reintroduced a GS to route 382 on 13th January 1965.

Between 1964 and 1968 a steady programme of withdrawing GSs from service was pursued, and where they were directly replaced with other buses it was always with RFs. In acknowledgement that the aim was to phase them all out as soon as possible the overhaul programme, which was now on its third cycle, was brought to a halt with the last to be dealt with, GS 42, going to Chiswick on 9th November 1965. The completion of its overhaul on 10th January 1966 meant that just twelve of the class had received a third overhaul.

In theory the new Thames tunnel linking Dartford with Purfleet should have provided a much sought-after public transport link between Kent and Essex, but it was not to be. The third attempt to provide a service via limited stop route 399 failed and Grays-based GS 34 was carrying a typical load when photographed on the southern approach road to the tunnel. At the time, the single GS on the 399 was the only one of its class still required to work on Sundays. The service ran for the last time on 12th May 1967. *Peter Mitchell*

The less than inspiring background of the Hicks Farm Estate at High Wycombe which GSs began to serve in October 1965 was far removed from the concept of bucolic country scenes that the memory of GSs normally invokes, but it was the last new venture that the class ever undertook. GS 28 arrived at High Wycombe straight from overhaul but did not stay right through to when RFs took over in February 1968, being replaced by GS 21 on 1st November 1967. *Peter Mitchell*

111

The dates when GS operations finally ceased at each garage were:

Stevenage (SV)	29th February 1964
East Grinstead (EG)	6th May 1964
Guildford (GF)	12th August 1964
Harlow (HA)	13th January 1965
Crawley (CY)	2nd October 1965
Hemel Hempstead (HH)	3rd October 1965
Windsor (WR)	31st December 1966
Dunton Green (DG)	31st December 1966
Grays (GY)	13th May 1967
St Albans (SA)	7th October 1967
Leatherhead (LH)	1st December 1967
High Wycombe (HE)	17th February 1968
Dorking (DS)	5th October 1968
Hertford (HG)	23rd November 1968

In the case of the GSs at Hemel Hempstead and Guildford, these had been active on the last two remaining services that London Transport had operated jointly with other operators. On 6th May 1964 London Transport handed route 316 in its entirety to Rover Bus, although a single GS was retained at Hemel Hempstead for a spasmodic residual working 316B at the New Town end until 3rd October 1965. Soon after giving up the 316, route 448 at Guildford became solely a Tillingbourne Valley working on 12th August 1964, and the latter company also took over the running of Guildford local service 448A to Pewley Way. The most unusual feature of the 448 had been that, since 1963, Tillingbourne Valley had purchased GSs direct from London Transport for operation on it in its own maroon and grey livery, so its takeover of the full 448/A operation resulted in no change to the type of rolling stock used. The withdrawal of Crawley's last GS coincided with the abandonment of the 852 inherited nearly eleven years earlier from Hants & Sussex, and the demise of Dorking's last GS on 5th October 1968 coincided with the withdrawal of the long established but lightly patronised route 433 (Ranmore–Dorking–Coldharbour), the Coldharbour end of which was henceforth covered by a replacement service operated by Surrey & Sussex Coachways.

At the close of 1968, only five GSs were still licensed for public service, GS 36 and 54 at Northfleet and GSs 15, 17 and 33 at Garston. A further five were still in active use, but as staff buses, at Plumstead (GS 10, 66) and Reigate (GS 12, 45, 62), while GS 34 was also licensed, but as a trainer, at Garston.

Sales of surplus GSs took place every year between 1963 and 1969. All were direct sales to new owners wishing to use them for a variety of purposes with the sole exception of GS 65 which went to Wombwell Diesels specifically for scrap in July 1969 in damaged condition incurred whilst operating from Hertford garage in May 1968. One further exception to the rule was GS 82 which was transferred to London Transport's service vehicle fleet in February 1964 and renumbered 1311CD, its role being to replace a former 4Q4 as a Civil Defence vehicle. A government decision in 1968 to stand down its Civil Defence Corps resulted in the sale of 1311CD to Tillingbourne Valley in December 1969 who restored it to operational use as a bus, one of twelve GSs that eventually passed through its fleet.

Subsequent to finishing work at Dorking in June 1962, GS 82 was converted just over eighteen months later into a poison gas decontamination training unit for London Transport's Civil Defence Corps with service vehicle fleet number 1311CD, and is seen in this guise at Parliament Square. By December 1969 it was back in service as a bus in the Tillingbourne Valley fleet.

On 4th October 1969 the last two GSs remaining at Northfleet were replaced by RFs leaving Garston as the sole operator of the class on stage carriage work. Even here, the main GS operations had ceased in February 1969 and the sole remaining scheduled commitment was the single bus on route 336A outstationed at Loudwater. It was now only a matter of time before the Country Bus & Coach department was to be split away from London Transport to form the new London Country Bus Services, and when this occurred on 1st January 1970 the dividing-up of assets saw the remaining GSs allocated as follows:

London Transport   GS 10, 13, 28, 52, 62 (total 5)
London Country   GS 12, 14, 17, 33, 36, 42, 45, 55, 64, 66 (total 10)

The five London Transport vehicles were all in active use as staff buses, their allocation at the time of the split being GS 10, 52 and 62 at Reigate with GS 13 and 28 at Abbey Wood. GS 28 later moved to Reigate and GS 52 to Abbey Wood, and the Reigate ones remained outstationed there even though the premises were now owned by London Country. The garaging of GSs at Reigate finally finished in October 1973 and the final one at Abbey Wood, GS 52, was replaced by an RT on 1st April 1974. It was the last GS to remain in the fleet, and when it was sold to a preservationist on 16th August of that year London Transport's connection with the little Guy Specials was brought to a close.

By the start of the nineteen-seventies and the transfer of London Transport's Country Bus & Coach department to London Country Bus Services, the only remaining scheduled GS operation was the single vehicle on route 336A which on this occasion was GS 17. It is seen at the Loudwater Village stand with its new fleet name and the removal of the former owner's enamel plate from the top of the radiator grille. GS 17 did not last until the final closure of the service, having fallen by the wayside in March 1971, but it later saw use with Sampson's Coaches at Cheshunt between 1973 and 1978.

The very last GS in London Transport ownership was GS 52 whose final days as a staff bus ceased at the end of March 1974. It is seen here in happier times when allocated to Dunton Green where it remained until this garage lost its last GSs in December 1966. It is seen passing the 4 ton weight restriction sign on Cudham Lane as it approaches the Green Street Green roundabout. *Alan Nightingale*

Seven of the London Country GSs were delicensed at the time of the Company's formation and stored at various locations. Five of these (GS 12, 14, 45, 64, 66) were destined never to be used by their new owner and, after having been gathered together in Garston garage for storage, were sold in June 1971. Two others, GS 36 and 55, were restored to use in April 1970 as a training bus and Reigate-based staff bus respectively. The only active vehicles at the time of takeover were all at Garston, GS 17 and 33 as the service bus for the 336A plus a spare, along with GS 42 which was officially a learner. In March 1971 the latter officially replaced GS 17 on the 336A. Up to 1971 this service had always relied on a regular driver, who since 1954 had been Harry Cross, but when he retired at the end of June (and received a cheque for £100 from the grateful Loudwater Bus Service Association), the outstationing at Loudwater ceased and the vehicle ran 'light' from Garston each day to start work. The 336A, which was now heavily loss-making, relied on a Council subsidy to keep it going, and when this ceased the service was permanently withdrawn.

On the last day of operation, Thursday 31st March 1972, both remaining GSs were put into service to cater for the large gathering of enthusiasts and well-wishers, with GS 42 performing the scheduled runs backed up by GS 33 as a duplicate. Subsequent to this GS 55 remained active in its staff bus role until August 1972 and GS 36 as a trainer until the following November. The last to be sold by London Country were GSs 17 and 36 on 15th March 1973.

The post-London life of the GS class has been well documented elsewhere and only needs summarising here. Approximately 40 of them found further employment with psv operators, either on stage carriage, express or contract work. West Bromwich Corporation, Corvedale Motor Company and Tillingbourne Valley have already been mentioned but another significant operator was B S Williams Ltd of Emsworth, Hampshire. This Company was controlled by the same Basil Williams who had formerly run the old Hants & Sussex empire, the remnants of which had been trading under the fleet name of Southern Motorways since 1962. Seven GSs passed through

A succession of GSs worked as useful members of the Southern Motorways fleet of B S Williams Ltd for a decade. GS 7 was an early arrival in June 1963 and served its new owner well until withdrawal in May 1972. Accompanying it in the Company's yard in Emsworth, overshadowed by the gasometer, in December 1964 are a one-time United Counties Bristol JO5G/ECW and a Bedford OB/Duple coach. *Ken Blacker*

the Southern Motorways fleet between 1963 and 1972 while an eighth ran for another Basil Williams company, Glider & Blue Motor Services of Bishops Waltham. Much later, odd commercial workings have occurred on specialist services such as the Sunday and Bank Holiday Surrey Hills Leisure Bus in the nineteen-nineties. Other GSs found new employment as works transports, welfare buses, scout and school transports, travellers' caravans and various other uses, and some of their owners have included such well-known names as British Railways, the National Trust and the St John Ambulance Brigade. A particularly notable disposal was that of GS 34 in October 1969 to the Motor Industry Research Association for use at its testing and research ground near Nuneaton until 1972.

Perhaps most significant of all was the high number that were bought, either directly from London Transport or from a previous purchaser, for preservation. The small size and attractive looks of the GS were no doubt major factors which combined to make it probably the most desired type of bus for preservationists in relation to its original fleet size that there has ever been. At least 30 of them have been the subject of preservation projects at one time or another, although a few of these are known to have since been cannibalised to provide spare parts for others. Some are believed to be still in existence but have languished unseen for many years while others may have fallen permanently by the wayside with their ultimate demise unrecorded. However a nucleus remains in capable and active hands, restored and in good condition, sometimes appearing at public events as a welcome reminder of a fascinating phase in London Transport's bus history.

The former GS 50 was, for a few years, the only full-sized bus serving the remote Outer Hebridean island of Barra where Alexander Macintyre used it on a mixture of school and public runs. It is seen here in June 1970 on the island's main circular road, the A888, departing from the village and ferry port of Castlebay at the start of a trip to the north end of the island. *Ken Blacker*

When GS 50 ceased running on Barra in December 1973 it was dumped, like all its predecessors, outside Mr Macintyre's house in the hamlet of Grean. Rescued for preservation some 20 years later, its corroded chassis was subsequently discarded and the body was mounted on a modified Ford Cargo chassis. Fitted with aircraft style seats, it toured with the Venture Reprieve charity to Romania and subsequently undertook an endurance rally to Morocco. It is believed to be still in existence. *Coach & Bus Week*

THE TWO-DOOR RELIANCES – THE RW CLASS

Looking very un-London-like but still sparklingly brand new, RW 2 stands in Hemel Hempstead bus station awaiting its departure time with its doors still firmly closed while some youthful passengers wait outside to board. When viewed from the offside it was readily apparent from the positioning of the glass cove panels that the majority of roof hoops did not line up with the side pillars in the normal manner. Ken Blacker

The tiny RW class, which entered service in the late summer of 1960, passed fleetingly through the annals of London Transport history leaving behind barely any trace of its short existence. It was significant, however, in at last introducing lightweight, 8ft-wide single deck service buses to the London Transport fleet several years after the concept of such vehicles had been adopted as the new standard by all other major operators. The Executive's obsession with achieving almost total fleet standardisation had left it with 700 heavyweight RFs based on the AEC Regal Mk IV chassis, which had become prematurely obsolete almost as soon as they were built, leaving no scope for reaping the substantial financial benefits that the new medium or lightweight models offered. All that London Transport was able to do was carry out its well-documented comparative trials of 1953/54 pitting the performance of three contemporary lightweight models – AEC/Park Royal Monocoach, Bristol LS and Leyland Tiger Cub – with that of the RF, and to note the results. By the time the last RFs entered service in March 1954, when experimental one-man operation of large single deckers commenced at Leatherhead garage, the 'lightweight' era was already well established.

The inspiration for the RW class was the small batch of four AEC Reliance/Willowbrook buses bought by Grimsby-Cleethorpes Transport in 1959. Grimsby 31 (KJV 996) was the first of them and the similarities to the RW class are clear to see. Both groups of vehicles ultimately achieved a similar, creditably long working life-span, the Grimsby-Cleethorpes Reliances remaining on their home territory until 1977 while the RWs, having gone to Chesterfield, remained together there until the same year.

With its plain front conforming to the standard BET body style of the time, the RW was not particularly stylish although the back end possessed quite a pleasant curve. The vehicles for both Grimsby and London had the words ENTRANCE and EXIT painted above the relevant doorways in exactly the same manner, although the style of livery application by London Transport was very different from the Grimsby-Cleethorpes blue and cream. Both had the same unusually shaped upturn to the roof of the front destination box, but the removable front panel for towing purposes was a specific London Transport requirement. *London Transport Museum*

However, aspirations lingered in some areas of management for fleet augmentation through the acquisition of more up-to-date and economical single-deckers than the RFs, and in April 1957 the influential Operating Managers of both operating departments – J B Burnell on Central Road Services and Geoffrey Fernyhough of Country Buses & Coaches – submitted a joint paper proposing the purchase of 45 new single deckers, allegedly to meet fleet requirements up to 1959. In doing so they were probably mindful of a statement by A A M Durrant some years earlier, when discussing the new lightweight designs then becoming widely available, that the achievement of a reduction of 2 tons in weight would result in a saving in fuel consumption to the equivalent of some £100 per annum per vehicle. He had gone on to say that: "Whereas this could not be taken into account insofar as the present commitments of up to 700 single deckers were concerned, an additional number would be called for in the 10-year programme, and in view of the fuel economy to be secured there might be justification in providing for not less than 50 of this new type single deck vehicle". In fact, despite his earlier pronouncement, Durrant now disagreed with his colleagues over the purchase of new vehicles and insisted that existing T and TD vehicles were mechanically sound and should be retained, despite their low seating capacity and their unsuitability for one-man operation. It was his view that finally prevailed and the purchase of 45 new vehicles was not authorised. However this did not stop an examination being arranged later in the same year of one of a batch of six Burlingham-bodied AEC Reliances then being delivered to Reading Corporation Transport to which reference had been noted in the influential weekly journal "Modern Transport" issue of 7th September 1957. These were of two-door layout with loading at the front door and alighting at the centre, and this was of special interest to the operating departments in offering a potential reduction in time spent at stops which could be particularly useful and cost-effective on one-man operated services.

No immediate outcome resulted from inspecting the Reading Reliance, but another opportunity arose just over a year later when the two Operating Managers were offered the chance to view another new Reliance then being constructed to the same two-door configuration. The vehicle inspected this time was one of a batch of four being built in the Willowbrook factory at Loughborough for the Grimsby-Cleethorpes Joint Transport Committee, and it may have been through Willowbrook's sales staff that the initial contact was made as they were actively working to secure new orders at the time. The inspection by the Operating Managers took place in January 1959 and their subsequent joint report led the rolling stock department to decide, on 16th February, to go and see the vehicles for themselves and to prepare a report on them from the engineering point of view. The outcome was a decision to mount a trial in the Country Bus & Coach fleet of just three new vehicles, for which a firm order was placed in March 1960 for delivery within six months.

Fortuitously Grimsby-Cleethorpes had placed a further order for five more Reliances identical to the first batch, four of which were due for delivery in June 1960 with a fifth to follow after exhibition at the Earls Court Commercial Motor Show later in the year. AEC agreed to make three Reliance chassis available for quick delivery. At London Transport's request these would be of the 2MU2RA model with 'Monocontrol' transmission and air brakes and not the 2MU3RV favoured by Grimsby-Cleethorpes which had synchromesh gearboxes and triple servo vacuum brakes. Willowbrook was happy to extend its construction programme to include three additional vehicles provided these were identical in all major structural respects to the Grimsby-Cleethorpes specification. The first completed vehicle, RW 1, was received from Willowbrook on 30th August 1960 with RWs 2 and 3 following on 1st and 15th September respectively. Registered 495-497 ALH, they were the first London Transport buses to carry reversed registration numbers, and they belatedly introduced 30ft long x 8ft wide single deck service buses to the fleet long after most other major operators had begun running them.

The chassis were powered by AEC's AH470 7.685 litre engine with 112mm bore and 130mm stroke which was the standard fitment for Reliances at the time. These had 'wet' cylinder liners and were of 'monobloc' construction with cylinder head and crankcase cast as one. The 'Monocontrol' air-operated direct acting epicyclic transmission was similar to that currently in use on the Routemaster but without the fully automatic over-ride, and the RWs were the first two-pedal vehicles in the single deck fleet to feature this. The Willowbrook lightweight metal-framed bodies were built to basic BET Federation body design suitably adapted to accommodate twin driver-controlled 2ft 7in wide doorways. The two-door layout resulted in shorter-than-usual side bays, but other customary features were retained such as the upright front with recessed driver's windscreen to reduce night time glare and a pleasantly-rounded rear end incorporating a single window, the emergency exit being close to the rear on the offside. A specific Grimsby-Cleethorpes requirement was the fitting above the cant rail of glass quarter lights, three on the nearside and five on the offside, for the benefit of standing passengers. These roof lights and all the accompanying roof hoops complied with normal BET pillar spacing and, unusually, did not line up with the windows below. The bodies were finished in standard London Transport green and cream, but the latter colour was confined to a broad band below the windows, and there was no cream line above them as was the case with other single deckers in the fleet. London Transport's standard-sized single destination display was provided at the front, sitting rather uncomfortably within the large box specified by Grimsby-Cleethorpes, with a single route number box built neatly into the curved back dome. Features fitted to meet London Transport's specific requirements included Routemaster-type front trafficators and rear repeaters, a removable front panel for towing purposes, and the Executive's standard battery booster socket enclosed behind a flap under the driver's offside window.

For passengers boarding via the front doorway the RWs presented an unusually attractive and welcoming picture. This was largely due to the combination of Routemaster-influenced décor consisting of burgundy lower panels, grey stove enamelled window surrounds and yellow ceilings, all brightened by natural light from the glass roof panels, making a pleasant contrast to the rather gloomy interior of the RF. Although the seats were very basic and with thinly upholstered backs – obvious weight-saving measures – they looked attractive with their Routemaster-style moquette coverings edged in burgundy leathercloth. With the exception of a longitudinal bench for three immediately behind the central exit door, all 42 seats faced forwards. Ample ventilation was available through eight sliding windows, while the driver's side window slid forwards to open and his sloping windscreen could also be opened outwards at its bottom edge. There were ample handrails, both vertical and along the ceiling.

In motion the vehicles were reasonably quiet, and though lower powered than the RF their lighter construction contributed towards a generally more lively acceleration, but it also produced multiple body squeaks. Perhaps the biggest drawback from the passenger perspective was a tendency to vibrate when the engine was idling in traffic or at stops, sometimes causing the whole body to shake and rattle very severely.

RW was probably a combination of R for Reliance and W for Wide. They had AEC chassis numbers 2MU2RA3099-3101 and London Transport body numbers 9230-9232 but, as far as is known, no internal type coding system such as 1RW1 was allocated to them. Their unladen weight of 5tons 18cwt 2qrs marked a considerable reduction below the 7tons 10cwt of the standard bus-type RF, and although no records are now available to show their mpg results they would almost certainly have been far more fuel efficient than the RF.

The glass roof panels provide an excellent level of daytime lighting in RW 2 and highlight the Routemaster-style internal décor, including the use of the now familiar burgundy upholstery for the first time on new vehicles other than Routemasters. *Ken Blacker*

The Country Bus department's intention from the outset was to try out the three RWs on its busiest one-man routes where the dual door layout would theoretically be of the greatest advantage, spending long enough on each route (or group of routes) to glean really meaningful results. Their first attachment was at Hemel Hempstead garage to work on routes 322/A (Hemel Hempstead–Watford), where RW 1 arrived for type training on 7th September 1960 followed by RW 2 on the 16th and RW 3 on the 21st. This basic system of sending in a trainer first prior to the commencement of full operation by all three was continued throughout the programme, the subsequent sequence being:

Garage	Route(s) operated		1st RW allocation
Addlestone	427/437/456	Weybridge–Woking by various routes	20th January 1961
Reigate	440/440A	Woldingham–Salfords/Redstone Estate	7th June 1961
St Albans	355	Harpenden–St Albans–Borehamwood	10th November 1961
Hertford	333/333B	Hertford–Chapmore End/Ware Pk Sanatorium	6th September 1962

A view looking towards the front in RW 3 shows the general layout adjacent to both doorways and also the plentiful lighting provided for after-dark operations with rows of bulbs above the glass cant panels augmented by further lamps under jellymould covers in the centre of the ceiling. Notices adjacent to each door read: "Experimental two-door bus. This bus is fitted with two doors. Passengers are asked to enter by the front and leave by the central door". *London Transport Museum*

The New Town bus station in Hemel Hempstead was frequently a hive of activity with three independent operators regularly terminating there in addition to London Transport, and the arrival of RWs on the 322 in September 1960 added still further to its interest. On this occasion RW 3 meets up with a Thurgood-bodied Bedford SB on Charles Knight's Bream Service while GS 80 picks up passengers on the 316 service worked jointly with Rover Bus. The GS served Hemel Hempstead only until October 1962 when it was put on the sales list and the RWs' withdrawal on 1st October 1963 left Bream's Bedford as the only one of the three remaining for any length of time. *Ken Blacker*

The first of the RWs' planned moves took them to Addlestone in January 1961 where they became a regular fixture for the next four to five months on the 427/437/456 group of routes. As previously at Hemel Hempstead on the 322, they worked alongside – and made an interesting comparison with – the regular RFs. RW 3 is seen at its terminus near 'The Ship' in Weybridge. *Michael Dryhurst*

The three RWs spent the summer of 1961 at Reigate on the 440 and 440A. On a hot day the driver has opened the windscreen on a lightly loaded RW 1 to let in the cool air and all the side window sliders are open, but there is still the likelihood that, on a day like this, the glass roof panels could still make the interior uncomfortably hot. Specified by Grimsby-Cleethorpes to provide a useful aid to standing passengers, there is little chance of the glazed roof panels being used for this purpose on routes such as the 440A. *Mick Webber*

As a general rule the three RWs accompanied each other on each assignment, the only exception to this being when RW 3 left Hertford on 26th September 1962 to work from Stevenage garage on route 383 (Oakfield Estate–Hitchin–Weston), an operation which lasted less than three months and ended with RW 3 rejoining the others at Hertford on 12th November. There were occasions when at some – possibly all – locations RWs appeared on services other than those shown above, probably in accordance with vehicle availability at the time.

The vehicles' performance was closely monitored at each garage, particularly to assess the value or otherwise of the two-door layout, and the conclusion was that it was an unnecessary complexity, offering little or no advantage over the normal single-door arrangement. Any potential value in speeding-up boarding and alighting could only be achieved on services with stops where heavy movements in both directions – both on and off – took place simultaneously, which was seldom the case on Country Bus services even at the busiest stops. Despite being pleasant enough to drive, they were not much favoured by drivers, many of whom viewed having to operate and oversee the central doors as an unnecessary chore, while in rural areas difficulty was sometimes experienced in positioning vehicles at stops to avoid passengers alighting into hedges or other obstructions.

A big problem with the RW was that the AEC Reliance chassis did not live up to its name. Despite the popularity of the model in terms of numbers sold, it was nowhere near as reliable as it should have been especially when employed on busy, stop-start stage carriage work, and in terms of lost mileage the RWs reflected poorly in comparison with the RF. Design shortcomings resulted in an inadequately sized radiator and sandwiched the flywheel between the engine and gearbox where it received little ventilation, inevitably resulting in frequent flywheel overheating problems. Also, the AH470 engine itself was not really up to the task. Despite the Reliance having been in production since 1954 this engine was still the only option offered at the time the RWs were purchased even though it had a widespread reputation for cooling problems causing overheating and excessive head gasket failures with all the consequences – some of them serious – that all this caused for maintenance staff. Later, AEC made the much-improved and slightly more powerful dry-liner AH505 available, but this came too late for the RWs.

The only RW to undertake a solo adventure anywhere was RW 3 which moved away from route 333 between August and November 1962 to work from Stevenage garage with its main focus on route 383, now a much shorter operation than in earlier days. Passengers wait to board the local service to Walsworth in the familiar surroundings of the bus stand in St Mary's Square, Hitchin.

Having done the rounds of potentially suitable services around the country area the RWs returned in June 1963 to where they had started, Hemel Hempstead garage on routes 322/A, RW 3 on 6th June and the other two on the 19th. Having served their purpose, and being non-standard, it was now decided to dispose of them while a good price could still be obtained. All three were delicensed on 1st October and moved a couple of days later to Garston garage for storage.

The purchaser was Chesterfield Corporation in whose fleet they became nos 18-20. The official sales dates were those on which they were collected by Chesterfield staff, RW 2 on 14th November, RW 1 on 25th November and, finally, RW 3 on 4th December 1963. They served Chesterfield well – a full 14 years in all three cases – with the last one of all, the former RW 1, being withdrawn from service in March 1978. The latter vehicle subsequently went for scrap, but the other two still survive. RW 2 was adopted as a preservation project by the London Bus Preservation Group shortly after withdrawal while RW 3, which saw further service in Somerset as part of C P Knubley's Brutonian Bus Company fleet until 1987, was also saved and is now active on the preservation scene.

The fourth operational garage for the RWs was St Albans where they spent ten months on route 355. RW 2 has arrived on a scheduled short working journey at Radlett. Signs of the changing times are that the via points on the destination blind are now in lower case lettering (first seen in November 1961, the month in which the RWs made their appearance at St Albans). *Simon Butler*

Green and cream are still the basic colours adorning the RWs under the ownership of Chesterfield Corporation although the application is now somewhat different. Nothing much else appears to have changed except that the London-style trafficator ears have been removed in favour of more conventional flashers. The former RW 2 is seen arriving with a fair load in the centre of Chesterfield. where the three vehicles spent a full and active life after leaving London Transport. *John Cockshott*

REAR-ENGINED DOUBLE DECKERS – THE XAs

The arrival of the nineteen-sixties found London Transport's bus operations in a parlous state. From the position of pre-eminence that it had occupied a few decades earlier, when it was a sharply managed and well-regarded organisation staffed from top to bottom by employees proud to work for it, the opposite now applied. Severe staff shortages adversely affected the standard of service being provided and public discontent over London Transport's performance was rife. Outside factors, such as the relentless rise in car usage causing passenger loss and traffic jams, had of course to be contended with, but an overriding problem lay within the organisation itself. Many of those now occupying top echelons of management were less sharp and entrepreneurial than their predecessors, which inspired less confidence among middle and lower ranks, especially when the latter witnessed management bending to unreasonable trade union pressure and acquiescing to a string of restrictive practices which made effective service provision even harder than it otherwise would have been.

The construction of 50 Atlantean bodies was a prestigious order for Park Royal to receive, and a production line for them was set up during the spring of 1965. Two are seen here in a fairly advanced state of construction. External panelling is taking place, and the one-piece glassfibre front and rear domes are already in position. *Leon Daniels collection*

Low wages for busmen lay at the root of the staff shortage problem. From being one of the highest paid trades in London before the war, inspiring loyalty for London Transport and keen competition for employment within it, pay restraint introduced in the wartime years and pursued afterwards in line with government policy had brought the job to its knees. One aspect that particularly rankled was that bus drivers, despite the arduous nature of their work, were paid a full 11% less than their motorman counterparts on the Underground.

Something had to be done, and in November 1963 the Conservative government announced the setting-up of an independent public inquiry under the chairmanship of economist Henry Phelps Brown to thoroughly examine London Transport's bus business and to come up with recommendations for turning the situation around. The Phelps Brown report, published in April 1964, was far reaching and concentrated the minds of the London Transport Board and the trade unions towards positive steps for planning a better future. Recommendation for improved pay levels obviously featured highly in the report, but several new operational features to raise efficiency were also recommended. One of these was that the use of a front entrance double deck bus with doors would be preferable to London Transport's standard openplatform Routemaster as the driver could control boarding, thus leaving the conductor free to collect fares, an option which many other operators had already been using for several years. The seed for the purchase of 50 Leyland Atlanteans for the XA (Experimental Atlantean) class was sown.

With the passage of time the days of coachbuilding at Park Royal are today a dim and distant memory. Former times are recalled here with brand new RCL 2247 and XA 6 standing in adjacent doorways. Although already obsolete in context before it has even started work, the Routemaster is undoubtedly the better built of the two and the difference in quality is clear. *Capital Transport*

The precursor of times to come, Leyland Atlantean demonstrator SGD 669 was tested at Chiswick Works for a couple of days in September 1964 to enable London Transport to finalise its own specification for the 50 vehicles of the same model that it intended ordering. A former Glasgow Corporation vehicle, SGD 669 had been repainted into an eye-catching yellow and cream livery with appropriate advertising material on the sides and back, and travelled widely as a demonstrator. A few weeks before coming to London, It was seen at work in Bradford city centre on the Corporation's trunk service to Huddersfield via Brighouse.
Roy Marshall

A formal order was placed on 8th July 1964 and in September a demonstration vehicle arrived at Chiswick Works. This was SGD 669, a striking-looking 78-seater with Alexander bodywork incorporating wrap-around windscreens at the front of both decks, adorned in a bold yellow and cream livery with black mouldings separating the two main colours.

Originally licensed for service in January 1963 it was, in fact, one of a sizeable fleet of identical vehicles supplied to Glasgow Corporation in 1962/63, who had subsequently sold this particular one back to Leyland specifically to undertake demonstration work on the chassis manufacturer's behalf.

SGD 669 spent two full days at Chiswick, on

Tuesday and Wednesday 15th and 16th September 1964, undertaking steering and brake tests. These were carried out in both unladen and fully-laden condition on the Chiswick Works internal test circuit which started from outside the experimental shop and, with five sharp left-hand turns and the same number of right hand ones, plus a westbound run through the famous 'dip', ensured that vehicles were thoroughly put through their paces. Kerb tests were also carried out, which consisted of pulling out from behind a stationary vehicle in order to overtake it such as often happened with a bus moving off from a stop. The results were duly tabulated and compared against those from four of London Transport's own vehicles which were similarly tested. Two of these, RT 3995 and RM 8, were permanently allocated to the experimental department and not used in public service, but the other two, RM 510 and RML 881, were taken from the normal operational fleet. In the case of the Routemasters, RM 510 was tested without power assistance to the steering and RML 881 with it, while RM 8 was tested in both conditions.

The demonstration Atlantean did not have power steering, and the conclusion from the tests was that steering effort on it, though comparable to standard London Transport vehicles in unladen condition, was considerably higher when laden. This led to a subsequent decision to specify power assistance when ordering the London Transport batch. The braking tests proved inconclusive because it was found that, to comply with Glasgow's specification, SGD 669 had been fitted with linings that were non-standard for Atlanteans, although it was decided that an air-assisted handbrake would need to be included in the London Transport specification.

Following the SGD 669 tests, the final specification for the 50 London chassis was quickly drawn up and issued on 26th October 1964. They were to be based on the Atlantean PDR1/1 16ft 3ins wheelbase chassis powered by a vertically-mounted 0.680 direct injection engine flexibly mounted complete with fluid flywheel, gearbox and radiator on a readily removable sub-frame at the rear of the chassis. The rear chassis extension formed a substantial cradle to carry the complete power pack on its sub-frame, and Leyland demonstrated that, under test conditions, the whole pack could be removed and replaced within the incredibly short time of 24 min 15sec, but since this presupposed the availability of a replacement power pack and of a fork lift, it would hardly have been relevant in normal London Transport garage circumstances. With 5 inch bore and 5¾ inch stroke, the 0.680 had a cubic capacity of 11.1 litres and was derated, in accordance with normal London Transport policy, to develop 130bhp at 1800rpm.

Many standard Leyland items featured in the specification including front and rear axles, radiator and fan, fluid flywheel, chassis lubrication, angle-drive unit and compressed air braking system using air supplied by an engine-driven compressor, with separate reservoirs for brakes and auxiliaries. The gearbox was to be a standard Leyland pneumo-cyclic air-operated unit in conjunction with a fully automatic change system to suit London Transport's requirements. A Marles cam and double roller type steering unit was specified with power assistance. The rear axle was of the spiral bevel type, and the suspension consisted of 4-inch wide semi-elliptic leaf springs.

Meanwhile, a body specification was agreed with Park Royal Coachworks which, since 1962, had been a subsidiary of the Leyland Motor Corporation. Park Royal contracted to provide bodies which, by agreement with London Transport, would follow a basic specification drawn up for seven vehicles supplied in May 1964 to Stockton Corporation Transport as its nos A 1-7 (BPT 511-517B), with a further seven identical vehicles A 8-14 (EPT 908-914B) following later in the same year. A special feature of these bodies was that a step was provided from the boarding platform instead of half way along the lower saloon, which lifted the floor from the bottom of the front wheelarches, thus providing a wider entrance to the saloon and giving a completely level floor within it.

It was arranged that the seats and general internal décor would be as close to Routemaster standard as possible. The bodies were heated by exchanger and blower units mounted under the upper saloon rear passenger seat and directed to both decks by way of ducting to various outlet slots. The double-folding GD Peters doors were electrically operated under the control of the driver. In contrast to normal London Transport practice the opening windows were of the sliding variety, those on XA 1-25 being of the Hallam Sleigh & Cheston 'Famco' type while XA 26-50 had Beclawat 'Zephyr' units. The driver's cab was provided with a full-depth locker for the use of the crew, and a demister unit was provided with two outlets to each windscreen and one to the driver's feet, while a fresh air inlet grille was also provided below the windscreens and was visible on the outside of the vehicle just above the bullseye motif.

Park Royal was, of course, busy building RMLs at the time, but these were very different and visibly much better quality bodies than the XAs and were built in another part of the factory. The Atlantean incorporated a steel framed structure with frameless, fibreglass front and rear domes of a style first initiated by the BET group ten years earlier. The Stockton vehicles were 74 seaters (41 upstairs and 33 down), but London Transport specified 72 seats to keep in line with the RML, with only 31 on the lower deck where a luggage rack was placed adjacent to the entrance platform instead of a seat for two.

The 50 chassis were supplied more or less in numerical order, the first being that of XA 1 (chassis no L23982) which arrived at Park Royal's factory on 1st February 1965. XA 2 and XA 3 (L25061 and L40195 respectively) followed on 12th February, and thereafter a steady though sporadic supply was maintained until XA 50's chassis arrived at the coachbuilders on 13th October. Interestingly, the majority of chassis from XA 10 onwards appear to have been built in pairs (or, on a couple of occasions, in batches of four), presumably to suit Leyland's busy production schedule, with chassis numbers reaching as high as L42857 with XA 50.

Each vehicle was described by London Transport as costing 'roundly' £8,000. The first completed ones arrived at Aldenham from the Park Royal factory in the form of XA 2-5 on 14th June 1965. XA 1 followed on 17th June, after which a fairly steady flow was maintained up to the arrival of XA 33 on 11th August. Many were delivered directly to Fulwell garage where there was ample space to store them until they could be accommodated at Aldenham for their initial delivery checks. A two month gap then occurred before deliveries resumed once again on 28th October culminating in the receipt of the final pair, XA 49, 50 on 21st December. All carried standard Central Bus red livery relieved by a grey central band which was notable in being considerably wider than on the RT and RM classes.

June 1965, and newly-completed XA 6-12 are neatly lined up in strict numerical order in readiness for their official photograph to be taken. London Transport was not yet ready to put them into service and they were delivered direct to Fulwell garage for storage prior to making their service debut some four months later.

Externally the XAs were disappointingly bland in appearance when compared with Alexander's inspired design on SGD 669. The plain, flat front of the bodywork lacked any artistic flair, and the frameless front dome section was rendered even more utilitarian-looking than usual by the disfiguring raised ridge that ran vertically through the centre of it as a means of enhancing rigidity. Their only saving grace was at the back with its nicely rounded dome and where shrouds were fitted which curved around and partially overlapped the engine compartment, giving a smooth rear-end appearance and avoiding the untidy bustle effect so often associated with the Atlantean. A three-piece destination display was provided at the front using standard Routemaster parts, but there was no side blind and only a route number aperture was provided at the rear.

At 30ft 4ins the XA was greater in length than the 29ft 10½ins of the RML but it was slightly lower in unladen height (XA – 14ft 4¾ins: RML – 14ft 5⅛ins). A major difference between the two was in unladen weight where, at 8tons 15cwt, the XA far exceeded the 7tons 15cwt of the RML, so it was handy that the 11.1 litre capacity of the XA engine was available to maintain the same level of road performance as that of the 9.636 litre RML. Despite its much shorter wheelbase (16ft 3ins compared with 19ft 2ins on the RML), the XA was the much less manoeuvrable of the two with a swept turning circle of 71ft 0ins, a full 3ft longer than the RML.

The Chiswick classification for the XAs was 1XA1 and they were allocated body numbers in a new series A 1-50. Registration numbers were reserved for them as CUV 1C upwards but these were applied only as far as XA 37. XA 38 onwards were not licensed for road use until 1st January 1966 which, being the start of a new year, required a change in registration number sequence and appeared as JLA 38-50D.

Now adorned with blinds for route 24, on which it never actually ran, and with Chalk Farm running number plates, XA 1 is posed at Aldenham still in pristine condition. XA 1 was, in fact, the very last of the class to enter service, at Stamford Hill, in July 1966. Totally unlike anyone's normal idea of a traditional London double decker, these vehicles looked bland and boxy when viewed from the front. *London Transport Museum*

Views inside XA 1 show the completely flat floor running the length of the lower saloon with the exception of the usual raised platforms over the wheel arches. The use throughout of Routemaster décor gives a London 'feel' to the interior, and a London-style bell cord has even been provided, albeit now on the offside rather than over the nearside seats. Fluorescent lighting is, however, a new feature. *London Transport Museum*

The upper saloon showing the seating arrangement and the positioning of the staircase. Although the latter does not impinge too much on gangway width, a single seat has been installed at the top of the stairs to facilitate passenger circulation. The roof is double-skinned except in the areas of the one-piece domes. *London Transport Museum*

The XAs were arguably more attractive when viewed from behind thanks to the sleek curvature of their rear domes and the use of engine shrouds, which overcame the untidy 'bustle' effect that disfigured so many provincial Atlanteans. At its second photographic session, on 18th June 1965, XA 1 still carries its route 24 blinds and CF garage running plates, but advertising material has now been applied including a reminder that unlimited travel could be had on country bus routes for a mere six shillings a day thanks to Green Rover tickets. *London Transport Museum*

The XAs were introduced to the trade press and other interested bodies at Stockwell garage on Monday 17th June 1965, followed by a run on XA 2 over some of the routes it was contemplated that they might run on. Some of those present, aware that London Transport had encountered difficulties in persuading the trade union to accept these vehicles, were perplexed at the mixed message emanating from senior staff at the unveiling. Introducing the XA, the Central Bus Operating Manager, M J McCoy, described its introduction as an experiment, predicting that by employing the vehicles on a route which passed through central London they would make a "pretty good impact" on the general public. However, K G Shave, the Chief Mechanical Engineer (Road Services), expressed the view that he did not regard the new vehicles as experimental in the sense that they were not up to London Transport's normal standards, and that if Mr McCoy's department's efforts proved successful, buses of similar layout but based on Routemaster principles would have to be built. This was hardly a vote of confidence in a vehicle which had yet to enter service.

It took almost five months after the press jaunt on XA 2 to get the new vehicles into passenger service. Lengthy and sometimes difficult negotiations took place with the unions over their introduction, and it was not until 7th November 1965 that the XAs finally made their service debut amid huge publicity on route 24 (Hampstead Heath–Pimlico) worked by Chalk Farm garage. Thirty-one were provided, a figure optimistically thought to be sufficient to cover the 30 scheduled duties and to provide engineering cover. These were XA 2-4/6-33 one of which, XA 20, had been licensed there from 21st October for driver training purposes. The remainder had mostly been in store in nearby garages at Holloway, Highgate and Finchley awaiting their call for duty.

London Transport's stated intention was to test this type of bus in the rigorous operating conditions of the West End and City against the conventional London Transport double decker with its open rear platform, and the partner service for this initial test was route 76 which had recently been equipped with a fleet of new RMLs in place of RTWs in readiness for the trial. Tottenham garage worked the 76, and it was London Transport's plan that the XAs would come here in due course with RMLs passing in the opposite direction to Chalk Farm. The 76 had not, in fact, been the original choice. This was the Monday-Saturday route 7 (Kew Green (Sats)–Acton (Mon-Fri)–London Bridge) operated by Middle Row garage, but this plan had to be abandoned when it was realised that the cramped and outdated premises at Middle Row were not suitable for housing Atlanteans. The 76 was an unusually complex operation focussed, in the main, between Victoria and Tottenham. However there was also a secondary service which diverted from the main route at peak times to link Victoria with Liverpool Street Station. Further than this, at its northern end, the 76 was extended from Tottenham to Lower Edmonton in Monday to Friday peak hours and for part of the day on Saturdays, with a few Monday to Friday factory journeys projecting into the far northern suburbs at Brimsdown. From here, some buses operated as route 34B to Walthamstow in a rare case on Central Buses of vehicles transferring directly from one route to another as part of their scheduled duty.

Under the renowned barrel-vaulted roof of Stockwell garage, XA 2's bonnet cover is raised to show the engine installation to representatives of the press on the big 'unveiling' day, 17th June 1965. Several locally-based RTLs can be seen in the background while, on the right, the BBC has sent along one of its television outside-broadcast units. *London Transport Museum*

It was planned that, once the 24 had been stocked with XAs, the remainder would go initially to Highgate garage for operation on route 271 (Highgate Village–Moorgate). Its 'partner' route, to which they would be transferred in due course in exchange for RMLs, would be the 67 (Northumberland Park–London Docks) worked from Stamford Hill garage. The 271 and 67 had both formerly been trolleybus operations (numbered 611 and 647 respectively) on which higher capacity 70-seat vehicles had once been the norm prior to their conversion to RM operation in 1960/61.

Once in service on route 24, all did not go well with the XAs whose mechanical frailties added to everyday operating problems such as late running which often caused severe disruption to scheduled meal reliefs. On this occasion, the inspector in charge at the Harmood Street stop in Chalk Farm Road, the closest to the garage, deals with the delayed arrival of the replacement crew for XA 25 while, on the other side of the road, XA 4 has already been curtailed at this point in the knowledge that the next crew would not be available, and now XA 31 has arrived, showing Hampstead Heath as its destination but with no staff available to take it onwards from here.
Michael Beamish

The mechanical unreliability of the XAs frequently meant that replacement vehicles of other types had to be provided. On this occasion, XA 29 prepares to depart from the stand at Hampstead Heath (although its destination blind hasn't yet been changed to read PIMLICO), but the next departure will not be a scheduled Atlantean; instead it will be veteran RT 4273. Although the two vehicles could not look more different, a feature they share in common is that both carry bodies built by Park Royal.
Capital Transport

Stage 2 of the experiment began on Saturday 1st January 1966 when Highgate received the 17 highest numbered Atlanteans (XA 34-50) for route 271. This route had been of particular interest in trolleybus days when it had required special vehicles with coasting and run-back brakes because of the steepness of Highgate Hill, which would test the hill-climbing capabilities of the XAs to the full.

Meanwhile, preliminary testing by Rolling Stock department staff at Chiswick had already begun (including trial runs on Reigate Hill) to ascertain the performance of the new vehicles using XA 2 and XA 33. The results, published internally within London Transport on 26th January 1966, announced that from a maintenance view the XA could not be considered as accessible as RM types, but concluded that the Atlantean compared favourably with RMs for mechanical and auxiliary equipment performance while acknowledging that no overall assessment could truly be made without extensive service performance. And, as was soon to become abundantly clear, service performance of the XAs would quickly demonstrate that they had many shortcomings. In fact operation of them became problematic and at times nightmarish, badly affecting service reliability and causing a collapse of confidence by staff and passengers alike.

The litany of problems with which the engineers found themselves confronted is dealt with later in this chapter.

Alongside its service trials with the Leyland Atlantean, London Transport was also experimenting with eight examples of its close competitor, the Daimler Fleetline, a small batch of which had entered service in the country area at East Grinstead on 15th September 1965, almost two months ahead of the XAs. A detailed examination of XF 1-8 is contained in the next chapter, but a mention of the XFs cannot be avoided here as their history while with London Transport is inextricably linked with that of the XAs. Although at the time of their purchase, there was no intention that either model would ever become a regular member of the London Transport fleet, it was inevitable that both the engineering and operating departments would want to study the merits of the two and to seek out and compare their various strengths and weaknesses. After experiencing a catalogue of problems with the Atlanteans, the inside staff at Highgate probably viewed with mixed feelings the news that their job was to become even more complex and that they were to receive the eight XFs to run alongside XAs for fuel consumption and other tests.

Unlike route 24, the 271 was not a West End service but it served, instead, the City of London where XA 21 is seen arriving at its terminus in Finsbury Square, Moorgate. Behind it, a more typical London bus of the era, New Cross garage's RT 1723, prepares for its long run south to Sidcup on route 21. XA 21 was not one of the original Atlanteans on the 271; it was a one-off transfer to Highgate from Chalk Farm in April 1966. *Alan Nightingale*

XA 36 was the lowest numbered of the eight XAs transferred to East Grinstead on 16th April 1966 in exchange for Daimler Fleetlines. Quickly adorned with front advertisements for a pram and cot dealer in East Grinstead, it looked very much at home passing through Horley on route 424 despite its red livery. *Ken Blacker*

On the evening of 16th April 1966 East Grinstead's eight XFs were despatched to Highgate to begin work on the 271 the next day. The eight Atlanteans which went in the opposite direction were XA 36-39, 42, 44, 47, 49. As the move was only a temporary one for experimental purposes, the sixteen vehicles retained their original livery and the red XAs soon became an accepted feature on route 424 (Reigate–East Grinstead).

June 12th 1966 was the date on which the first XA/RML exchange was due to take place, with Chalk Farm's XAs from route 24 moving eastwards to Tottenham to take up their new role on routes 76 and 34B. Their stay at Chalk Farm had lasted just over seven months, but the XAs were destined to be a feature of the Tottenham scene for very much longer than this, becoming the mainstay of routes 76 and 34B for the next 2½ years. The situation was further enlivened when they were joined by FRM 1, London Transport's own effort at designing a rear-engined double decker, which made its inaugural public run as a 34B on 26th June 1967 and remained working alongside the XAs until it was delicensed on 1st August 1969. During the XAs' tenure, route 76 was cut back from its long-established terminus at Victoria to Waterloo on 22nd March 1969 apart from some peak hour journeys which now terminated at Horse Guards Avenue.

XA 45 was one of the vehicles that introduced Atlantean operation to Tottenham garage on 12th June 1966. A feature of route 76 was that it crossed the Thames twice on its inner London section, and on this occasion XA 45 has just left Blackfriars Bridge and is now arriving in Stamford Street to find its compulsory bus stop temporarily closed due to nearby building works.

The second of the two XA/RML swaps was scheduled for 10th July 1966 but was complicated by the fact that eight out of the fifteen rear-engined double deckers at Highgate on the 271 were the green-liveried Fleetlines, XF 1-8. These were not initially required at Stamford Hill for route 67 (although they would be tried out there later), and were returned to East Grinstead whose eight XAs moved overnight to Stamford Hill. Also of note amongst the Stamford Hill contingent was XA 1, which was the only Atlantean not so far used in public service having been used up to then mainly as a trainer. This now became part of the 18-strong XA fleet initially provided to cover the same number of scheduled workings on route 67 which, incidentally, covered common ground with the XAs on route 76 over the very busy stretch of road between Tottenham and Dalston through Stamford Hill and Stoke Newington. Inevitably, with no spare XAs to call on to cover scheduled maintenance or breakdowns, RMs could frequently be found working alongside the newer vehicles. Not long afterwards, on 31st December 1966, Stamford Hill's XAs opened up new bus territory when route 67 was extended beyond its old London Docks terminus to Wapping, a largely unknown and unvisited area of dockland London at that time.

Nine months after XAs arrived on route 67, the second of the two XA/XF exchanges took place on 13th May 1967. A two-way move was arranged for the XAs destined to go to East Grinstead, its purpose being to avoid the same ones returning that had worked from there previously. Eight XAs were transferred from Stamford Hill to Tottenham and this enabled XA 5, 6, 8, 14, 15, 29, 30, 41 to go to the country area for the first time. This second incursion by Fleetlines to the central area was destined to last much longer than the first, and found the eight XFs working at Stamford Hill for not far short of two years during which time they all received an Aldenham repaint but retained their green livery. This longer spell of dual operation gave a better opportunity to compare the merits and demerits of the two types of vehicle, and it is fair to report that the Fleetline once again proved almost unanimously the more popular of the two, both with engineering and driving staff, being more reliable in operation and less prone to breakdowns. Interestingly, the XAs were seen to perform better at East Grinstead than on central area service, probably because their work on the 424 was less onerous than the stop/start conditions prevailing in central London, a fact which did not go unnoticed by London Transport's senior management. Their stay at East Grinstead lasted until 1st March 1969 when the comparative trial ceased and the two batches of vehicles returned home.

At all four Central garages to which they were allocated the XAs produced a host of mechanical problems, causing inevitable lost mileage and necessitating frequent substitution by vehicles of other classes. A senior member of the Chiswick

The only major projection into new operating territory by the XAs during their Central Bus career was when route 67 was extended into the heart of Wapping on the very last day of 1966. With only a temporary 'dolly' stop on hand to notify its presence, Stamford Hill's XA 44 stands at the terminus in Wapping High Street just across the road from the Metropolitan Line station which had hitherto provided the only public transport access into the area. Thanks to the huge Docklands redevelopment of recent times, Wapping looks nothing like this today. *Ken Blacker collection*

engineering staff, Colin Curtis, was given the task of collating and examining all these problems, and on 29th January 1968 he produced a full, 11-page report on every aspect of the XAs' performance. In the conclusion to his report, Colin noted that, compared with the Routemaster, the Atlantean had some serious problems and remarked that it had been disappointing to London Transport that these were still present on a vehicle which had already been on the market for several years. However, he gave credit to Leyland Motors' service department at Borehamwood, under the direction of Mr F Margetts, which had given invaluable service to London Transport in trying to keep the vehicles on the road. Regular meetings had been held with Leyland and many tests carried out. He rightly suggested that more development work by Leyland under true service bus conditions would bring better reliability, and this is what subsequently occurred, culminating in the AN68 version of the Atlantean which made its debut in February 1972 and retrieved the reputation for Leyland that the PDR range had badly tarnished, not just in London but with operators elsewhere too.

In no particular order of importance, some of the problems that beset the XAs in London service can be summarised as follows:

Overheating Almost as soon as the class entered service overheating became a serious and constant problem. It was associated with the fluid flywheel which was a fully enclosed unit, and being sandwiched between the engine and the gearbox there was no way that heat could be dissipated when idling or left stationary in gear, which was London Transport's standard procedure at the time. Flywheel glands failed, leading to the necessity for gearbox removal. It was observed that on the XFs, where the flywheel was not enclosed, under-bonnet temperatures were found to be as much as 50% lower than on the XA.

Further flywheel failures In addition to the overheating problem, frequent breaking-up of the ball race at the back of the flywheel caused serious damage to the flywheel itself, while further failures occurred because of oil leakage due, in the main, to the use of an easily-damaged aluminium rear casing.

Engine A major fault, often experienced, was that severe end thrust could occur on the crankshaft which led, in several cases, to failure of the crankshaft itself.

Fuel system Non-starts were a constant problem with the XAs right from the beginning due to the fuel running back from the fuel pump. Despite a number of modifications this problem was never really solved.

Gearbox Excessive band wear, especially on third speed, resulted from over-high operating temperatures causing a severe drop in friction of the brake liner material leading to excessive slip. The higher temperatures also seriously affected oil viscosity. Several cases also occurred of worn out top speeds, possibly influenced by the absence of shims to take up plate wear.

Steering The two-spoke steering wheels supplied on earlier vehicles at Chalk Farm quickly buckled and had to be replaced by the four-spoke variety as used on RTLs and RTWs. The power steering was sometimes found to be inadequate because the header reservoir was too small, and a larger tank had subsequently to be fitted.

Air pressure system The extremely high underbonnet temperatures caused various problems with the air pressure system requiring two complete campaign changes to be carried out.

Cooling system Considerable difficulty was experienced early on with radiator leakage and necessitated a design change, but continued difficulty was experienced in keeping the radiator tight in its mountings. Boiling of the system occurred, especially in summer. With the engine, flywheel, gearbox and transfer box plus the radiator situated in a common chamber, an abundance of heat could be expected, but attempts to introduce more air by additional louvres on the bonnet top were unsuccessful.

The report contained some statistical information which clearly indicated how the 50 vehicles had needed time-consuming unit changes far in excess of what would reasonably be expected in a fleet of its size still less than three years old, namely: fluid clutch/flywheel 116, starter motor 45, radiator 37, gearbox 30, air compressor 18, engine 9.

The comparative trials between the XA and the RML had indicated clearly the superiority of the latter in terms of mechanical reliability and overall operating costs. Fuel usage, which on the RML averaged 7.8 miles per gallon on central London service, reduced to a disappointing 6.6mpg for the XA on similar work. Increased boarding times caused by the doors further impeded their performance compared with the open platform RML. A reappraisal of the future of the XAs was obviously necessary, and it was concluded that they would be better employed on less stressful, suburban work with fewer stops and starts and where higher operating speeds could be achieved.

Meanwhile an overhaul programme for all 50 vehicles was devised with a trial run commenced at Aldenham on XA 7 starting on 1st February 1968. Being an 'off the shelf' model, the Atlantean could not be accommodated within the normal Aldenham overhaul system due to its semi-integral nature where the body was not designed to be separated from the chassis, and XA 7's overhaul, which was very much of an exploratory nature, took almost nine months. It was recorded as being complete on 21st October 1968, allowing the vehicle to be relicensed for service at Tottenham on 1st December. Meanwhile a second vehicle, XA 2, was taken into the works on 11th October 1968, and a regular process encompassing the rest of the XA fleet commenced in February 1969. Each vehicle was delicensed for the period of its overhaul and the time spent on each one varied but was usually between two to three months.

When the inevitable decision was taken to move the XAs on to suburban work, it was also decided that they would also be employed in future as one-man operated vehicles, for which they were best suited. From October 1969 onwards, vehicles emerging from overhaul were no longer put back into service at Stamford Hill and Tottenham with the result that the number of XAs in service on the 67 and 76/34B began to steadily dwindle as increasing numbers of ordinary RMs became ever more apparent. Already-overhauled vehicles were being delicensed too, and returned to Aldenham to be prepared for the next phase in their London career. By 1st November 1969 the number of XAs at Tottenham had dwindled to 9 and at Stamford Hill to 12, while from 1st January 1970 only one remained at Tottenham and four at Stamford Hill. The theoretical final day of XA operation at both garages is believed to have been 20th January 1970 with XA 45 still available for work at Tottenham and XA 7 and XA 50 at Stamford Hill.

The XA overhaul programme of 1969 found XA 10, freshly ex-works, shunted from Aldenham to Chiswick in May as a guinea pig in the trial of a new, modern-looking fleet logo. The bullseye motif has gone from the front, and on the side an open white roundel sits where the traditional and stylish LONDON TRANSPORT gold lettering formerly appeared. This was, in fact, approved as the new standard except that the LONDON TRANSPORT name was added to the cross bar, and this became the norm for overhauled XAs henceforth. It lasted only until a plain, infilled white roundel replaced it in 1973, but all the XAs had gone from the fleet by then.

Meanwhile the stock of XAs on Central Buses had decreased by three. The Country Bus & Coach department was about to introduce a brand new style of operation under the title of 'Blue Arrow' in Stevenage New Town for which three of its Daimler Fleetlines were required, and these were replaced by three XAs. XA 47 and 48 were transferred there from Tottenham on 1st November 1969 followed four days later by XA 46 when it was released from training duties, and all three were immediately placed in service at East Grinstead. Two of them were new to the garage, only XA 47 having served there previously. In the opposite direction, RMLs 2321, 2441 and 2443 were transferred to central area stock and were repainted red before re-entering service in December.

XA 46-48 left London Transport's books just two months later on 1st January 1970 upon formation of London Country Bus Services Ltd although, like all former London Transport stock absorbed into that company, they were destined to retain their former London Transport identity and to remain initially under the wing of Aldenham works and the rolling stock department at Chiswick pending the opening by LCBS of its own new central works at Tinsley Green, Crawley in January 1976. None of the three had received an overhaul prior to transfer to London Country, but after London Transport's own XAs had all been dealt with these three were despatched to Aldenham for similar treatment in March 1970, returning to East Grinstead in May and June in green and yellow livery.

The first move towards a new future for the 47 XAs destined to remain with London Transport occurred on 25th October 1969 at Croydon garage when XA 25 arrived there from Tottenham to take up training duties, joined from 1st November by XA 22. The latter made history on Saturday 22nd of the same month when it entered passenger service on route 233 as the Central Bus department's first one-man operated double decker. Previously worked by a single RF, the 233 was a shuttle service between West Croydon bus station and Roundshaw introduced as recently as 31st May 1969, which had rapidly taken off and already required a larger vehicle than the RF. Within a few days XA 28 had been made available as a spare joined by XA 24 at the end of the month. From 19th December these were joined by FRM 1 which found itself running alongside XAs once again, albeit now in omo mode.

Following on from this tentative start, the future plan was for Croydon's allocation of XAs to be massively increased with the majority of the class being based here in future. However, bodywork modifications were required before the vehicles could be one-man operated including provision of a periscope to enable the driver to view loadings (and passenger behaviour) on the upper deck. To make the periscope effective the upstairs mirror had to be re-sited from above the top of the staircase where, with no conductor on board, it no longer served any purpose. Its new position was on the offside corner of the front dome. The latter, being of frameless construction, had to be drilled right through to take the mirror supports, leaving a tell-tale sign visible from outside that it had been converted for omo. A reversing light, inserted at the rear immediately above the existing rear lamp cluster, was another requirement. In most cases the work of preparing the XAs for omo was carried out at Aldenham while they were going through overhaul.

The autumn 1969 conversion of the XAs for one-man operation necessitated the installation of a fairly substantial box-like arrangement at the upstairs front to accommodate the driver's periscope. This work was carried out at Aldenham along with the repositioning of the mirror into the offside corner of the frameless front dome where it could be viewed by the driver using his periscope. *London Transport Museum*

The flat-fare 'Johnson' boxes, which proved almost universally unpopular, were installed within clear view of the driver, up against the now blanked-off fare chart holder. In a 2nd December 1969 view a make-believe passenger (perhaps a member of staff?) demonstrates dropping a 6d coin into the top of the box, with the driver releasing it into the container below. A later photo, taken on 4th January 1970, shows the instruction notices provided to inform passengers on how to use the system. *London Transport Museum*

However, before Croydon began receiving its large batch of XAs, a small secondary operation was established at Peckham garage on 24th January 1970 where, as part of the grand 'Re-shaping' programme introduced in response to the Phelps Brown report, RM-operated circular route 173 linking Peckham with Nunhead was converted to omo using XAs and renumbered P3. The P3 was designed as a flat-fare operation using automatic fare collection machines known within London Transport as 'Johnson' boxes and the majority of the forthcoming Croydon XA fleet was also planned to operate with this method of fare collection. The 'Johnson' box was fitted just inside the vehicle on the left of the entrance door, obscuring the former fare chart holder which was no longer needed on a flat fare operation. According to an internal summary of the omo fleet dated November 1971, 45 out of the 47 XAs were equipped with these boxes.

In preparation for the start of the P3, XA 29 was based at Camberwell between 25th and 29th October 1969 to provide mechanical training for Peckham's inside staff, while XA 30 was available at New Cross from 1st January onwards for driver training. At the start of operation, seven XAs were allocated to Peckham (XA 2, 3, 14, 19, 30, 32, 33) to cover the six scheduled workings, and three days later these were joined by XA 23 and XA 28.

A suburban scene in Nunhead soon after the introduction of Atlantean-worked flat fare service P3, with XA 30 approaching on the clockwise leg of the circular operation and XA 3 disappearing into the distance. At this stage XA 30 still carries the original style of fleet names. Both vehicles were among those that introduced XA operation to Peckham garage on 24th January 1970, remaining in service there until early 1973. *Peter Mitchell*

Large scale operation of XAs at Croydon began a little later than originally anticipated. Staff reaction against the introduction of one-man operation, and the Re-shaping plan in general, meant that things did not move forwards as quickly as management hoped, and a result of this was that 26 XAs that were relicensed for service at Croydon on 1st March 1970 could not immediately be put to use. They were part of a total of 28 needed to work partly as conventional omo vehicles in place of RTs on route 234 (Selsdon–Hackbridge), but mostly to cover a range of new flat-fare, farebox services linking West Croydon bus station with New Addington, augmenting but not entirely replacing the established route 130, and incorporating elements of express operation in peak hours. These were to be C1 (Mondays to Fridays and Sundays) terminating at Homestead Way in New Addington, C2 Monday to Friday to Salcot Crescent, C3 Saturdays to Homestead Way and C4 Saturdays to Salcot Crescent. Pending their delayed entry into service the newly-licensed XAs had to be stored somewhere, and though a couple were housed at Croydon itself the rest were hived off to a number of garages that had space to spare, principally Bexley but also New Cross, Fulwell, Edmonton and Stamford Hill.

The rolling stock department managed to rustle up 34 XAs to add to the few already at Croydon by the day that new schedules finally started operation on 18th April 1970. Now approaching five years old and having been thoroughly overhauled once, the XAs had all been subjected to various small modifications with the aim of improving on their original dire performance. Their new sphere of operation was clearly better suited to their abilities, but in fact they remained troublesome and Croydon's inside staff were said to have felt overwhelmed by having to keep so many of them on the road. As at the other garages to which they had previously been allocated, the XAs demonstrated that London Transport's standard engineering staffing and skills levels, which had been based on the much vaunted reliability of the RT, RF and RM classes, were inadequate to cope with the additional complexity, not to mention the in-built unreliability of the Leyland Atlantean.

An additional route was added to the XAs' roster from 31st October 1970. This was a Saturdays-only operation on route 234B (South Croydon garage–Selsdon) which previously had run only on Sundays worked by RFs, as it continued to be on that day of the week even after the introduction of XAs on Saturdays. Thereafter the XA era at Croydon and Peckham lasted relatively unchanged throughout 1971 and 1972 and into 1973 except that the one-bus working on route 233, which had often been covered by FRM 1 anyway, was lost on 27th March 1971 when the service was revamped with SMS-type single deckers. Thereafter the FRM worked alongside XAs on route 234 but not on the C routes, having been deemed unsuitable for conversion to farebox operation because of its high driving position.

An early casualty during this period was XA 20 which was prematurely delicensed on 14th September 1971, possibly as the result of an accident, and was subsequently sent for storage at Finchley. Although it returned to Croydon in January 1973, presumably now repaired, it did not run in London again. Others of the class fared better, however, and starting with XA 6 in July 1972 a programme of repainting began at Aldenham which had encompassed at least 24 of the class before ceasing five months later.

A cheerless and litter-strewn West Croydon bus station is still a hub for XA operation on the local flat fare services in January 1973, but not for very much longer. DMSs will soon begin drifting in, and the XAs are now destined for a new life in Hong Kong. XA 13 on route C4, and XA 49 behind it on the C3, were both withdrawn from service on 1st April 1973. *Ken Blacker*

Route 233 earned a place within the annals of London bus history when it became the first double deck Central Bus service to become one-man operated. Photographed some time afterwards, XA 8 was not one of the original vehicles on the 233, but was one of the large number resuscitated at Croydon for the New Addington flat-fare operation on 18th April 1970. The top of the new periscope fitting can be glimpsed at the foot of the offside front upper deck window.

The reason why the repainting programme had drawn to a premature halt was soon made clear. A report published in the trade journal 'Commercial Motor' on 12th January 1973 revealed that London Transport was about to sell all its Atlanteans to a "buyer as yet unnamed, but thought to be in the Far East". The article revealed that each vehicle had covered less than 350,000 miles, and that replacement by Daimler Fleetlines and single deck vehicles would commence within the next week. It quickly became common knowledge that the purchaser was the China Motor Bus Company, based on Hong Kong island. This company, which was the main franchisee for bus services on the island, had found itself with a desperate need to acquire additional high seating capacity double deckers subsequent to the opening on 2nd August 1972 of the new Cross Harbour Tunnel between Hong Kong island and the mainland at Kowloon. It had approached Leyland for advice on companies willing to sell used Atlanteans and a few had been obtained from National Bus Company operators Trent and Western Welsh, but London Transport was suggested to CMB as a likely source for a much larger quantity of such vehicles.

For its part, London Transport welcomed the opportunity to dispose of the XAs which were otherwise destined to remain a non-standard thorn in its side. The marked superiority of the XFs over the XAs under service conditions had resulted in the placement from 1968 onwards of a succession of orders of new Daimlers to form the DMS class, and subsequent to the first DMSs entering service on 2nd January 1971 vehicles of this type had quickly become a familiar feature throughout much of London.

1973 began with 44 of London Transport's 47 XAs still in active service, 35 at Croydon and 9 at Peckham, but this situation was destined to change rapidly. The first big hit came at Croydon on 20th January when 10 were permanently delicensed with the conversion of routes 234 and 234B to DMS operation along with substitutions commencing on a one-for-one basis of DMSs for XAs on the C routes. FRM 1 was also delicensed on the same date. Next, on 17th February, all of Peckham's XAs were replaced by SMS single deckers, and by this date the number of XAs still licensed at Croydon had diminished to 19.

Another event to record on 17th February was the introduction of a new Monday to Friday between-peaks local service within New Addington numbered C5 and worked by vehicles from the C1. In most cases the C5 journeys were covered by DMSs but at least two XAs are known to have been fitted with the appropriate blind displays and were seen at work on it on their very last days with London Transport.

From 31st December 1970 onwards a trio of XAs was required each Saturday to cover new route 234B. On this occasion XA 12 erroneously displays a 'via' blind for the long-established route 234, although in all probability no-one noticed and the error remained uncorrected all day. XA 12 was taken out of service on 17th February 1973 on which date 13 XAs were withdrawn, the largest number to cease operation at any one time. *Peter Mitchell*

The once-familiar frontage of East Grinstead garage, notable for its varying doorway heights and now adorned with new LONDON COUNTRY signage, forms the backcloth in February 1973 to two very different ex-London Transport vehicles, RF 209 and XA 48. Within a few days XA 48 will be delicensed preparatory for its sale to Hong Kong while RF 209, which was already 13¾ years old when XA 48 was built and well past its prime, will soldier on in London Country service until June 1974. *Ken Blacker*

Such was the influx of new DMSs that by 1st March only nine XAs remained licensed and this was destined to be their final month of operation. The very last one recorded in service was XA 22 which was observed on route C2 on 29th March. On 1st April it and four others (XA 13, 21, 49, 50) were delicensed and London Transport's unhappy experience with the Leyland Atlantean was at an end.

In addition to the 47 London Transport XAs, China Motor Bus also purchased the three belonging to London Country. Since passing into new ownership, XA 46-48 had remained working from East Grinstead garage and in May and June 1970 had been re-liveried during overhaul at Aldenham into London Country colours. At the same time they were converted for one-man operation and reclassified 1XA1/1, although this was purely a paper manoeuvre for London Transport benefit as their new owner did not use the classification system. Rumours that these XAs were about to be sold circulated towards the end of 1972 and were strenuously denied by the company, but all three were delicensed on 27th February 1973 and passed into CMB ownership in April, with three new Atlanteans ordered to replace them. When they arrived at Southampton docks on 30th April they were, in fact the last of the 50 XAs to leave the UK.

During March and April 1973 China Motor Bus despatched all the XAs on the long voyage to their new home where work began to prepare them for their new existence. All were repainted into CMB's half-red half-cream livery with the moulding below the upper deck windows picked out in black, and initially looked very smart. Their London fleet numbers were retained. Prior to departure, London

The XAs probably worked harder in Hong Kong than they had ever done in London and could sometimes be found carrying huge passenger loads. Still wearing its original red and cream CMB livery, XA 30 displays its former London fleet number prominently above the driver's windscreen and again over the doorway. The destination blinds have white lettering on a red background.
Dave Stewart

China Motor Bus's later blue livery did not perpetuate the fleet number display and there is no obvious sign that the vehicle on CMB route 10 was, in fact, XA 16. The tramway vehicle of the left that it is just about to pass is roughly contemporary in age with XA 16 and was one of 20 four-wheel single deck trailers supplied to the Hong Kong tramway by Metal Sections of Oldbury which outlived the XAs and remained in service until April 1982. *Dave Stewart*

Transport had replaced the luggage rack adjacent to the doorway with a passenger seat increasing their capacity to 75, and the CMB workshops, in acknowledgement of the climatic conditions there, installed tropical style full-depth sliding windows extensively in each vehicle. Most side windows were re-glazed in this way, as were the upstairs and downstairs windows at the back and also the upper deck front. New windscreens in anodised aluminium frames were fitted which had push-out sections at the bottom of both windows, and the protruding London Transport-style trafficator ears were replaced by ones of a more conventional design. The first XAs are believed to have started work in Hong Kong in January 1974.

CMB worked the XAs hard in Hong Kong, where high ambient temperatures and the hilly terrain exacerbated their tendency to overheat even though an additional and quite large ventilator aperture was cut into the rear bonnet cover. In 1975 a cooler-running Gardner 6LX engine was fitted into XA 44 with XA 25 and XA 48 subsequently treated likewise, but cost considerations coupled with short life expectancy mitigated against any expansion of this programme. Although a few XAs subsequently received CMB's mid-1970s radically revised livery of blue and buff, a major withdrawal of the class took place in 1979 with the last few being disposed of in 1981.

It was rumoured that a scheme had been launched to preserve XA 4 in Hong Kong, but nothing came of it and all 50 vehicles are believed to have been scrapped on the island.

LONDON'S FIRST FLEETLINES – THE XFs

London Transport's prompt response to the recommendations of the Phelps Brown report, mentioned in the previous chapter, resulted in the purchase of eight Daimler Fleetline double deckers in addition to the fifty Atlanteans. They were to be known as the XF (Experimental Fleetline) class. Of similar concept to the Atlantean, with rear engine and front entrance, the Fleetline had been in series production since 1962 and had become a serious competitor to the Atlantean, not least because many operators were finding it the cheaper and more trouble-free of the two to operate. Its Gardner engine, offered in both 6LW and more powerful 6LX forms, endeared it to many purchasers, while its patented concentric-drive semi-automatic gearbox enabled the fitment as standard of a dropped centre rear axle which meant that it could accommodate low height bodywork with a centre gangway running the full length of both decks unlike the convoluted and very unsatisfactory layout necessary for the Atlantean when bodied in low-height form.

In contrast to the XAs, which were purchased specifically for operation with Central Buses, London Transport's plan for the XFs was to run them experimentally in the country area, initially as crew-operated vehicles but eventually in one-man mode as soon as the regulations were amended to make this permissible. In doing so the Board would be following another of the Phelps Brown report recommendations, while reaping the additional benefit of being able to compare the two makes of rear-engine double decker and to evaluate the strengths and weaknesses of each. It had been common knowledge for some time that the Ministry of Transport, under pressure from bus operators, had been leaning towards legalising the use of double deckers for one-man operation, and in November 1965 it produced draft regulations for operators to comment upon which were intended to permit this in a limited way. Subject to the necessary safety requirements, the Minister proposed to give operators scope to experiment with the use of one-

With their almost identical Park Royal bodywork the XFs look superficially like a green replica of the XAs, although their Daimler wheels and slightly longer rear bonnet with its prominent nearside access hatch were clear indications that, under the surface, things were very different. Along with the rest of the class, XF 2 started work at East Grinstead garage on 15th September 1965, almost two months before the first XAs entered service. *London Transport Museum*

man operated double deckers, either with the top deck sealed off when running in omo format, or even in certain circumstances (such as on services with few stops) with both decks in use.

Eight standard CRG6 Fleetline chassis were ordered from Jaguar group manufacturer Transport Vehicles (Daimler) Ltd. The 16ft 3ins-wheelbase Fleetline chassis came with air pressure brakes, fluid flywheel and 4-speed Daimler-SCG 'Daimatic' direct selection epicyclic gearbox and leaf springs. Power assisted steering was specified, and in common with the great majority of other Fleetline operators LT opted for the Gardner 6LX 10.45 litre engine, a well-proven unit which had been on the market since 1958 and had earned the reputation of being the most reliable and economic engine in its class.

The 72-seat bodies were built by Park Royal and looked exactly like those on XA 1-50 except that they carried standard country bus green and cream livery. In fact the bodies on the two classes were, in almost all respects, completely identical and used exactly the same components, even to the extent of having the same high lower-deck saloon floor which was totally unnecessary on a Fleetline and meant that the advantages of carrying a lower and lighter body were not obtained. Apart from livery, there were only two immediately discernible differences between the XA and XF classes. One was that, due to the extra depth of the Daimler-supplied engine compartment, the XF was 2 inches longer than the XA at 30ft 6ins and exhibited a slight bulge at the rear, and the other was noticeable internally where a door was fitted on the XFs at the foot of the staircase which could be locked in either the open or closed position. This was provided in anticipation of the vehicles being allowed to run in omo mode with the upper deck sealed off once the law had been changed to make this possible.

At the start of 1965 it was anticipated that the eight XFs would be delivered in June of the same year and this target was almost achieved. The first four (XF 1-4) were received at Aldenham on 23rd August 1965 and all eight were in stock by 2nd September, Park Royal having taken the opportunity to build them during the two months hiatus that occurred in Atlantean chassis deliveries from mid-August onwards.

The Guinea Pig public house on East Grinstead's Stone Quarry Estate is the location where XF 6 was photographed on 3rd February 1966. Light off-peak passenger loadings had identified route 424 as a prime candidate for the forthcoming trial of one-man operation at quiet times of day, and plans were already in hand to implement this. *London Transport Museum*

31 PASSENGERS SEATED IN LOWER SALOON

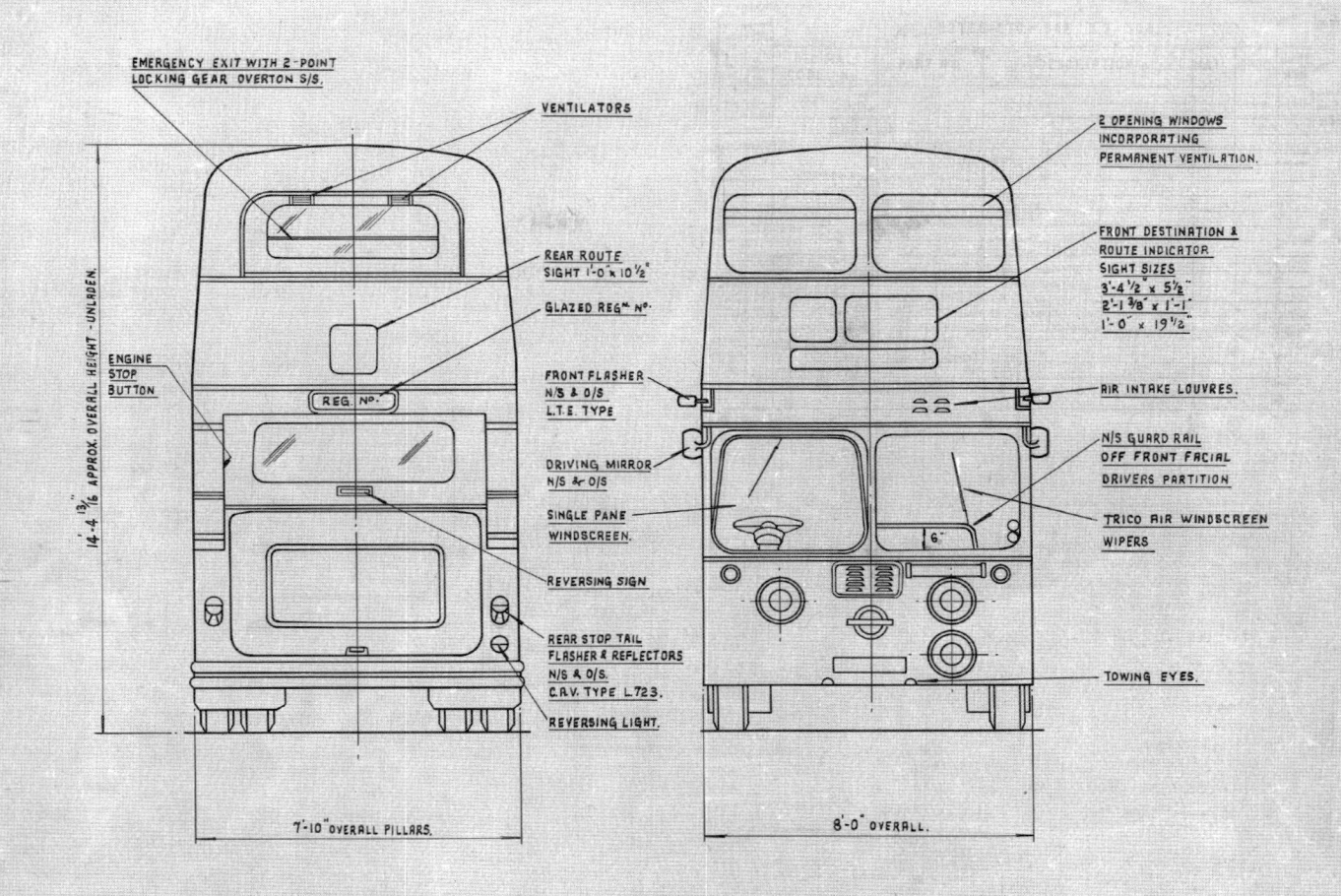

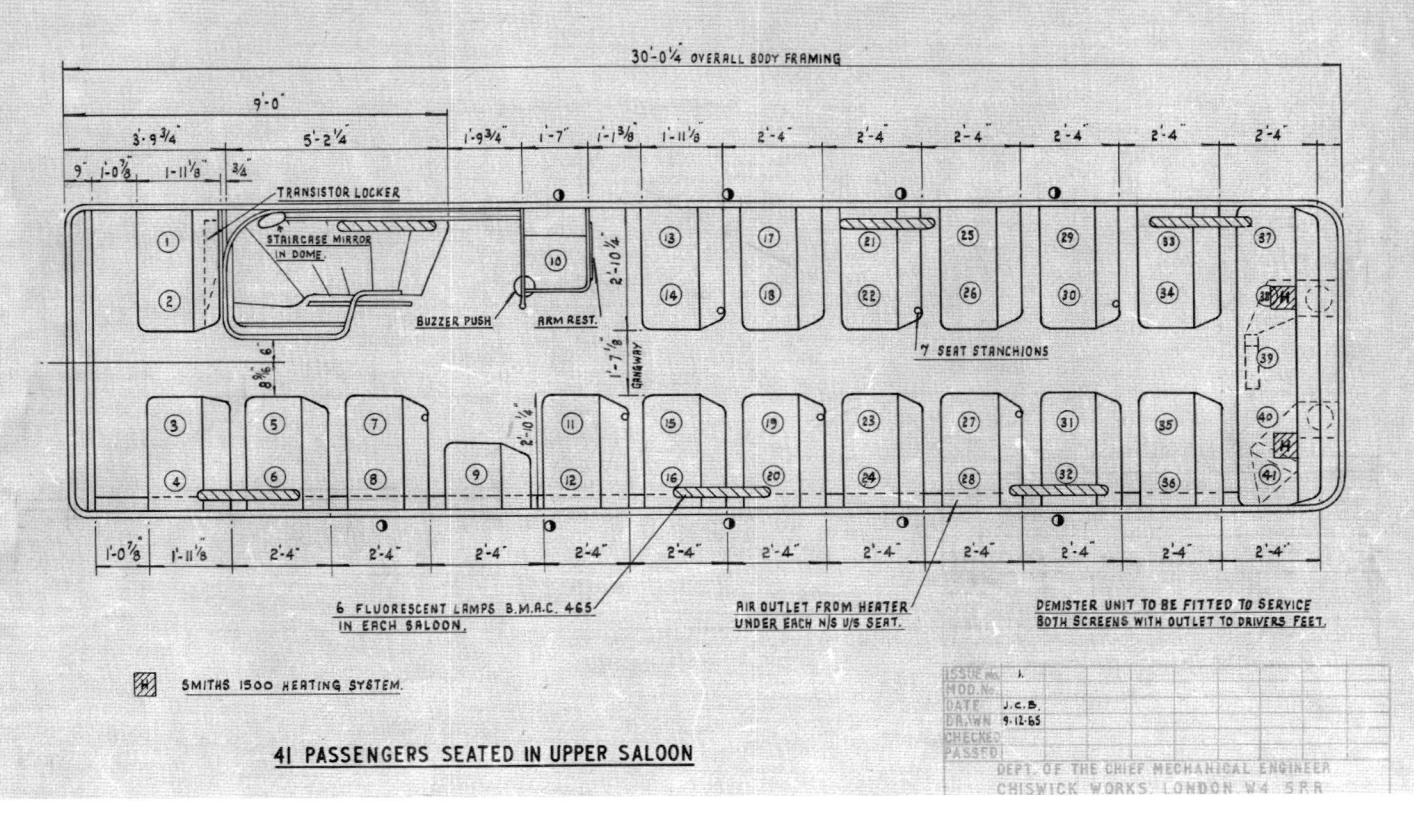

41 PASSENGERS SEATED IN UPPER SALOON

On 17th April 1966 the eight XFs were transferred to Highgate for route 271 which enjoyed a mix of red and green vehicles for the next 13 weeks. Like XF 1, RM 364 in the background at Moorgate is also working from Highgate garage on an ex-trolleybus service.
Alan Nightingale

Classified as 1XF1, the XFs carried Daimler chassis numbers 61205-12 but, having not been bodied in sequence, these numbers were completely jumbled up within the batch. London Transport body numbers were A51-58 (in order), and were a continuation of those on the XAs. Similarly, the allocated registration numbers CUV 51-58C followed on from the batch originally booked for the XAs but only partly used by them. At 8 tons 18cwt the XFs were 3cwt heavier than the XAs and they carried 35 gallon offside-mounted fuel tanks as compared with the 38 gallon tanks on the Leylands, but in anticipation of their better mpg performance the lower capacity probably made no difference.

The Reigate management decided that the XFs should operate from East Grinstead garage where they would displace RTs from route 424 (Reigate–East Grinstead via Horley) on a schedule which also included odd journeys on East Grinstead local service 435 and the 438 group of works services. The 424 was a long, largely rural cross-country route with an end-to-end running time in the region of 1 hour 25 minutes. It had 'grown up' over the years from being a purely single deck operation, and it still really only needed double deckers for a few busy peak hour and school journeys. After a week of familiarisation work on unlicensed XF 8, staff at East Grinstead were ready to introduce XFs to the 424 on the same day that they were licensed, Wednesday 15th September 1965. Without having so much trade union hostility to navigate, it had proved possible to get the XFs into service almost two months ahead of the first XAs. At the time, the 424 was still crew worked and the staircase doors on the XFs were firmly locked in the open position pending approval being received for one-man operation at a later date.

Right from the start, the XFs appear to have been well received by staff at East Grinstead and were popular with them, in stark contrast to the reception given to the XAs and certain other new classes introduced in the middle and late nineteen-sixties. Though by no means completely trouble free, they did not plague the engineers with constant road calls and in fact gained a reputation for showing a reasonable level of mechanical reliability. Some of this may have been a reflection of the favourable and not particularly onerous operating conditions on route 424 which were well suited to the Fleetine, but certain design features were soon noted as being an improvement over the Atlanteans. The Park Royal bodies were, admittedly, a bit rattly but this may have been aggravated by some of the bumpy country lanes that the vehicles traversed.

The first of the well-remembered exchanges between the XFs and the XAs took place on 17th April 1966, on which date all eight of the class started work at Highgate on route 271 (Highgate Village–Moorgate), with the same number of ex-Highgate XAs taking their place at East Grinstead. From the travelling public's point of view, this was merely a case of green vehicles running on the 271 instead of identical red ones, but for London Transport's management it was an essential move to determine the strengths and weakness of both chassis types when faced with identical working conditions, and perhaps even to indicate the path that future purchases might take. It took hardly any time at all to establish that the XFs were free of the severe engine overheating problems that plagued the XAs, the simple reason being that its transmission system was not enclosed as it was on the XA.

XF 3 had only been at Highgate for a few weeks when, on 2nd June, it was delicensed and despatched to the Daimler factory in Coventry where, by agreement with London Transport, an interesting experiment was to be initiated. Daimler's parent company, Jaguar, had become interested in building a joint venture with the American engine manufacturer Cummins to construct the latter's V6-200 engine in the former Henry Meadows factory in Wolverhampton. This engine, arranged in a V configuration with the six cylinders sharing a common crankshaft, was a compact, square unit in complete contrast to the Gardner 6LX, and required considerable work to install it into the Fleetline chassis where it would drive through the Daimler/SCG concyclic gearbox. As it happened, the plan to build V6 engines at the Meadows factory did not materialise and all of them – including the one in XF 3 – were imported from Columbus, Indiana.

After receiving its new engine, XF 3 spent much of its time off the road and, as a result, was not well photographed. This side-on view was taken after it started working from Stamford Hill garage in May 1967, where it remained until being delicensed with gearbox trouble in February 1969. *Alan Nightingale*

A fresh coat of green paint distinguishes the rear-end panelling and modified engine cover fitted to XF 3 to accommodate its Cummins V-profile engine. With its accessibility side panel removed, the engine pulleys, dynamo pulley and positive drive belt are revealed, but the most obvious modification is the projection of the bonnet cover that would disfigure XF 3 for the next few years. *Ken Blacker collection*

Whereas its original Gardner engine had spread-eagled across much of the engine compartment on XF 3, the square-shaped Cummins unit barely reached half way across. Other features visible in this general view of the engine compartment include the air intake filter, steering pump and reservoir, gearbox and fan drive. *Ken Blacker collection*

XF 3 returned to Aldenham on 5th August 1966 and, without even lifting the engine cover or listening to the noisy new unit in action, it was clear that XF 3 had undergone quite a major transformation in the engine compartment. Although the V6 unit was compact, its shape did not allow it to fit within the existing available space across the back of the vehicle, and the solution to this problem had been to construct a rather ugly extension which projected about 10½ inches beyond the main bodywork,. Thereafter, XF 3 stood out prominently from the rest of the class by virtue of its strange-looking rear end bustle.

While XF 3 was away, the seven remaining XFs stayed at Highgate for only three weeks longer before returning to East Grinstead on 10th July 1966 having spent less than three months with Central Buses. The Minister of Transport had now approved one-man operation of double deckers and London Transport set about making a prompt start with its proposed hybrid, part-crew and part-omo working to route 424. In peak hours the vehicles would run in normal crew-worked format with both decks in use, but at slack times and at weekends the top deck would be sealed off and the driver would be in sole charge. It was optimistically hoped that the lower deck alone would suffice at those times even though it contained only 31 seats. However, introduction of this arrangement did not come as easily as hoped because insufficient staff at East Grinstead could be persuaded to volunteer to work under the new arrangements. It was only after volunteers from Godstone and Crawley garages had been drafted in that operation finally commenced on Sunday 2nd October 1966. XF 3 had meanwhile returned to service with its new engine on 2nd September, so all eight XFs were available when the new arrangements began.

The XFs' part crew-worked and part one-man hybrid style of operation commenced on 2nd October 1966 and XF 1 was photographed working in omo mode towards Reigate soon afterwards. Brackets to hold the yellow 'PAY AS YOU ENTER' slip board have been attached to the front panel below the nearside windscreen in readiness for this. In theory at least, the board was removed when the bus was working in crew mode. *Peter Mitchell*

ROUTE 424

Starting on Sunday, October 2, the buses on this route will be worked by a driver and conductor during the busy periods on weekdays, but in the off-peak periods and on Sundays, the driver will collect fares and issue tickets as passengers board. At these times, the lower deck only will be used by passengers and the staircase to the upper deck will be closed.

On some journeys the conductor will leave the bus at intermediate points, and before closing the staircase will ask any passengers on the upper deck to continue their journeys on the lower deck. This slight inconvenience is regretted but is unavoidable. Passengers may smoke on the lower deck when the upper deck is not in use.

The new arrangement which has been made possible by the Ministry of Transport is experimental and is in the ultimate interest of passengers. As on many routes, the number of passengers using route 424 is falling, while costs of operation are constantly rising. This experiment will show whether it is feasible to dispense with the conductor during off-peak periods, and thereby reduce costs. The only alternative may be the reduction of the service.

Please give the experiment a fair trial. Everything possible will be done to avoid delay or inconvenience to passengers.

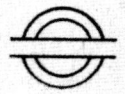

Despite early optimism, and much hard work by staff on route 424 to make a success of it, London Transport's unusual brand of one-man operation lasted only six months and the experiment was concluded on 1st April 1967 when the 424 reverted back to full-time crew working. Results from the trial had been inconclusive and with little scope for it to be widened to include other routes, there was no point in continuing it further. However, the other ongoing experiment, involving XF3's engine, continued even though the vehicle had already become noted for the extra noise and vibration emanating from its Cummins engine. However, it still had to be tested against the rigours of slow speed, stop-start in-town operation to which it was now about to be subjected.

The engineers wished to resume the Atlantean versus Fleetline comparison trials that had ceased abruptly and inconclusively in July 1966, and on 13th May 1967 all eight XFs moved back to the central area, but this time to Stamford Hill for operation alongside XAs on route 67. XAs were once again sent to East Grinstead as their replacements, and it was during their tenure that Sunday operation on the 424 ceased from the start of the 1968 winter programme on 5th October. The XFs' stay at Stamford Hill was largely uneventful, and while they were there XF 1-5 found time to visit Aldenham in August and September 1968 for a repaint, retaining their green livery.

The heavily built-up environment through which route 67 ran for most of its length could hardly have been more different from the bucolic nature of route 424. With its spell of experimental hybrid operation on the 424 at an end, XF 5 is now working from Stamford Hill garage and is held up at a zebra crossing in Kingsland High Street on its way to the docks.

Their stay at Stamford Hill produced much the same results that had earlier been demonstrated at Highgate, such as a major reduction in day-to-day problems such as overheating and non-starts compared with the XAs. This is not to say that the XFs displayed no weaknesses, especially in the area of the gearbox where wear on the 2nd and 3rd speed bands was particularly noticeable, and in the drive coupling, while oil leakage on the power steering pumps affected all eight vehicles. However it was while they were at Stamford Hill that London Transport placed the first of a number of orders for more Fleetlines to form what eventually became the 2,646 strong DM family of new double deckers. After almost two years on route 67 the trial finally came to an end, and all eight XFs returned to East Grinstead on 1st March 1969.

It was in the very final days of London Transport's operation of country bus services that the XFs recorded their greatest moment of fame, and in a location far removed from their normal operating haunts in rural Surrey. Back in August 1967 the Stevenage Development Corporation had conducted a cost/benefit analysis to determine long term traffic trends in the growing New Town, subsequent to which a working party consisting of the Development Corporation, London Transport and the Ministries of Transport and Housing & Local Government had developed plans for a bus-operated, taxi type service carrying pre-booked passengers in reserved seats at agreed times from their homes in the Chells area, across Stevenage to the industrial zone on the western side of town where they could be dropped off at or near their factory gates. Its principal aim was to keep car use to a minimum. The experimental 'Blue Arrow' service was sanctioned by the Ministry of Transport in the second half of 1969 and London Transport set about making arrangements to operate it using three XFs. Work was carried out at Chiswick and Aldenham in November 1969 on the three vehicles that had not been repainted a year earlier, XF 6-8, and all three were relicensed at Stevenage on 22nd December 1969 ready to start work as Blue Arrows exactly a week later. They carried a striking light blue and silver livery and, most notably, introduced the fleet name LONDON COUNTRY, the first public manifestation of the big split in ownership that was due to occur on 1st January 1970. A little pointlessly, in view of the fact that they were imminently due to leave London Transport stock, they were officially reclassified 1XF1/1.

The three XFs ran in their blue and silver livery for only three days in the ownership of London Transport before passing to London Country, whose fleet name they already carried in silver lettering. Free of advertisements and in an attractive new paint scheme, they were undoubtedly an eye-catching advertisement for the new Blue Arrow venture, a promotional poster for which is prominently displayed on the advertisement board adjacent to the garage entrance. Departing from Stevenage garage on the first day of operation, XF 8 contrasts vividly with the hum-drum appearance of the standard green London Transport vehicles that it has just passed. *Ken Blacker*

The public's introduction to Blue Arrow came on Saturday 13th December 1969 when XF 6 was put on view in the Chells area, and the accompanying publicity material heralded the buses as "personal taxis". XF 6 was still unlicensed at the time, having only arrived at Stevenage from Aldenham two days earlier. Starting day for the new operation was Monday 29th December and it comprised two services, numbered A1 and A2, both linking Chells to the factory area, the A1 to its northern section and the A2 to the southern. Each bus carried a female courier as well as the driver, and only two vehicles were required, the third being an engineering spare.

The Blue Arrow buses were fated to run for only three days under London Transport ownership. On 1st January 1970 the Transport (London) Act came into effect placing Central Buses (and the Underground) in the municipal sector under the control of the Greater London Council with the title London Regional Transport, while the Country Bus & Coach department remained in the nationalised sector under its new title of London Country Bus Services Ltd within the auspices of the National Bus Company. All 28 garages and two outstations passed to the new company. Its new fleet name, LONDON COUNTRY in gold block capitals had, as already mentioned, been publicly aired on the three Blue Arrow XFs, and it quickly appeared throughout the fleet. The difficult history of London Country in its early days has been amply described in other books, but it is relevant to note here that, out of 721 double deckers inherited from London Transport by the new organisation, no fewer than 501 (incredibly almost 70%) were 15 years old or more. Notably, only eleven double deckers (8 XFs and 3 XAs) were suitable for one-man operation which, by this time, was clearly where the future of the bus industry lay.

London Country adopted a policy of moving completely to one-man operation as quickly as possible, and the first stage of this embraced XF1-5 when route 424 was converted on 27th June 1970, double deck omo having now been legalised. All five had undergone a slight livery revision whereby the cream central band was overpainted in yellow, giving the vehicles an altogether brighter appearance. At about this time London Country's attractive and clever new yellow logo – unveiled in March as a worthwhile attempt at image building and subsequently widely nicknamed as the 'Flying Polo' – began appearing on vehicles in the fleet. Meanwhile, at Stevenage patronage on the Blue Arrows built up to a reasonably healthy level but began to be undermined by the introduction on 31st July 1971 of the first stage of the much-acclaimed 'Superbus' network using blue and yellow single deckers (SM class AEC Swifts and MS Metro-Scanias). The Blue Arrow service was reduced to single deck operation on 14th March 1972 when the three blue XFs were delicensed into storage at Hertford, and totally ceased in September.

With even its front wheel trims buffed-up to suitably impress, XF 6 is seen at work on route A2 carrying the 'LONDON TRANSPORT BOARD' legal lettering that it will lose on 1st January 1970. Although the front and rear number blinds optimistically carried provision for routes up to A6, A2 was the highest to which the Blue Arrow service ever aspired. *Capital Transport*

In common with many other former London Transport vehicles all the XFs, with the exception of XF 3, were sent to Aldenham for overhauling in the early days of London Country when the new company had no comparable facilities of its own. During the autumn of 1972 XF 7 continues to undergo bodywork renovation despite already having been in the works for at least six months and still carries the light blue and silver livery from its Stevenage days. It contrasts with the much darker Lincoln green on XF 5, which has arrived at Aldenham more recently. These were the first two XFs to be outshopped in the new National Bus Company corporate livery. *Capital Transport*

Now six years old, time was overdue for the XFs to receive their first full overhaul, and the availability of the three former Blue Arrows made this possible. Still heavily reliant on Aldenham Works, London Country delivered XF 6 there for overhauling on 29th March followed by the other two ex-Blue Arrows on 13th April. A combination of the lethargy that was now rumoured to be embracing the Aldenham system and a growing nationwide shortage of spare parts probably accounted for the fact that XF 6's overhaul took almost six months to complete and was not finished until 13th September. XF 8's completion on 30th October marked a stay of just over six months in Aldenham, while XF 7 left there exactly eight months after its arrival, on 13th December. XFs 6 and 8 emerged looking very attractive in London Country's adopted livery consisting of a pleasant shade of green which was somewhat lighter than London Transport's traditional Lincoln green, plus a greater area of yellow embracing the downstairs windows as well as the central band. In contrast, XF 7 was overhauled into the corporate colours adopted by the National Bus Company and imposed on all its subsidiaries from late October onwards. For companies running green-liveried vehicles these combined a rather insipid and quick-to-fade leaf green with a single white band and grey wheels, along with block capital white fleet names in standard 'house' style and NBC's double-N logo.

XF 1, 2, 4 and 5 subsequently followed suit between September 1972 and February 1973 and were the last XFs to be dealt with at Aldenham. Compared with XF 6-8, these overhauls were slightly speeded up and mostly took about 4½ months to perform, and all of course emerged in NBC corporate colours. Cummins-engined XF 3 was dealt with differently. In March 1975 it was despatched to Sparshatt's Ltd at Portsmouth for overhaul, and when it finally returned nine months later it had reverted to its original form with Gardner 6LX engine now reinstalled and its distinctive rear-end protrusion removed. The Cummins V-series engine had proved unsatisfactory, not just in XF 3 but generally within the industry in the many new Daimler Roadliner single deckers supplied to provincial operators, in which it had been installed. It had not only been found unsuitable for slow-speed stop-start work, but its roughness, noise and heavy smoke emission, coupled with various failures within the engines themselves, had badly diminished its reputation.

The XFs remained faithful to East Grinstead garage, sharing duties on routes such as 424,

Conversion to conventional omo has just come to route 424 on 27th June 1970, and XF 4 terminates at Reigate with its new "PAY AS YOU ENTER, Exact Fare Please" white lettering permanently displayed on the front of the vehicle. The same notice is also carried on the nearside to the right of the doorway. This view typifies the XFs in their early days of London Country ownership with the fleet name in Johnston-style gold block capitals and the central band painted in yellow to brighten up the vehicle's appearance.
Ken Blacker

Two of the former Blue Arrows were reintegrated into the fleet at East Grinstead carrying London Country's bright but short-lived version of its green and yellow livery which it was forced to abandon at the end of 1972 in favour of NBC's corporate style. XF 8 carried the new livery when it re-entered service at East Grinstead on 1st November 1972 and still looked quite smart when photographed almost two years later.
Mike Harris

428, 435, 438A and 438C with newer Leyland Atlanteans, but the late 1970s saw them gradually fade away. First to be withdrawn from service was XF 8 in December 1978, followed by five more in 1979. XF 5 remained in service until February 1980, leaving only XF 3 still operational. One of the 1979 withdrawals, XF 1, saw further use as a driver trainer in green and yellow 'learner' livery during 1980 and the early part of 1981, but it was sold, along with most of the other XFs, later in the year. Only XF 3 remained at the end, its last operational day being Christmas Eve, Thursday 24th December 1981, just a week before East Grinstead garage itself closed its doors for the last time. XF 3 had achieved the status of being the last former London Transport bus to remain in regular service with London Country, so great had been the transformation within its fleet since the company's formation just over a decade earlier.

It is fortunate that two of this small experimental batch of Fleetlines remain in private preservation today. XF 1 and XF 3 appear at rallies and special events from time to time to remind us of an interesting time of change in London bus history.

Newly emerged from overhaul at Aldenham in February 1973, XF 5 displays the corporate leaf green and white livery with grey wheels that would quickly bring a sameness to NBC fleets throughout England and Wales and would ultimately wipe out all sense of local individuality. The white fleet name, in approved style, is accompanied by the double-*N* symbol first unveiled in July 1972 and quickly imposed throughout the network in the hope of enhancing public awareness of the existence of the National Bus Company.

After lying at Reigate unused for 2½ years, XF 3 was dispatched to Sparshatt's at Portsmouth in February 1975 to be reunited with its Gardner engine, as a result of which it resumed the same physical appearance as its fellow XFs. Photographed at Rutherford Way, Crawley in May 1978, it was destined to outlive the rest of its class in London Country's passenger service fleet for almost two years, and it still survives in preservation to the present day. *Mike Harris*

A NEW LOOK FOR GREEN LINE – THE RC CLASS

"New Look for Green Line" was the headline in October and November 1965 across the pages of the various regular passenger transport journals of that time, heralding the entry into service on Sunday 28th November 1965 of new RC class coaches on route 705. At the time they broke new ground in being the longest and widest passenger vehicles ever operated by London Transport, so it was inevitable that they would attract great media attention.

News of their forthcoming arrival had first circulated at the start of the year with a press release from London Transport that fourteen coaches, to be called the RC (Reliance Coach) class, had been ordered and that they would hold 49 passengers on what were claimed to be the most comfortable seats to be fitted to a Green Line coach to date. Combining AEC Reliance chassis with Willowbrook steel-framed bodywork, the RCs were, like the XAs and XFs, part of London Transport's speedy response to the Phelps Brown report, one of the recommendations of which was that new coaches working as 'Express' vehicles should be used to update the image on the Green Line network which had been falling into a state of decline in recent times.

The version of the AEC Reliance chassis specified by London Transport on this occasion was known as the 4U2RA. It differed fundamentally from the unfortunate RW class in being of the maximum permitted width of 8ft 2½ins and length of 36ft on a wheelbase of 18ft 7ins. It was considerably more powerful than the RW by virtue of its AH690 horizontal 11.3 litre underfloor engine, which was mounted amidships between the axles and was expected to give a very lively performance. With a bore of 130mm and 142mm stroke, the AH690 was derated by 10%, in common with most engines used by London Transport, to produce 175 to 185 bph at 2,000rpm. The gearbox was a semi-automatic, electro-pneumatically operated epicyclic 5-speed unit with first gear intended only for emergencies. A compressed air twin-line footbrake system operated on all four wheels, with a mechanical handbrake connected to the rear wheels only. Air for the braking system was provided by a 13½ cu ft/min compressor through two reservoirs, the compressor also supplying the gearbox and air suspension reservoir. Dunlop bellows supplied air suspension to both axles.

The bodies perpetuated the precedent set by the RWs a few years earlier by being built similar

With their large size, modern styling and bright livery, the RCs looked unlike anything ever previously seen in Green Line service. When photographed outside the factory in Loughborough, the first one to be completed carried the fleet name GREEN LINE EXPRESS. Before entering service the word EXPRESS was removed, presumably in the realisation that, although route 705 was scheduled as an express operation west of London, this was far from being the case on its eastern leg.
Martin Fisher

Six weeks before entering service, on 12th October 1965, RC 1 participated in the official photo-shoot to record the class for London Transport's picture archive, using staff members in the role of 'passengers' for several of the scenes. The blue internal décor was unlike anything ever seen previously on Green Line and the high-backed seats and forced air ventilation were also new features. The seats were provided with arm-rests on both their gangway end and adjacent to the body side. *London Transport Museum*

A general view of the driver's cab of RC 1, taken on the same occasion, shows that it was not particularly spacious, while the steps up from the pavement to the level of the saloon floor appear to present a formidably steep challenge, especially for elderly or infirm passengers. *London Transport Museum*

in basic outline to the standard BET styling of the time. This had now developed into a very distinctive shape with curved screens at front and back surmounted by peaked fibreglass domes. Although the body shell was designed basically for bus work, a number of BET-owned companies and others had specified a modified design with double length 'panoramic' side windows, 7ft 7ins long, aimed at giving greater visual appeal to vehicles categorised as 'dual purpose' and used principally on limited stop, longer distance operations where full coach specification was not thought to be justified. Solid steel stress panels between the floor and waist were riveted to the main structural members on these bodies to help compensate for any loss of strength and rigidity resulting from the reduction in the number of full-height pillars.

Several manufacturers produced the BET standard body with little if any visible difference between them and it is not known why Willowbrook was selected as the supplier. With the exception of the three RWs, this was not a company with which London Transport traditionally did business, but it is possible that the promise of a favourable delivery date influenced the placing of the contract. When progress was reviewed on 14th February 1965, delivery of the completed vehicles was anticipated in June, but this target was eventually missed by several months. AEC did not succeed in delivering RC 1's chassis to the bodybuilders until 21st May with the remainder following between 2nd July and 10th September. The first complete coach, RC 1, was received by London Transport from Willowbrook on 13th October and all were in stock by 19th November.

The management team at the Country Bus & Coach department under Geoffrey Fernyhough were keen for the new coaches to make as much impact as possible, and they certainly stood out from the rest of the Green Line fleet in carrying an eye-catching new livery which was predominantly pastel grey. The traditional Lincoln green was relegated to a waistband below the windows which was fairly wide overall but much narrower at the front below the windscreens. The wooden route boards, which were a customary feature on Green Line single deckers, were retained but now carried black lettering on a yellow background instead of the other way round.

It was in their internal fittings and décor that the RCs differed most greatly from all other Green Line stock. The 49 seats, which all faced forwards, were high-backed in true coaching style with vinyl-covered fabric covers to the head-rolls. Unlike anything else on Green Line, the main interior colour theme was blue with seat moquette in dark and light blue stripes. The floor was given a blue and white marbled effect and the side walls, window surrounds and fibreglass luggage racks were in various shades of grey. The ceiling, in white plastics, was relieved by three translucent ventilating panels on which conductors were given instructions about how and when to activate them. The panoramic side windows were not capable of being opened, forced-air heating and ventilation being provided through two Smith's blower units serving outlets on the

Before entering service the RCs were provided with brackets on the front to carry a LIMITED STOP board. Unusually, no fleet number was displayed on the nearside of the vehicles. Dunton Green based RC 9 carries WR (Windsor) garage plates on a westbound run early in its service career. *P J Relf*

underside of the luggage racks and controllable by passengers through adjusting the telescopic nozzles through which the air was dispensed. Fluorescent lighting was provided and electrically-operated driver-operated folding doors were provided at the front.

Each complete RC weighed 8ton 6cwt unladen and was 9ft 11⅝ins in height. With a capacity of 48 gallons, they carried the largest fuel tanks of any London Transport vehicles at that time. Registration numbers CUV 59C-72C followed on from those of the XFs; likewise body numbers were A59 to A72, and the batch was classified 1RC1. Their AEC chassis numbers were 4U2RA5766-5779 but these were not in numerical sequence with their fleet numbers.

Extensive acceleration and brake performance tests were carried out at Chiswick on RC 2 during November 1965 prior to the entry into service of all 14 vehicles on the 28th of that month, with RCs 5 and 7 acting as training vehicles in the fortnight beforehand. The route selected for RC operation was Green Line 705 (Windsor–Sevenoaks) worked by Windsor and Dunton Green garages. It was selected because, since August 1963, its western section between Victoria and Windsor had operated on an express basis using the Chiswick Flyover, Great West Road and Colnbrook By-Pass, there being only 12 intermediate stops over this section. With speedy operation on its western leg and normal running in the east, the 705 was an ideal setting on which to trial the RCs under all manner of running conditions in order to test public reaction to them and to ascertain the lines on which Green Line services might be developed in the future.

Windsor and Dunton Green received seven RCs each for the start of the service, with RC 1-3, 5, 7, 10 and 14 at Windsor and the remainder at Dunton Green. They were certainly eye-catching when new, and with ten more seats than the RFs that they replaced on a one-for-one basis, passengers on the 705 benefited by the provision of 20 more seats per hour. Despite their rather steep entrance steps, public reaction to the new vehicles was generally favourable although, as proof that you can't please everybody, some complained about the seats and actually found them uncomfortable. Predictably driver reaction was mixed, with some traditionalists unhappy about the size of the vehicle. At 8½ins wider, 6ft greater in overall length, and with a much longer wheelbase than the RF it was inevitably less manoeuvrable, and this was particularly noticeable in tight places and in heavy in-town traffic conditions. Although the RCs' speed and smooth riding – especially when heavily laden – was fully appreciated, its combination of air suspension and power steering gave some drivers a feeling of insecurity and lack of full control. Overriding all this, however, was a growing awareness that they were not as reliable as they should have been resulting in numerous road calls and breakdowns, most of which were related to their brakes, and sometimes – though to a much lesser extent – to engine and suspension problems. Reliability on the 705 began to suffer badly.

The offside fleet number, as exhibited here by RC 14 as it picks up passengers at Eccleston Bridge, Victoria, was minuscule in size and just about visible on the grey offside panel just below the driver's window. While the basic grey livery looked striking when it was new and shiny, the vehicles began to look dowdy as the gloss wore off, while road dirt further disfigured them during rainy times. *C Carter*

Undoubtedly the RC's Achilles heel was its braking system which proved unsuitable for psv work. A system of dual air brake circuits, one for the front and the other for the rear brakes with both brought into operation by the footbrake, quickly led to uneven braking applications with drivers unsure whether the vehicle was going to pull to the nearside, the offside, or straight ahead! Rapid wear on either front or back brake liners, or both, could lead to inadequate braking or, occasionally, none at all. Handbrakes were sometimes found to be ineffective too, and the fact that the vehicles had a semi-automatic gearbox only made matters worse as this meant that the driver could not use the engine to retard the vehicle. The point arrived when brake liners failed to last more than a week and brake adjustment became necessary on a daily basis, or even at the end of each journey, putting great pressure on garage engineering staff. Inevitably confidence in the vehicles plummeted, and after persevering with them for a fraction over two years, they were all taken out of service and delicensed on 2nd December 1967 when replacements in the form of RCL class Routemasters became available as a result of cuts elsewhere to replace them on the 705.

All fourteen were placed into storage, mostly at Reigate and Garston, pending a decision on what action to take with them. Further operation involving negotiating the dense traffic of central London appears to have been ruled out, and a niche for them was finally identified in the lowly role of Monday to Friday duplicates to the regular RFs on peripheral route 725 (Gravesend–Windsor via Croydon and Kingston). The 725 was scheduled to be worked by no fewer than four garages (Windsor, Staines, Dartford and Northfleet), but as the duplicates were not expected to run west of Croydon, only the two garages at the eastern end of the route were fated to receive RCs. As they would be working alongside RFs, the decision was taken to repaint the Reliances into the standard Green Line style now carried by recently refurbished RFs, which in fact suited the RCs and was generally perceived as an improvement over the original pastel grey which had not weathered particularly well. Between 29th January and 6th June 1968 all fourteen RCs were taken under trade plates to Aldenham for repainting into two-tone green livery, the first to appear in this style being RC1 on 7th March with RC 14 the last on 28th June.

Even in their revised colours, the RCs still had the miniature-sized offside fleet numbers. This side-on view demonstrates the peaked glassfibre domes carried by these vehicles at both front and rear ends, perpetuating a popular design feature of the era, as well as emphasising the length of the panoramic side windows. RC 4 demonstrates how well the revised livery suited this particular style of bodywork. Although the side route board covers the full length of the 725, the RCs seldom if ever ventured west of Croydon.
London Transport Museum

Newly repainted RC 3 was relicensed and spent a week at Northfleet in March 1968 but it was not until 1st August that operation on the 725 is thought to have actually commenced when RC 3-5 were licensed at Northfleet. Northfleet's connection with the RCs lasted only until 28th August when they were transferred to Dartford, which then remained the sole garage operating RCs until the need for them ceased when route 725 was converted to one-man operation on 15th February 1969. Vehicles were interchanged quite often during Dartford's spell of operation depending, presumably, on their serviceability, but no more than three were ever licensed at one time (reducing to two from 1st January 1969). Six out of the fourteen (RC 7-9, 11-13) were not used at all during this spell of operation.

Once again all fourteen coaches found themselves out of service. Being nearly new, and still retaining a high book value, this was a situation that could not be allowed to continue. The decision was taken to fully investigate, and replace if necessary, the braking system which was the main cause of their unreliability, and also to convert them for one-man operation on a service suited to their abilities. One of the coaches, identity unknown, was sent to the experimental shop at Chiswick where S-cam brakes as used on the Routemaster were installed and tested, with a reasonably satisfactory result achieved at the time. As a result of this, it was arranged for the remainder to be similarly converted at Aldenham while they were there for the conversion to omo. The route on which they were planned to operate was the busy, orbital 727 between Luton and Crawley which served Heathrow and Gatwick airports. In addition to adding a reversing light and indicator at the rear of the vehicles, internal alterations were also made. With the expectation of large quantities of passengers' luggage they were downseated to hold only 43, the seats immediately behind the driver being removed to accommodate a full-height luggage rack. The first coach, RC 8, was sent to Aldenham for conversion on 16th April 1969 with the last converson fully completed on RC 12 on 27th May .

167

To: DIVISIONAL ENGINEER, COUNTRY BUSES AND COACHES

From: MECHANICAL ENGINEER (ROLLING STOCK - ROAD SERVICES)

r Ref: C.16/3/5

Date: 13th March, 1969

CONVERSION OF "RC" COACHES TO ONE MAN OPERATION

Commencing on Wednesday, 16th April, RC Coaches will be sent into Aldenham Works for conversion to O.M.O.

Vehicles to be ready for collection by Works Drivers at 07.30 hours on the dates shown, and will be returned to the garages indicated for storage until required for service.

					RETURN TO:
Wednesday	16th April	RC.	8	WY	RG
"	23rd "		13	WY	RG
Friday	25th "		11	RG	RG
Monday	28th "		14	RG	RG
Wednesday	30th "		1	RG	RG
Friday	2nd May		2	RG	RG
Monday	5th "		3	GR	GR
Wednesday	7th "		4	GR	GR
Friday	9th "		5	GR	GR
Monday	12th "		6	GR	GR
Wednesday	14th "		7	GR	GR
Friday	16th "		9	GR	GR
Monday	19th "		10	GR	GR
Wednesday	21st "		12	GR	RG

By February 1969 all 14 coaches were again out of service, lying unused in Addlestone, Reigate and Garston garages. This is the instruction circulated to interested parties on 13th May in preparation for their conversion to one-man operation.

Taking no chances, London Transport tested each converted RC over the length of route 727 before returning it to service. The RCs began to drift on to the 727 from 17th May 1969 with two relicensed at Reigate and one at St Albans, and from 1st June all fourteen were operational with seven allocated to each garage. With a scheduled requirement of only eight coaches on the 727 – four from each garage – this gave a spares ratio of 75% which should have been far more than adequate to cover any mechanical problems that might arise, but it was not. Reports from drivers of inadequate braking, poor road holding and other faults still prevailed, on top of which the vehicles were being heavily worked, and with a requirement for each to cover some 2,000 miles per week seemingly endless brake adjustments became necessary. The only answer was to bring back the trusty RFs which, though fifteen years older than the RCs, could be relied upon to provide an acceptable level of service. On 6th September, after less than four months on the 727, all except four RCs were removed from it and a full service of RFs was reinstated. The few RCs that remained were kept to serve as late-running stand-bys and were probably used in this capacity as little as possible.

The RCs' final fling under London Transport ownership was as one-man operated coaches on Green Line 727, and Reigate based RC 10 is seen in St Albans 30 minutes into its 3hr 28min run from Luton to Crawley. RC 10 was one of only four members of the class still licensed for service when ownership passed to London Country on 1st January 1970. *Ken Blacker*

Six of the vehicles taken out of service on 6th September were delicensed, but apart from the four kept as spares for the 727 another four were despatched to Dartford with a return to the 725 in mind, presumably to resume working the Croydon shorts but now in omo mode. It seems likely that staff resistance doomed this new venture as all four were delicensed after only five days, and it is quite possible that they never returned on the 725.

The RCs all passed into the ownership of London Country Bus Services with the great shake-up of 1st January 1970. With GREEN LINE being retained as a brand name, no immediate change took place in the external appearance of the vehicles apart from revised legal ownership wording and removal of the bullseye motif from the front. Only four were active at the time (RC 6, 10 at Reigate and RC 8, 11 at St Albans), with two rostered as stand-bys for the 727 and the others serving as spares for the first two. The remainder, as had so often happened in their short career, were unlicensed and back in storage.

The early days of London Country saw little change for the RCs which just about eked an active existence with three or four licensed at any one time for occasional use on Green Line 727. However, with the whole of the Green Line single deck coach fleet time expired by National Bus Company standards except for the RCs, it was probably inevitable that London Country would find itself under pressure to put the latter back into full-time service. It is not known why route 711 (Reigate–High Wycombe) was selected for their renaissance, especially as it went through the heart of the West End with all the traffic delays that this entailed and which London Transport had wisely avoided since the class's original and unfortunate debut on the 705. Perhaps the fact that one of its termini was Reigate, where extensive maintenance facilities were available, influenced the decision, coupled to which was the advantage that many Reigate staff were already accustomed to the RCs and their various foibles. The same did not apply at High Wycombe garage, which shared the 711 on a fifty-fifty basis with Reigate, so RC 2 and RC 9 were taken out of storage and licensed there for staff training purposes on 1st September 1970.

RC 8 spent from October 1970 to August 1971 as part of the High Wycombe contingent on route 711. Still in the Green Line colours inherited from London Transport (and with several signs of paint coming away from the edges of its glassfibre front dome), it now carries London Country's imaginative but short-lived 'flying polo' motif on its front panel in place of the original bullseye.

The 711 schedule required seven vehicles from each garage to fulfil its Monday to Saturday obligations (slightly less for Sundays) and each garage was supplied with an allocation of seven RCs. This inevitably meant that the venerable RFs could still often be found in action on the 711 covering scheduled maintenance commitments and the inevitable breakdowns after the service was officially converted to RC on 16th October 1970. The sporadic RC operation on the 727 ceased at this time, and the two RCs latterly held at St Albans were transferred to become part of the High Wycombe contingent.

It was while working on the 711 that tragedy struck RC 11. A major failure of its A690 engine caused the Reigate-bound vehicle to catch fire at Lower Kingswood, the conflagration becoming so great it caused some of the bodywork fittings to melt, with little remaining of the vehicle that was re-usable. On 16th August 1971 its road fund licence was cancelled and it was finally written off London Country's books at the end of the year, its remains being dismantled at Aldenham in January 1972. The complete demise of the RCs on the 711 followed fairly swiftly after the fire and on 26th August, they were removed from it and RFs returned to restore stability. Despite their badly tarnished reputation the RCs remained in all-day service after being ejected from the 711, albeit once again on purely suburban work far away from the slow-moving traffic of London's West End. Perhaps surprisingly, they were transferred back to the 727 on which their earlier performance had, at best, only been mediocre. Reigate retained six of them for the 727, while High Wycombe's contingent of seven passed back to St Albans.

Since the RCs' last tenure on route 727 it had developed into an exceptionally busy operation. A March 1971 extension in Luton from the station to the airport resulted in it now serving three major airports, with so much passenger traffic being generated that relief coaches were frequently needed. On this occasion the RCs were only fated to remain for a little under four months, and on 18th December 1971 they were all taken out of service and sent across to Grays in preparation for the next and last phase of their Green Line saga at the start of 1972. Their replacements on the 727 were the first of the new RP class which, although also AEC Reliances, were an altogether different proposition and were destined to prove infinitely more reliable than the unfortunate RCs.

RC 11 met a fiery end while working as a Reigate based coach on Green Line 711 in August 1971. Its remains were ultimately sent to London Transport for dismantling at Aldenham in January 1972.

The RCs' final spell of Green Line operation – which was also destined to be their longest – began at Grays on 1st January 1972 when route 723 (Tilbury–Aldgate) was converted to one-man operation. All thirteen remaining RCs were available on the start date except for RC 4 which was away at Aldenham being overhauled, the remainder having stood at Grays licensed but unused over the Christmas period of 1971 awating their next call to duty. For the first time in their lives the RCs were scheduled to serve London's East End, and though 13 vehicles were theoretically more than ample to cover requirements on this relatively short route, the usual problems remained and RFs were often called upon as substitutes. It was during the RC era, on 5th May 1973, that the 723 was removed from its traditional eastern terminus at Tilbury and cut back to terminate at Grays.

During their time at Grays the physical appearance of all of the RCs changed as they passed

A gloomy day in March 1972 finds RC 14 resting in the garage yard at Grays between trips on route 723. Alongside is RF 40 which has been pressed back into Green Line service despite Grays holding its full complement of RCs. RCL 2234, on the left, has now been demoted to bus duties and is destined, in times to come, to be sold back to London Transport. Side route boards were not carried on the RCs at Grays, and shortly after this photograph was taken the rear wheel discs and their supporting brackets were removed from all of them. *Ken Blacker*

through overhaul. For just over two years from the start of 1972 a spasmodic programme was pursued of sending them to Aldenham for overhaul and a total of eight were dealt with there. During 1972 itself vehicles emerged from overhaul with the traditional Lincoln green replaced by London Country's attractive lighter shade, while from 1973 onwards the NBC corporate image was applied using apple green on the lower panelling and white on the window and roof areas in the manner officially approved for so-called local coaches. Other overhauls were carried out at Sparshatt's in Portsmouth and at Grays and Romford garages, and the output from these was usually in bus-style overall NBC green with a single white band amidships. Wherever the overhaul was carried out, the airport-style internal luggage rack was removed and seats installed to bring the vehicles' capacity up to 47, just two short of their original 49.

In May 1974 it was announced that new SNC class Leyland Nationals would be taking over operation of the 723 at a date yet to be announced and that the RCs would be transferred to bus work. The takeover date turned out to be 3rd August 1974 by which time arrangements were well in hand for the RCs to transfer to Hertford where RC 14 had been present since 29th July for staff training. The actual takeover date from RFs on a whole host of rural bus services operated from Hertford was 10th August, allowing a week in which to transfer all the remaining RCs from Grays except for RC 5 which had been delicensed with mechanical problems since 21st March 1974. In the interim, it had probably been heavily cannibalised to keep others going and was found to be in no fit state to be moved. In fact, it never ran in service again and was effectively the second RC to be withdrawn after the fire-damaged RC 11.

The photos on these two pages, taken in the summer of 1974, illustrate the mix of liveries in which the vehicles now appeared and capture some of the run-down appearance that had befallen what had once been a proud and prestigious operation. RC 2, photographed at the Aldgate terminus, had not received a complete coat of fresh paint since April 1968 and had now become unique in being the only one retaining the luggage racks installed in London Transport days for route 727, still clearly visible through the first saloon window. The same location finds RC 7 in the standard NBC semi-coach style applied at Aldenham in January 1973 and now – thanks presumably to panel replacement – disporting various shades of green at the front. Unlike most of the class, RC 3 arrived at Hertford already carrying NBC corporate bus livery. It had been repainted in this style in May 1974 while it was still at Grays, and had operated in this within its last few weeks on route 723 with no outward pretense of still being a Green Line coach.
Mike Harris/J G S Smith

173

Prior to their arrival at Hertford garage, notice was given to the local staff that the RCs should only operate on ten specific running numbers on Mondays to Fridays and eight on Saturdays. They were instructed that it was imperative that these should be strictly adhered to and, under no circumstances (with the word no underlined) should an RC vehicle be allocated to any other number. There was no Sunday work for them. The garage's operations through rural Hertfordshire and into Essex were extensive with a considerable amount of interworking, and the RCs found themselves with primary responsibilities for the main groups of routes 327/331/337 and 390/392/393 but with appearances also on 308, 333, 350, 351 and 384, all of which they shared with other types of vehicle including RF and, later, BN (Bristol LH) and SNB (Leyland National). By mid-1976, which was destined to be the RCs' last full year of operation, the Hertford network of single deck services was scheduled for coverage by 10 RC, 6 SNB and 4 BN.

The same mixture of livery styles and fleet names latterly displayed by the RCs on route 723 was perpetuated during their early days on bus service at Hertford. In this instance RC 6 displays the NBC version of Green Line livery as it passes the Rose & Crown at Aston on its way to Stevenage on its first working day at Hertford. *Mike Harris*

RC 9 broke down in April 1975 and was never restored back to life, and most of the others visited Sparshatt's at Portsmouth at various times for engine overhauls and, where necessary, for repainting into standard NBC bus colours. The only one to arrive from Grays still carrying a full set of luggage racks installed for the 727, RC 2, was converted into a 47-seater while it was at Sparshatt's in November 1975. One vehicle that stood out for a while from all the others while at Hertford was RC 7 which, in August 1975, received an all-over advertisement for house agents Jeffrey King & Company of Hoddesdon. Depicting houses and gardens on a white background, it ran in this form, primarily on routes 392 and 393, until September 1976.

The RCs' somewhat inauspicious operating career came to an end on 29th January 1977 when the last ones to remain in active passenger service (RC 1-4, 6, 8, 10, 12-14) were all delicensed. Another of the class, RC 7, was theoretically serviceable but had not been reactivated after being repainted out of advertising livery at Hertford in October 1976.

The January 1977 date also marked the end of scheduled RF operation elsewhere in the London Country fleet, so the RCs would have been the next for withdrawal anyway. More Leyland Nationals made surplus by cuts elsewhere were drafted in to replace them.

It had been decided in advance that most of the RCs would be disposed of, with only four (RC 6, 10, 12, 13) to be retained for possible use in covering shortages elsewhere. The two completely unserviceable ones, RC 5 and RC 9, which had not been used since 1974 and 1975 respectively, had been sold for scrap just four days before the main batch ceased work. Seven more went to Booth's of Rotherham for scrap in June 1977. None of the four that were retained ever returned to passenger service. RC 6 and RC 10 served temporarily as staff canteens at Epsom racecourse in 1977 while RC 10, 12 and 13 acted as short-term driver training vehicles at various times between July 1977 and January 1980. Three of the four went to Wombwell Diesels in July 1979 and the last to survive, RC 10, was sold to the same scrap merchant in May 1980.

The age of applying all-over advertising material as a revenue earner, at the expense of disfiguring the vehicle's appearance, was in full swing by August 1975 when RC 7 received this predominantly white scheme for Jeffery King & Company, It was photographed in Hertford bus station and ran in this form for just over a year. *J G S Smith*

These fourteen coaches, which had started out with such high hopes pinned on them, had totally failed in their original purpose of heralding a start to the upgrading and re-imaging of the Green Line network. Under the National Bus Company, the Green Line image had not been uplifted as the RCs' original protagonists had hoped; instead it had been brought deliberately downmarket with a huge influx of Leyland Nationals. The great irony is that, on the very day that the last RCs were taken out of service, a start was made in rectifying the folly of the NBC era with the introduction of what was to become a large fleet of proper luxury coaches, the RB and RS classes, in a belated attempt to restore the status of Green Line back to where it should always have been.

As for the RCs themselves, they suffered a disastrous reputation for unreliability which was undoubtedly deserved, especially in their earlier days. Wherever they were sent to work, this reputation preceded them and perhaps doomed them to be judged more harshly than they otherwise would have been. It is not particularly surprising that, after their withdrawal from service by London Country, not a single one of them found further use anywhere and all went immediately for scrapping.

RC 1 is also in Green Line livery, NBC style, but in this instance it displays a larger area of white than its contemporaries. Whereas it proved necessary for the RCs at Hertford to have part of their front blind boxes masked to accommodate all the required displays, this was not the case at the rear where only a few route numbers needed to be accommodated. *J G S Smith*

ORIGINAL
AC ACE & COBRA

ORIGINAL
AC ACE & COBRA

Rinsey Mills

Photography by Mick Walsh
with John Simpson and Ned Scudder

Edited by Mark Hughes

Bay View Books

Published 1990 by Bay View Books Ltd
13a Bridgeland Street
Bideford, Devon EX39 2QE

Text © Copyright 1990 by Rinsey Mills

Colour illustrations © Copyright 1990 by Bay View Books Ltd

Designed by Peter Laws

Typeset by Lens Typesetting, Bideford

ISBN 1 870979 14 1
Printed in Hong Kong

Most of the photographs in this book were taken by Mick Walsh. Cobras in the USA were photographed by John Simpson and Ned Scudder. Karl-Heinz Will in Wiesbaden lent a photograph of the badge of his Cobra 289. John McLellan lent the black-and-white chassis photographs, courtesy of AC Cars. To all of these, the author and the publisher offer their warmest thanks.

Contents

Introduction	6
AC Past and Present	8
AC Ace and Aceca	**19**
Optional Extras	56
Colour Schemes	56
Ace (AC engine) Production and Export Figures	57
Ace (AC engine) Engine Types	58
Ace Bristol Production and Export Figures	58
Ace Bristol Engine Types	59
Aceca Bristol Production and Export Figures	59
Aceca Bristol Engine Types	60
Ace RS 2.6 Production and Export Figures	60
Aceca 2.6 Production and Export Figures	60
Leaf Sprung AC Cobra 260 and 289	**61**
US 260 and 289 Cobra Optional Extras	77
US 260 and 289 Cobra Colour Schmes	77
US 260 and 289 Cobra Production Figures	77
European Cobra 289 Colour Schemes	77
European Cobra 289 Production and Export Figures	78
427 Cobra and AC 289	**79**
427 Cobra Competition Specifications	92
427 Cobra Semi-Competition Specifications	92
427 Cobra Colour Schemes	92
427 Cobra Production Figures	93
AC 289 Colour Schemes	93
AC 289 Production and Export Figures	93
Buying Guide	94
Clubs and Specialists	96

Introduction

When my friend and publisher Charles Herridge mentioned that he was thinking of adding a book on AC Aces and Cobras to his successful 'Original' Series, I greeted this idea with mild amusement, explaining that these were not mass production cars like the others already dealt with. My amusement turned to apprehension, and then horror, when it began to dawn on me that it might be me who had to write it.

Now, six months and many miles and telephone calls later, it is finished. In reality, of course, it is not finished, as there is much more that could be said and doubtless someone will find some mistakes, but a deadline had to be set and when it arrived the information before you was what had emerged.

Many people are unaware of what an AC is but perhaps have heard of a Cobra. A conversation which I and surely other owners have had runs something like this:

"What make of car is it?"
"An AC".
"Yes, but who made it?"
"AC's".
"Who?"
"Have you ever heard of a car called a Cobra?"

If the answer is "Yes" you are home and dry and can tell the enquirer it was made by the same people; if "No" you have some further explaining to do!

A few words of explanation are perhaps necessary from me regarding the, at times, unfamiliar titles given to the different models in this book, especially Cobras. One of the first discoveries I made when beginning my research amongst the remaining original documents at the factory was that the various designations or names that I and most others had always used to describe the various Cobra models were in fact incorrect – at least the factory ledger kept as the cars were built would have it so. Therefore what I had known as MkI and MkII Cobras became USA Leaf Sprung or European Leaf Sprung Cobras, early cars even being called Ace Cobras. This makes sense, as the whole run was merely a development of the same theme: the 260 engine being enlarged to 289, Bishop Cam steering being replaced by rack and pinion, and so on. The 260 Cobra is popularly called the MkI but in fact the largest changes came around the introduction of rack and pinion steering some fifty cars later. The car known as the MkIII is thus the true MkII, and the factory ledger calls it just that, 'MkII Coil Sprung

INTRODUCTION

Cobra', the European coil sprung car being named the 'AC 289'. I have respected the manufacturer's own designations throughout the book.

ACs have always been rather special cars. Founded in the very first years of the twentieth century by the unlikely combination of a butcher named Portwine and an engineer named John Weller, the firm of Autocarrier, as it was then named, began by making three-wheeled, single-cylinder delivery vehicles, with a passenger variant called the Sociable. Four-wheeled cars of either 10 or 12hp appeared shortly before the First World War; these had the gearbox in unit with the rear axle, a feature that was to persist until the Hurlock era. The six-cylinder engine used in the Ace and Aceca was designed by Weller in 1919 and was in production from the early 1920s, pioneer motorist and former head of Napier cars S. F. Edge owning the firm during this period. Under his aegis the company was very successful in competition, as Napiers had been almost twenty years previously. In 1922 a 1½-litre four-cylinder AC became the first car in its class to cover 100 miles in an hour, and in 1926 a six-cylinder car was the first British car to win the Monte Carlo Rally.

The Hurlock family bought the company at the beginning of the 1930s after it had gone into receivership, and from then on until the Second World War the two brothers, William and Charles, oversaw the production of a few hundred cars ranging from Aero saloon to Competition two-seater. These had many proprietary components such as ENV axles and Moss or ENV gearboxes but still used the 2-litre alloy engine, which now produced some 90bhp in rare supercharged form. The story after the War is related in the next chapter, but AC cars still retained the individual 'persona' that only hand built cars can have.

When the time drew near for the cars to be photographed, Club registrars and owners were contacted, and in some cases the 'one owner, totally original' car was found to be in a hopelessly neglected state, painted an extraordinary colour or fitted with a non-original motor. In any event I hope that the cars finally selected from those available give a good cross-section of the various models.

I would like to thank the following owners for their patience and general good humour whilst their treasured possessions were subjected to both my criticism and the inquisitive eye of the camera: Barry Howsley, who owns almost the first Ace (AE24); arch-AC enthusiast David Hescroff, owner of the superbly original white Ace; long time Frazer Nash exponent Brian Heath, for turning out on a rainy day with his Ace Bristol (BEX 1033); Maurice Knight, who has owned ACs for very many years and whose Aceca (AE 777) I was very pleased to use, David Hescroff's Bristol engined car (BE 790) being the dark green version of the coupé. For the RS 2.6 I can make no excuses as it is my car (RS 5020), reluctantly selected because it is unrestored yet fairly presentable; the Weber-carburettor engine is fitted to Peter Kirby's 2.6 (RS 5003). Gary Hullfish owns the fabulously original early 289-engined Cobra (CSX 2099) – oh that all cars could have remained in this condition. Nick Green kindly let his scarce right hand drive 289 (COB 6020) be used, and Karl-Heinz Will photographed the badge on his car (CSX 2013). Ned Scudder's S/C 427 (CSX 3042) is rare and desirable in any company, the red 427 (CSX 3117) is owned by Harvey Siegal, and last but not least the Black Pearl AC 289 (COB 6101) has been in the family of the owner Philip Corn since new.

Many other people kindly gave their time and knowledge to assist in the preparation of the book: Brian Angliss, owner of AC cars, under whose auspices spares availability is now better than for many a year and who generously allowed me access to company records; Lesley Webb, his cheerful secretary/administrator, Eugene Carter, still working for the company after more than forty years (and who was responsible for much of the chassis fabrication on all models); Brian Gilbart-Smith, Chairman of the AC Owners' Club, who has probably driven and raced his Ace Bristol as much as anyone, for throwing open his files; Ace Registrar Tom Gibbon, Aceca Registrar Austin Weltman and Cobra Registrar Andy Shepherd.

Ned Scudder, Cobra Registrar of the SAAC, and Nick Green restorer, and racer, gave most generous amounts of their time to help me get the Cobras 'right', and I owe them particular thanks.

Mark Hughes, the editor, translated the original text into something that you the reader would find more palatable. Photography of cars in England was very ably taken care of by Mick Walsh, those in the USA being covered by John Simpson and Ned Scudder.

Past owners usually remember their Ace, Aceca or Cobra with affection. To these people, especially those who bought their cars new at not inconsiderable expense, thus creating and maintaining a demand for such cars, to Charles and Derek Hurlock and their staff at Thames Ditton who worked so hard to produce such beautiful cars, and finally to Caroll Shelby and those who worked alongside him to turn his dream into reality, I dedicate this book, for without them there would be no ACs.

AC Past and Present

The timeless elegance of the Ace: this is AE 24, one of the very first cars sold to the public, which left the factory on 22 May 1954. Originally this car would have been fitted with drum brakes at the front. The battery carrier is visible behind the front wheel. All early cars had the flat windscreen.

The AC factory entered the dowdy post-war world with its stolid but well-made 2-litre saloon, which was powered by AC's own evergreen six-cylinder engine. As the 1950s dawned and people began to feel a little more emancipated from the burden of the previous decade, two trends developed in the motoring world: Americans discovered English sports cars and began to want to buy them; and motor sport, after a shaky immediate post-war start, began to gain momentum.

For the moment the AC factory continued making the saloon at the rate of some four a week, and also engaged the Buckland Body Works to produce a few rather unlovely tourers on the same chassis. Perhaps AC was aware – or perhaps not – that it was about to be left behind producing outmoded cars and lacking the resources to develop a new model from scratch.

Meanwhile, an ebullient London motor dealer, Cliff Davis, was beginning to have some success with a Barchetta Ferrari styled sports racing car powered by a 2-litre Bristol engine, coming ninth in the BARC race and winning the Brooklands Trophy in 1953. The chassis for this car was designed by John Tojeiro, another keen motor sport enthusiast, and consisted simply of a pair of 3in tubes with a single cross member, and a suspension tower at either end carrying transverse leaf springs and wishbones. Fabricated uprights carried Morris Minor hubs, while rack and pinion steering from the same source was employed; alloy road wheels were fitted.

At around the same time a motor engineer, Vincent Davison, built another Tojeiro, powered by a 2½-litre four-cylinder Lea Francis engine, which he endowed with a similar body. Through Ernest Bailey of the Buckland Body Works, both of these cars were brought to the attention of AC's Charles Hurlock and his nephew, Derek, who were beginning to find themselves in a quandary about what AC should do next. The upshot of this was that Vincent Davison's car was demonstrated to the Hurlocks and their senior staff by Cliff Davis. After some hasty decision-making, this car was purchased from Davison and he himself was hired as development engineer.

Throughout the late summer of 1953 the stark Tojeiro was transformed into a more civilised sports car for the London Motor Show in the autumn. The interior was fully trimmed and a hood and sidescreens were added; perforated Alfin brake drums,

· AC PAST AND PRESENT ·

splined hubs, chromium wire wheels and an AC engine and gearbox all went together to make the car look more professional for the exhibition. In another part of the factory a chassis which was to become the first true AC Ace, AE 01, was built up, although when it was exhibited on the stand next to the revamped Tojeiro it was neither capable of running nor in its final form (it had rack and pinion steering and a saloon radiator).

The new AC was up against stiff competition for attention at the show. Jaguar had won Le Mans that year and had the victorious C-type on its stand, Triumph displayed a modified TR2 which had exceeded 120mph in Belgium and Aston Martin had its DB3S. Added to these were many cars, open and closed, which could attain or exceed 100mph. The Ace stood alone among its sports car competitors, however, in being the only one with all-round independent suspension. It cost £915 against such cars as the Austin Healey 100 at £750 and the Jaguar XK120 roadster at £1130.

When the show chassis was later completed, gone were the rather droopy lines of its predecessor. In one move AC had pulled the whole shape into a tight yet flowing form to create the body that was to remain in production virtually unchanged for nearly ten years. As cars began to be sold, the first Ace, now registered UPJ 75, and a pair of stablemates were entered by the factory for the 1954 Alpine Rally. No spectacular success came their way – a fifth in class was the best placing – but this and other competitive events set the scene for the future.

Meanwhile, not content to rest on its laurels, AC was planning a coupé version of the Ace; the result, built on Ace chassis number AE 56, appeared at the 1954 London Motor Show. Described by *The Autocar* as "Quite one of the best looking cars at Earls Court", the Aceca, as it had been called in a revival of the name given to the AC that had won the Monte Carlo Rally nearly 30 years before, looked stunning in brilliant blue.

With the Aceca, the factory transformed what was a spartan sports car into a two-seater GT coupé, to use that now often abused term. Its basic price was expensive at £1215 but compared favourably with other coupés such as the Alfa Romeo 1900SS at £2500, Bristol 404 at £2350, Porsche 356 at £1260 and Aston Martin DB2/4 at £1925. Only Jaguar undercut

A colour scheme popular in the United States. This Ace, chassis AEX 1076, was sent there on 5 May 1959. Drum brakes were still used on some cars late in the production run, the cars being so light they were not much of a disadvantage for normal road use.

9

One of the last AC Acecas made (above and left), chassis AE 777, which left the factory on 8 July 1960, is painted in the same shade of green as that worn by the factory Le Mans cars. With its short, sloping tail the Aceca is one of the less cumbersome GT coupés of the period. The line of the front wings was higher towards the rear than on the Ace to merge with the doors and rear wings.

them all with an amazing £1140 for the XK140.

Although the Ace was raced at club level with verve and enthusiasm on both sides of the Atlantic, its engine was not really suitable for serious competition, fourth place in the 2-litre class at the Sebring 12 Hours in 1956 being its only success in a major international event; the consensus was that the car could benefit from a more powerful engine option.

Ken Rudd, the enthusiastic Sussex AC agent who was to have no small effect on the fame and fortunes of the marque, rendered his 1954 Ace more competitive for racing by returning to the Bristol power unit which Cliff Davis had used in his Tojeiro with such success, the improved performance giving Rudd the 1956 *Autosport* Production Sports Car Championship. This was a good start for the new marriage of Ace and Bristol engine, but more was to come. Over the next few years the Ace Bristol, as it was officially called, became arguably the most successful 2-litre production sports car racing in the late 1950s.

In 1957 at Sebring an Ace Bristol came third in the sports car class behind a pair of sports racing Ferraris. This may have encouraged Ken Rudd to have a go at Le Mans. With little or no prospect of an official factory entry, though, Rudd had to buy an AC-engined Ace factory demonstrator, fitting it with a Bristol engine and making slight body modifications. In early June he drove his car out to the Sarthe circuit, circulated at 97mph for 24 hours, came second in class behind a Porsche RS and tenth overall, then drove home. To round off the Ace Bristol's first full year of competition, Colonel Robert Kuhn captured the SCCA Class E championship with an Ace Bristol in the USA.

Towards the end of 1956 the Aceca too had been given the opportunity of being propelled by the Bristol engine, and indeed the second car built was raced in the last tragic Mille Miglia of 1957. It did not do at all well, splitting its petrol tank and using

AC PAST AND PRESENT

Sold new in France, this Ace Bristol, chassis BEX 1033, left the factory on 23 January 1959. By this time the short boot was used and the curved screen was a popular option, as were the front disc brakes.

over 200 gallons of petrol in the process.

The following year, 1958, saw another championship title for the Ace Bristol in the SCCA's class E, and Le Mans was revisited with two cars – a special Le Mans AC designed by John Tojeiro and an Ace. Both Bristol-powered, they came eighth and ninth overall and second and third in their class.

In 1959 came the Ace Bristol's finest achievement amongst the pine trees of this famous circuit. Ken Rudd acquired a secondhand example from an AC owner and enthusiastic supporter, and after careful preparation drove the car to the circuit. In one of the hottest Le Mans races for years, the little Ace Bristol left all its rivals in the 2-litre class (and much of the larger exotica) abandoned by the roadside to win the class and finish seventh overall. Coincidentally, the race was won by a certain Carroll Shelby (teamed with Roy Salvadori) in an Aston Martin DBR1.

Ace Bristols won the SCCA championship once again in 1959, so to try to counter their invincibility the organisers elevated them to Class D for 1960. They promptly won again, which led to them being upgraded once more, into Class C; the next year they won that as well....

Amid all this activity a letter arrived at the AC factory one morning with some bad news. Bristol was about to switch to V8 engines for its cars and so would be ceasing manufacture of the 2-litre six-cylinder unit; but fortunately enough engines were available to continue producing Ace and Aceca Bristols for a while.

What to do next? The Ace engine, in the midst of its 40th birthday celebrations, was given its final update to CLBN form, but this was not really the answer. Ken Rudd, the long time Ace exponent and also a Ford tuning specialist, saw the plight which the Hurlocks might once again face and suggested the Ford-powered Ruddspeed Ace. And so the RS 2.6 was born, with the only major styling change during the Ace's life – the tapering bonnet and longer nose with smaller nacelle allowed by the shorter Zephyr engine. With the introduction of

· ORIGINAL AC ACE AND COBRA ·

The RS 2.6 Ace became more aggressive looking with the redesigned nose. By this time drum brakes had been abandoned. Chassis RS 5020 was sold on 1 September 1962. The first owner was a Mr Armstrong, owner of the shock absorber company.

Chassis CSX 2099, shipped on 20 March 1963, the 100th Cobra built and given as a wedding present to its first owner! Cars were only available in red, white or black at the time, so a black one was purchased and immediately resprayed dark green, which was considered the only suitable colour for a British sports car. Up to chassis CSX 2159 Cobras had these narrower wheel arch flares, and this car of course has no side vents in the front wings.

this new model, AC, under the auspices of Ken Rudd, inadvertently set a pattern of using Ford engines for all its subsequent models.

At £1468 in its most potent form, the RS 2.6 was cheaper than the £1550 Ace Bristol as well as being faster and more tractable. Since both were nearly twice the price of an Austin-Healey 3000, however, trade began to drop off. So when another letter arrived at the Thames Ditton factory, it was read with more interest than might have been expected. That letter was written by Carroll Shelby, who had now retired from racing and was intent on building his dream sports car – a machine that he was later happy to tell people would "blow Ferrari's ass off".

In October 1961 Shelby visited the Hurlocks and a deal was struck for a prototype to be built. Shelby returned to the US and arranged for a pair of Ford Fairlane engines, selected because of their light weight, to be sent to AC. Ford had shown interest in the project due to its desire for a more sporting image to attract young customers, and had agreed to supply these motors.

Shelby himself returned with blueprints, and AC's staff, including Vin Davison, soon produced and tested a running car. After some minor alterations it was airfreighted, less its engine, to the US. CSX 2000 arrived at Los Angeles airport and was taken to the workshop Shelby shared with his friend Dean Moon, the engine tuner. The entire staff set to and within a few hours had installed a 260 engine and were sampling the result of the Anglo-American partnership. During the next few months the new car appeared at various shows and was often road tested by magazines; it sported different colour schemes, probably to make it appear that more than one car existed.

By the late summer of 1962 cars were beginning to arrive in some numbers. Some were shipped to New York to be completed in Pittsburg by Ed Hugas, a well-known racing driver who was Shelby's East Coast distributor, a handful went to Tasca Ford, and the rest were sent to California, to be completed at first in the Santa Fe Springs workshop and later at the larger Venice plant to which Shelby moved, partly to be near to Los Angeles airport. These first cars had many minor – and undocumented – running changes incorporated in them; because the chassis numbers left the factory out of sequence, these changes are also apparently haphazard.

Shelby was quick to instigate racing activity, the first Cobra to race being car CSX 2002 at Riverside, California, in October 1962. Driven by Billy Krause, it walked away from the opposition until sidelined by a broken rear hub. Appearances followed at Nassau, Riverside (where Dave MacDonald gave the Cobra its first victory in January 1963), Daytona, Sebring and Le Mans (its first foray into

ORIGINAL AC ACE AND COBRA

· A C P A S T A N D P R E S E N T ·

The size and shape of the wheel arch flares on this rack and pinion steering 289 car distinguish it as having the second or larger type fitted to roadgoing leaf sprung cars from chassis CSX 2160. This car, chassis COB 6020, is one of the handful of right hand drive leaf sprung Cobras manufactured.

The most brutal of all roadgoing Cobras, the S/C, looks quite peaceful amongst the fallen autumn leaves of New Jersey – this is chassis CSX 3042, which left AC on 19 February 1965. All 427s had a much larger radiator nacelle with oil cooler intake below and of course increased wheel arch flares. Semi Competition 427 Cobras came from the run of cars produced for FIA homologation and so, although rendered street legal, look much more the racing car.

· AC PAST AND PRESENT ·

Europe). Two Cobras competed at Le Mans: one car, CSX 2142, driven and entered by Ed Hugas and Peter Jopp, blew its engine almost halfway through the race, whilst the other, CS 2131, a right-hand drive car entered by the AC factory and driven by Ninian Sanderson and Peter Bolton, came seventh.

Towards the end of 1963, a small run of left- and right-hand drive European Cobras was embarked upon; these were made entirely at the AC factory at Thames Ditton, all of them bearing either COX or COB chassis numbers. At Earls Court that autumn the Cobra was priced at £2030, a figure which, although it may seem cheap now, looked high against the E-type coupé at £1583 or the Austin-Healey 3000 at £865.

For 1964 Shelby enlarged his racing programme and built several Daytona Coupés on leaf-sprung chassis. Le Mans produced a fourth place for one of these, but AC's own special coupé – the car that achieved notoriety by being tested at 180mph on the M1 before the race – crashed disastrously after seven hours. Several wins did come their way but Ferrari still retained the Manufacturer's GT Championship.

Finally, in 1965, Shelby was to attain his dream. In spite of a not too successful Le Mans, where the highest-placed Daytona was eighth, Shelby secured the World Sports Car Championship at the next race, the Rheims 12 hours, where Daytonas came first and second in their class.

Amid this frantic activity, Shelby, in conjunction with Ford and AC, was busy redesigning the Cobra. The 427 was developed as his final answer for the GT Championship; although it had been intended to homologate the model early in the year for the 1965 season, this was not to be because Shelby – and Ferrari for that matter – could not muster a sufficient quantity of new cars for the April deadline. This meant that both protagonists had to

Normal roadgoing 427 Cobras lost the outside exhausts, bonnet scoop and roll bar but acquired bumpers. This is chassis CSX 3117, which left the factory on 24 November 1965. The horizontal air splitter in the nacelle should have a chrome trim.

17

race the previous season's cars.

The 427 competition cars, however, were dominant in the SCCA production class for some years, taking their last win in the early 1970s. Unsold competition cars, with minor modifications to make them street legal, were sold off as Semi-Competition models, Shelby realizing that soon there would be no more money from Ford for racing. Ford's own GT40 programme took precedence over the Cobras, and in any case the day of the front-engined sports racing car was really at an end in international events. Shelby had achieved what he set out to do, the curtain coming down with the crashing roar of the racing Cobras still reverberating in people's ears. As a realist, he knew that he might be able to beat Ferrari again, but not the might of Ford.

Shipment of normal road 427s started almost as soon as the 1965 homologation fiasco was over and continued until production stopped abruptly in December 1966. The AC factory, meanwhile, finished producing its small run of European coil spring cars, now called AC 289s; although the now Ford-owned name of Cobra was available, the factory decided not to use it on these last cars. As the final trickle of cars left the works in 1968, AC's next car, the Frua-bodied 428, was already in production.

Throughout their 15-year lifespan, the Ace and the Cobra had always been appreciated by those motorists who wanted to own something rather special – something almost intangible, hand-made and scarce. The rarest version was the RS 2.6 Aceca with a total of just eight cars, the most prolific the US leaf-sprung Cobra 289 at 518 cars. The last figure may appear large in this context, but one should remember that this represents considerably less than half the number of export E-type roadsters made by Jaguar in only the first year of production – and all the ACs covered by this book totalled less than the export E-type roadsters in the second year of production.

Very soon after the last Cobras had been built, owners began to cherish them, probably because they realized that their like would never be seen again. They were outmoded yet fabulous, just like the huge chain-drive racing cars of 60 years before. Aces and Acecas, perhaps through being more refined than their more spectacular relations, took rather longer to become recognised generally as the spritely thoroughbreds that they are, although many owners, past and present, have always known this.

All of these cars, even though the youngest is approaching 25 years old, can be maintained, driven and enjoyed in exactly the same way as they were intended to be, apart from restrictions imposed by speed limits and greater traffic density.

In the ownership of one family from new, this AC 289, chassis COB 6101, is the very first one made, leaving the factory on 27 June 1966. The use of the narrower of the two rear wing patterns and wire wheels for this model renders it rather more sleek than the 427. Pedal box and brake master cylinder can be seen on the underside.

AC Ace and Aceca

CHASSIS

The Ace chassis frame is constructed of a pair of 3in diameter steel tubes of 14swg which run parallel from front to rear, with a cross member of the same material linking them near the centre. At each end of these two tubes is welded a suspension box fabricated from 10swg steel sheet. Each suspension box takes the form of a flat-topped triangle, the flat tops being necessary to accommodate the transverse leaf springs. The front assembly is inclined very slightly rearwards to provide castor angle, is drilled to accept wishbones and has mountings for shock absorbers. There is also a V shaped bracket at the front to support the steering idler; this bracket can be a weak point and should be checked periodically for fractures.

The front ends of the main chassis tubes are closed by welded circular plates. Between the front suspension mountings and the central cross member are fabricated mountings, welded directly to the main chassis tubes, for the engine/gearbox assembly. On the right-hand side – or directly opposite on a left-hand drive car – are two further fabricated assemblies welded to the main chassis tubes; these support the steering box and carry the hydraulic cylinders and pedals for brake and clutch. Also forward of the central cross member is welded the 1½in diameter tubular hoop which supports the scuttle. This hoop is braced by a pair of tubes which triangulate from the centre of the hoop down to the main chassis tubes; in addition a steering column bracket is attached to the hoop on the appropriate side.

The rear suspension box is made in such a way as to accommodate the differential, the nose piece of which is bolted directly onto the front face of the suspension box. This assembly is also drilled and fitted with the appropriate bracketing for the rear

The 1955 Ace Show chassis. Many components such as carburettors, exhaust manifold and shock absorbers have a 'show' finish. The springs have not been wrapped in tape.

Ace chassis (above) complete with its tubular body framework. The engine mountings and pedal box indicate that it is to become a right hand drive RS 2.6. The main chassis tubes of the Ace RS 2.6 were of the same wall thickness as the Aceca's, thicker than earlier Aces' at 12swg instead of 14swg.

Left hand drive Aceca rolling chassis complete with body tubes and glass fibre footboxes ready to accept the wooden door and tailgate frames prior to being panelled.

wishbones. The rear shock absorber brackets take the form of a tube welded crosswise at the top rear of this housing and supported by further tubes returning downwards to the main chassis. This construction also helps to support the bodywork at the rear. A pair of perforated and tapered channel-section outriggers support, at either end, the tube around which the base of the sill is formed; two further outriggers attach to this tube and support the seat frames and floor.

The Aceca chassis is broadly the same as that of the Ace but the main chassis tubes have a greater wall thickness of 12swg. Because the differential is rubber-mounted (in the search for silence and smoothness with the coupé body), there is no fabricated suspension and final drive carrier; instead there are brackets welded at the rear of the main tubes to act as a mounting for the differential and the wishbones. The rear ends of the main chassis tubes are closed by a cross member perforated by five holes.

The Aceca has a further 3in tubular cross member just in front of the differential brackets. The rear transverse leaf spring is bolted to a pad supported by two pairs of small diameter tubes rising up from the main chassis, each pair stiffened with a perforated web at the top portion.

Two substantial box-section outriggers project from the main chassis just in front of the rear cross member; these are tapered at their ends and also have large graduated perforations. There are three tapered channel-section outriggers (also with graduated perforations) projecting from the chassis tubes, two on the passenger side and one on the driver's side. In addition, there is a further small-section tube projecting from the main chassis either side of the central cross member. The outward extremities of all outriggers are joined by another small-section tube running fore and aft. All construction is welded as on the Ace and the smaller diameter tubes are of ¾in section. The whole of the chassis frame and subsidiary tubular framework were finished in black prior to assembly.

FRONT SUSPENSION

All-round independent suspension on a road car was something of a novelty at the time of the introduction of the AC Ace, but transverse leaf spring independent front suspension had been used pre-war on such cars as Alvis and Delahaye. The 37¼in long spring bolted to the Ace's suspension box

Engine mountings were welded directly to the main chassis tubes and were normally stamped with the chassis number, as on this AC engined Ace, AE 24.

had eight leaves until the introduction of the 2.6 model, which gained an extra leaf because of increased engine weight.

Very early cars had a plain, tubular A-shaped wishbone, but soon a sheet strengthening web was added. At first bronze bushes were employed in the suspension but from chassis no. AEX 128 all suspension pivots had rubber bushes. (Before attempting to remove wishbone pins at either front or rear, the ¼in BSF Allen locating screws must be removed, these being found in the outer face of the uprights.) Connecting the spring and the wishbone on either side is a fabricated steel box section upright incorporating a lug in which the king pin is mounted. Armstrong hydraulic telescopic shock absorbers were used unless an owner specified alternatives.

The wishbones, uprights and other suspension parts (apart from the springs) were finished in black, the shock absorbers in manufacturer's colour. The springs were wrapped in Drevo tape; it or its equivalent Denso tape is available from plumbing suppliers.

REAR SUSPENSION

The rear leaf spring is a little longer than the front at 41in and has only seven leaves. Apart from these differences, it is mounted in the same way as the front spring. As at the front, the tubular wishbones have bronze bushes on the earlier cars and rubber bushing from chassis no. AEX 128 and on all Bristol-engined cars. The fabricated steel uprights differ from the front ones, of course, in that their construction allows for the rear hub to be mounted on them and the driveshaft to pass through.

Steel parts are finished in the same manner as those at the front, shock absorbers are again in manufacturer's finish and the spring is also wrapped in glutinous brown tape.

The factory handbook for both Ace and Aceca suggests greasing the spring shackles and wishbones at both front and rear every 500 miles. While it is not essential to rigorously adhere to this procedure, it is strongly recommended that these points receive regular attention. Wear can occur rapidly and, apart from anything else, the handling of the car will deteriorate dramatically. Rear-end steering and various clonks are a sure sign that suspension bushes need attention.

STEERING

By the time the Ace was on sale to the public it was equipped with a Bishop Cam steering box, but when the show chassis was exhibited at the 1953 Motor Show it was fitted with rack and pinion, from the Morris Minor. Many Aces and Acecas have been subsequently fitted with rack and pinion, but having driven cars with and without the original steering I have yet to be convinced that rack and pinion is an all-round improvement. The reason is

Almost all AC and Bristol engined Aces had this large centrally mounted, and awkward to use, fly-off handbrake. Note the original steering wheel and adjuster. The long cranked gearlever denotes an AC engined car with Moss gearbox.

A woodrim wheel (below) was an option: this correct type has been repaired at its centre with extra rivetted plates. The strange 'tonneau' behind the windscreen was supplied by request on light coloured, curved windscreen cars to cut reflection during night driving.

All cars fitted with Bishop Cam steering had this steering idler (right). This is a right hand drive car and has just been greased.

The disc brake caliper, always mounted forward of the hub on Aces and Acecas, can be seen behind the 16in wheel of this Aceca. The sills and front valance on this car have had bitumen paint applied by the owner to stop paint chipping.

probably that the steering arms are of a length designed for the steering box.

The Bishop Cam steering box fitted as original equipment is adjustable for play by way of a screw with locking nut in the cover. The trick is to obtain the minimum amount of free play without this resulting in excessive stiffness. A worn box can sometimes, after adjustment, become very stiff on either lock, the reason being that there is less wear in these portions of the gear and the play has been taken out of the central worn section.

A stator tube runs through the box and column to the trafficator and horn controls in the centre of the steering wheel. The wheel itself is black with three sprung chromium quadruple wire spokes. The position of the steering wheel is adjustable for reach by a normal telescopic adjuster with large knurled ring on the column and expanding spiral dust cover, and for height by means of the bracket up behind the dashboard. The steering box drop arm is connected via the idler and split track rods to the steering arms.

The factory handbook gives the following settings: wheel camber, 1–2° positive; wheel toe-in on rim, 1/16in; castor angle, 5°; King pin inclination, 9°. All steel parts on the steering assembly are finished in black.

BRAKES

From the start of production, both front and rear brakes on the Ace were 11in × 1¾in Girling hydraulic with Wellworthy Alfin drums. Early cars had alloy back plates at front and rear, but in 1954 steel ones were standardised at the front. Those at the front had twin leading shoes, each shoe being operated by its own wheel cylinder; this system gave a certain amount of servo effect. The rear brakes had a single wheel cylinder each and sliding shoes. There are two adjusting nuts on each front back plate and one on each rear; turning these clockwise takes up wear in the linings. These brakes were also used on some Austin Healey 100s and Austin A70s.

Most cars nowadays have their handsome Alfin aluminium brake drums either bare aluminium finish or polished, but it is the author's opinion that originally these would have been unpolished aluminium, or matt black on some cars. Manufacturers seldom polished metal surfaces that needed to dissipate heat as this process cuts down surface area dramatically and therefore cooling capabilities.

All models had these cast aluminium pedals. The ones on this car are in need of replacement non-slip rubbers. The correct dipswitch is a Lucas FS22.

Chrome wheels were always an option. These are the second type with double row spokes.

Double laced 15in wheels were available from the late 1950s onwards. This Aceca Bristol, chassis BE790, was delivered on 9 June 1960, and has the roof mounted aerial fitted to the majority of cars with radios.

As a result of racing experience, disc brakes were offered first as an option on Aces then later as standard equipment. These 11in disc brakes were the same as those fitted to the Triumph TR3. Quite a number of cars went back to the factory to be fitted with these brakes, and doubtless other cars have been modified over the years by enthusiastic owners. Fitting the correct type of disc brakes is, I would say, a quite acceptable but not strictly original modification, especially if the car was manufactured before the date when they became an option. The first car to leave the factory fitted with disc brakes was chassis no. BEX 289 on 1st August, 1957, bound for Switzerland, and the first home market car so equipped was chassis no. BE 369 in November, 1957, consigned to Ken Rudd.

The 2.6 Ace used the same rear brakes, but at the front discs of 11¾in diameter were fitted in conjunction with the same calipers as other Aces or Girling three-piston calipers. The caliper is type 17/3J and the pads required are type GD522, which were also fitted to the Cobra, Aston Martin DB5 and pre-1972 Jaguar XJ6. A Girling MK2 vacuum servo unit was fitted to some 2.6 cars and was mounted on a fabricated bracket bolted to the driver's footwell.

Final Drive

A conventional Hardy Spicer propellor shaft transmits the drive from the gearbox to the ENV HP110 differential mounted directly to the fabricated housing which constitutes part of the chassis. Short flanged shafts emanate from either side of the differential and are in turn bolted to the universally jointed shafts which connect with the hub shafts. These hub shafts run in two ball bearing races, clamped to the shaft through distance pieces by the driving flange retaining nuts. The 42mm splined wheel hubs also have internal splines into which the hub shafts are pressed and retained by circlips. The standard rear axle ratio was 3.64:1, but 3.91:1 and 4.3:1 were optional.

As with the suspension, regular attention with the greasegun is advised in the various universal joints which make up this final drive assembly. The Aceca's differential is mounted on a three-point rubber mounting, two below and one above the casing, instead of being built into the rear chassis suspension box. The oil capacity of both Ace and Aceca differentials is three pints. Differentials and propshafts were finished in black.

Wheels & Tyres

From the beginning, the Ace and later the Aceca were fitted with centre-laced, 48-

spoke 16in diameter road wheels with 42mm splined centres, carrying Michelin X tyres. These early X tyres, although long ago surpassed in terms of grip, give a very long life together with the good roadholding enthused over in contemporary road tests, although recent owners of ACs view these now archaic Michelins with suspicion.

By 1957 double-laced wire wheels fitted with 56 spokes made their appearance on both models, still with 16in diameter; by 1959 15in wheels were an option offered by the factory. In the author's view an Ace or Aceca looks more attractive on 16in wheels but many people like the lower and more modern look imparted by the 15in wheels; certainly the variety of tyres available in the smaller size makes it attractive.

One can safely say that the majority of cars had painted wheels, but certainly some were fitted with chromium wire wheels from new. If painted, the standard factory options were silver, cream and red, but other colours could be specified by customers.

Engine

By the time the Ace was announced at the 1953 Motor Show, the 1991cc, 65mm × 100mm, six-cylinder AC engine had been in production for some 30 years and once again was pressed into service for the new model.

Apart from the water pump now being mounted on the side of the block, the adoption of bronze-backed white-metalled main bearings (instead of diecast white metal) and a repositioned vibration damper, the engine was very much as it had been before the war. In addition the harmonic balancer that had been integral with the flywheel now lived out in front on the crankshaft pulley and the front engine mountings were altered, but these modifications had appeared on the immediate post-war saloons some seven years previously.

The first Aces, up to chassis number AE 59, had the identical UMC series engines with 2000 series numbers. The engines gradually became uprated through the life of the Ace and Aceca from 85bhp to some 105bhp in the CLB series motors. First came the CL, with 2100 series numbers, which had a larger diameter crankshaft and gave 90bhp. Then came the CLB with around 102bhp, and finally the CLBN in some late Acecas was rumoured to develop

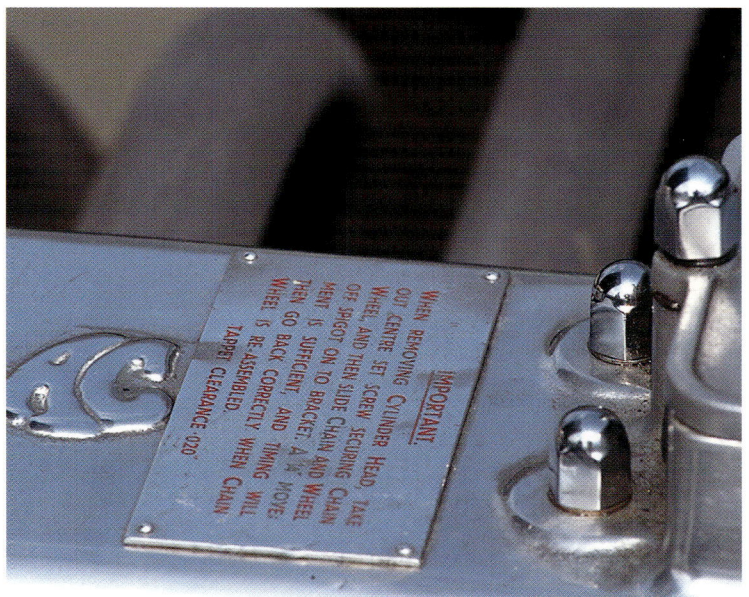

The red plug leads and the breather pipe from the camshaft cover are non-original on this AC engine. The inner wings should be bare aluminium and not painted. Concise instructions for cylinder head removal were on a plate rivetted to the camshaft cover.

nearly 110bhp; these are 2400 WT series motors.

The basis of this trusty powerplant is a cast aluminium crankcase and water jacket which carries a five main bearing crankshaft. This unfamiliar configuration for a six-cylinder is due to there being two rear main bearings sandwiching the sprocket for the duplex chain driving the camshaft, the large bronze helical gear to drive the cross shaft being directly in front of the forward of these two bearings. The main bearing caps are in aluminium, topped by steel plates, and brass unions are screwed into each one between the studs; the unions are attached to a pipe which feeds oil to the crankshaft.

The main bearings are of equal size with the exception of the rearmost one, which is of a greater diameter in order to carry the adaptor for the flywheel and camshaft drive. This adaptor is keyed onto the tapered end of the crankshaft and secured by a large nut and tab washer. At the front of the crankshaft are mounted the vibration damper (innermost), then the pulley for the water pump and finally an aluminium pulley for the fan. CL engines have bi-metal

This engine has acquired red plug caps as well as leads. The front breather on the camshaft cover is correct; the rear one on the oil filler lid is correct but is not always present. The Otter Controls thermoswitch for the choke is visible in front of the carburettors, as are the two separate, different size, fan belts. The accelerator cross shaft passes behind the cylinder head. SU carburettors on all Aces should have brass dashpot caps.

main bearings but the CLB units have a nitrided crankshaft with lead indium main bearings.

The cast iron liners are a push fit into the base of the aluminium cylinder block and are sealed with 'figure of eight' gaskets. The connecting rods are quite slender and are of H section with two bolt caps, the white metal bearings being uprated to lead indium in the CLB engine. The pistons have two compression rings and one scraper ring, while the gudgeon pins are located by circlips. The compression ratio was initially 8:1, rising to 9:1 in CLB form. Removal of a piston has to be carried out with its liner due to the fact that the big end is too large for the bore and the piston will not clear the crankshaft.

A conventional copper/asbestos gasket is fitted which will only seal correctly providing the flange on the liners protrudes slightly above the block; the amount the liners stand proud should reduce to some .008in under compression of 40lb ft as the cylinder head is tightened. The cast iron head has slightly inclined valves activated by rockers carried on a shaft above the camshaft. These rockers have rollers that bear on the camshaft lobes, and the shaft itself runs direct on the head and four iron caps. The earlier engines have valve clearances of .020in (hot) and those after CLB 2457 have .013in clearances.

This engine is designed to enable the cylinder head to be removed without disturbing the valve timing, and to this end the chainwheel for the camshaft drive is located on the shaft by two off-centre pegs and secured by a large bolt. Upon removal of this bolt it is possible to prise the chainwheel from the camshaft and then sit it on a special bracket while the head is removed; the off-centre pegs ensure that the chainwheel only fits back on the shaft in the same position.

Oil is added to the engine by way of the large pivoting cover on the aluminium camshaft cover. The cast aluminium sump houses the oil pump in its base, on the exhaust side, driven by the cross shaft gear. It is possible to gain access to the pump by removing the steel cover at the outside base of the sump. Oil pressure should be at least 60psi hot at 2500rpm; if the pressure falls below this point and the bearings are in good condition, the cause is likely to be wear in the pump, which can be reconditioned. The oil pressure relief valve is situated to the rear of the oil filter cover in the vicinity of the external oil main feed pipe which runs from sump to block at the rear of the engine on the exhaust side. Later engines are fitted with a Purolator external full-flow oil filter. From the CLB engine onwards a higher capacity oil pump was used.

The engine number is found stamped on the top flange on the defunct dynamo mounting, which is to the rear of the block on the exhaust side. Prior to the Ace and Aceca models, the dynamo had been mounted at right angles to the block and driven from the cross shaft, but the block casting remained the same until the end of production.

The aluminium cylinder block and other aluminium castings were left bare, while the iron cylinder head was finished in black.

COOLING SYSTEM (AC)

The total capacity of the cooling system is 2¼ gallons and the water is circulated by a belt-driven water pump located on the side of the engine block underneath the front carburettor. The water is drawn into the pump from the bottom of the radiator (manufactured by Marston) and then passes into the block, circulating therein, percolating upwards through the head

The old AC engine is definitely the most aesthetically pleasing of any of the engines fitted to Aces, Acecas and Cobras. The coil fitted to this car is a more modern replacement and the camshaft cover is probably shinier than it was when new. If heat resistant paints like Sperex had been in general use in 1954 AC would probably have used them, as the owner of this car has on his exhaust.

The fan assembly (right) is completely separate from the water pump. The drive belt is adjustable by pivotting the whole on the through bolt. This spring is wrapped with the correct tape, and one horn is just visible forward of the radiator header tank.

gasket, around the cylinder head, out from the front into the thermostat housing, and back into the radiator header tank. Running into the thermostat housing from the pump is a by-pass hose into which is inserted a thermo switch (manufactured by Otter Controls of Buxton) for the auxiliary starting carburettor.

The idler carying the five-blade cast aluminium fan is bolted to the front spring mounting. Because it is driven by a separate pulley from water pump and dynamo, it is possible to disconnect it or remove it entirely in suitable conditions. The water pump was not painted.

Exhaust System (AC)

The exhaust manifolds are a pair of fabricated units, each having three mild steel pipes converging into a single outlet. This pair of pipes, with flexible inserts, run into a silencer with twin inlets and outlets and finally exit at the rear on the right.

Carburettors & Fuel System (AC)

The triple SU 1¼in type H2 carburettors are mounted on cast aluminium manifolds, the centre one having a thermostatically controlled starting carburettor. This is an automatic device activated by the ignition and set to cut out once the water temperature reaches 35°. In old age, however, these units seem sometimes to develop a mind of their own, so it is not uncommon to find a manual switch fitted into the circuit.

Petrol is fed to the carburettors by an SU electric fuel pump located in the boot and drawing from a 12 gallon steel tank under the boot floor. The tank is supported by a pair of tapered steel-channel outriggers; these and the tank were finished in black.

Transmission (AC)

A single-plate Borg & Beck 9 A6.G clutch, type BB9/186 A, was fitted as original equipment to the Ace and was operated hydraulically. A Moss gearbox was fitted to the large majority of cars; the main casing is of cast iron, the bell housing and tail piece of

The correct Vokes air filters obscure the Solex carburettors of this Bristol engined Aceca. The shallow V-shaped steering idler bracket is visible forward of the spring. The heater unit is the earlier 'round' type. The chassis should strictly not be finished in light grey, but this serves to highlight it in this picture. An oil filter conversion made by Bristol engine specialists TT Workshops has been fitted.

The later or 'square' Smiths heater unit is fitted to this Aceca. The washer bottle is of a later type. The more rounded edges of the glassfibre footwells are just visible as a contrast to the aluminium ones in the illustration opposite.

aluminium. If a car is fitted with a Moss gearbox it is recognisable by the long cranked gearlever. Standard ratios were as follows: first, 3.390:1, second, 1.98:1; third, 1.368:1, top, 1:1.

A rare option was the Moss SH gearbox, which had a slightly more rearward gearlever, but the same ratios. It could also be ordered with closer ratios, as follows: first, 2.981:1; second, 1.751:1; third, 1.209:1; top, 1:1.

Later, AC produced a lightweight gearbox which consisted of Triumph TR3 gears in a special aluminium housing, with a remote gearchange and a straight 6in gearlever. This gearbox first appeared on Ace chassis number AEX 1136, and the ratios were as follows: first, 3.38:1; second, 2:1; third, 1.325:1; top, 1:1. This gearbox uses a TR clutch centre plate because of its larger splines.

All types of gearbox could be fitted with a Laycock de Normanville overdrive, and this was offered by the factory as an option from 1956, the overdrive operating on second, third and top gears. Gearbox oil capacity is three pints. The short propshaft is fitted at each end with Hardy Spicer type K5 L4 universal joints.

The gearbox casing was finished in black, while the bell housing, tail piece and top were not painted.

Engine (Bristol)

In 1956 a version of the Bristol engine, which was a BMW design acquired at the end of the war, began to be fitted into the Ace and Aceca. Although the design dated back some 20 years and did not have an overhead camshaft, it was extremely sophisticated, constructed of the very highest grade materials and assembled meticulously. Furthermore, in its most developed form this engine had proved itself in international competition when fitted to racing cars such as the Cooper Bristol.

The six cylinders each had a bore and stroke of 66mm by 96mm to give a capacity of 1971cc. The cylinder block was cast in chrome iron, the dry liners were of nickel alloy steel, and the nitrided crankshaft was carried in four main bearings. The

The Ace Bristol had different engine mountings welded to the chassis tubes. Rubber sheet is attached by pop rivetted aluminium strips to the arch in the inner wing through which the spring passes. Short tunnels for the cross pushrods are visible at the base of the carburettors. Interestingly, Ace Bristol exhaust manifolds use the same method of construction as Bugatti did many years earlier.

The owner forgot to replace the greasegun in its Terry clips! A steel strap running from the steering box to the front spring clamp has been added to this left hand drive car.

connecting rods were of forged steel, and both big end and main bearings were of the thin wall lead bronze type; the crankshaft can be reground to minus .020in only on the big end journals but will reduce to .040in on the mains. Small end bushes were phospor bronze and the floating gudgeon pins were retained by circlips.

The pistons had four rings – three compression and one oil control. A duplex chain drove the camshaft, which had four pressure-fed bearings. The cylinder head was of aluminium alloy with austenitic alloy steel inserts for the valve seats and bronze inserts for the sparking plugs, the hemispherical combustion chambers being polished. The valves were inclined at an 80° angle and actuated by vertical pushrods to the inlet side and crosshead ones to the exhaust side, all pushrods being of duralumin. Tappet clearance is set with the engine cold at nil, or, for practicality .002in, but opens out to a working clearance of .012in due to the different expansion rates of aluminium head and iron block. In order to be able to fit between the valves, sparking plugs of 10mm are used, the original type being KLG long-reach.

Lubrication is by a Hobourn Eaton type oil pump driven by a helical gear in the centre of the camshaft and circulated via an external full-flow filter on the left-hand side of the engine block, this having provision for plumbing in an oil cooler. Oil pressure should be 60psi at 3000rpm or more, but it does tend to fall quite rapidly below this speed. It is worth noting that high revolutions should not be employed until the oil is fully warmed, which takes some time with the well-cooled 12 pint sump. To reduce pressure build-up within the crankcase, there is a large breather pipe leading up from the sump, over the oil filter and returning downwards behind it to exit at the base of the engine.

The dynamo is also mounted on the left-hand side of the engine and is belt-driven from a pulley on the front of the crankshaft, which incorporates a torsional vibration damper. In addition, on the same side of the engine are found the drive for the rev counter at the base of the distributor (the whole being driven off the camshaft), the oil pressure gauge feed and the small pipe feeding oil to the rockers. The starter motor is on the right hand side of the block.

The majority of engines supplied to AC were the 100D2 (9:1cr) version which developed 128bhp at 5750rpm; the C type (8.5:1cr), giving 125bhp at 5500rpm was fitted to some early Ace Bristols; and the less powerful B type (8.5:1cr), which produced 105bhp at 4750rpm, was also available. The 100B and 100C had a Girling crankshaft damper, the 100D2 a Holset damper. The B type had less radical valve timing.

The rocker cover and valve chest cover were stove-enamelled black; various items such as dynamo, starter, breather and oil filter bowl were also finished in the same colour. The engine block was grey with a slightly green tinge. The engine number is stamped on the top of the flange for the bell housing on the exhaust side.

COOLING SYSTEM (BRISTOL)

A water pump with a cast aluminium two-blade fan is driven by the dynamo drive belt and the flow controlled by thermostat, this opening at around 75°C. The radiator is the same as that fitted to cars with AC engines, the rubber hoses connecting it to the engine being of 1⅜in diameter.

EXHAUST SYSTEM (BRISTOL)

A pair of fabricated exhaust manifolds emanate horizontally from the engine, each one merging into a single pipe (with triangular reinforcing web) before curving downwards and rearwards. As with AC-engined cars, there is a double inlet and outlet silencer with twin tail pipes.

CARBURETTORS & FUEL SYSTEM (BRISTOL)

Three multiple jet downdraught Solex carburettors, type 32.PB.16, were fitted, complete with air cleaners. Petrol was supplied by an AC mechanical fuel pump driven off the camshaft (the AC component factory had no connection with the car manufacturer). The petrol tank was the same as on other Aces and Acecas.

TRANSMISSION (BRISTOL)

Borg & Beck supplied the type BB 8/81 clutch; its 8in diameter plate was 1in smaller than that used with the AC engine. It was again hydraulically operated by a master cylinder with integral reservoir.

The gearbox was also of Bristol manufacture and had closer ratios than the Moss 'box: first was 2.92:1; second, 1.8:1; third, 1.292:1; top, 1:1. The casing, bell housing and tail piece were all cast in aluminium. AC cars were always fitted with type BW gearboxes, normally models CR9 and CR12. The Bristol freewheel gearbox was also occasionally fitted – quite why I cannot imagine.

Laycock de Normanville overdrive was a popular option, and although the factory literature did not recommend its use with the D series motor it proved the be popular and desirable, and was used with the CR9 gearbox. The propellor shaft was the same as the AC-engined cars.

ENGINE (FORD)

The MkII Ford Zephyr 206E engine was fitted to the 2.6 Ace; the instigator of this model, Ken Rudd, offered various stages of tune. This engine was one of Ford's first over-square designs, the bore and stroke of 82.55mm by 79.5mm giving a capacity of 2553cc in six-cylinder form (the same dimensions were used for the four-cylinder Consul engine).

Four main bearings supported the cast iron crankshaft, which had hollow flying webs and crankpins, the latter to reduce the weight of counterbalance; the main bearing journals were 2.375in and the big ends 2.12in. These were hefty dimensions for the period, but the Achilles heel of this engine is its weak main bearing caps, which can fail when the engine is very highly tuned. The later version of this engine, the 213E, fitted to the MkIII Zephyr/Zodiac range, had detail improvements, so any owner wishing to buy a spare engine for his Ace might do better to choose one of these, as visually it is almost identical to the 206E

Ignition and choke control knobs are to the left of the PLC switch on left hand drive cars. The Bristol gearlever was similar to the Moss one but shorter and slightly less sharply cranked.

unit. All main and big end bearings are Vandervell shell type, the connecting rods are just over 5in long and the gudgeon pins are floating type, retained by circlips. The pistons have two compression rings and one oil control ring.

The cylinder head and block were of cast iron. The slightly inclined valves were operated by shaft-mounted rockers and pushrods, and the camshaft was driven by a chain with a spring tensioner. This camshaft, on the right-hand side of the engine, drove the distributor and oil pump via skew gears, while the AC-Delco petrol pump was driven by a lobe on the camshaft. On this same side of the engine was a replaceable oil filter contained in a housing just behind the timing case.

The valve chest cover was a steel pressing, with a breather pipe pointing vertically downwards by means of an elbow. The rocker cover was also a pressing and the filler cap was an AC-Delco item incorporating a breather; these components were finished in black. The engine block was painted dark turquoise, while the rest of the engine (including the pressed steel sump) was finished in black, except for any aluminium castings.

Few, if any, Ford-engined Aces or Acecas were delivered with the engine in standard form as these models were offered from the start with various states of tune, as follows.

Stage 1
Modified Ford cylinder head, opened out and polished porting, larger inlet and exhaust valves. Triple inlet manifold with three H6 1¾in SU carburettors giving 120bhp at 5000rpm.

Stage 2
As stage 1, but with lightweight pistons and pushrods, which gave an extra 5bhp (125bhp at 5500rpm).

Stage 3
Special six-port aluminium cylinder head (made by Rubery Owen at Bourne, Lincolnshire) known as a Raymond Mays head. Special lightweight pistons and lightweight pushrods, these pistons being some 4oz lighter than standard. All this, with triple SU H6 1¾in carburettors, combined to produce 155bhp at 5500rpm.

Stage 4
As Stage 3, but with three Weber DCOE2 carburettors which pushed power up to 170bhp.

The radiator was of a different type for the 2.6 Ace, now made by Gallay instead of Marston as on previous models. Multiple carbs and aluminum head do something to disguise the motor's humble parentage but the rocker cover gives the game away. The radiator top hose is of the correct pattern, also used on Bristol-engined cars.

The 2.6 was the only Ace with a battery mounted high up under the bonnet (it has been removed here for visibility). The original aluminium heater pipes have survived, some of the pipework for the carburettors being of the same material.

Either individual pancake air filters or these bellmouths could be fitted to the SUs on the 2.6. The electric choke is on the centre carburettor, all of which retain their brass dashpot caps.

The ultimate state of tune for the RS 2.6 was the triple Weber set-up on this car. The Ruddspeed aluminium rocker cover was an attractive but now unobtainable option. AC changed to cable throttle operation for these Ford engined cars.

A further option in Ken Rudd's pamphlets – but not in factory literature – came between Stages 2 and 3; if considered official, it would upgrade the latter two states of tune to Stages 4 and 5. This consisted of the Raymond Mays head, but with twin SU H6 1¾in carburettors and only the lightweight pushrods. Rudd advertised this engine as giving 140bhp at 5000rpm.

There are, in fact, several types of Raymond Mays cylinder heads for six-cylinder Ford engines. The correct one for ACs is the Mk3, which is immediately identifiable by the rocker cover being secured by set screws around its circumference as on the standard head; the earlier heads have three central studs to hold the rocker cover down. The water pump bypass hole is cast directly into this head rather than having an adaptor plate under the thermostat housing, as on the Mk2 head. The rocker cover fitted to these converted engines could either be a normal chromium-plated Ford item or a cast aluminium finned one with the Ruddspeed logo, a filler cap with ball-ended T-bar and provision for a breather. Oil capacity for this engine is 8½ pints.

COOLING SYSTEM (FORD)

The normal Ford water pump was retained, and even if an aluminium head is fitted the water circulation is the same: from the bottom of the radiator into the water pump,

The overdrive switch on this 2.6 is the same as on any AC fitted with overdrive. Below it are the switch and warning light for the auxiliary electric petrol pump, and the cigar lighter, which would not have been fitted as standard. The rattle inhibitor for the door is also evident, its rubber grommet now somewhat perished.

from there through the engine's waterways, then out to the top of the radiator via an aluminium manifold bolted over the thermostat in its housing at the front of the head (the bypass hose below this carrying the flow until the thermostat opens). Radiators for the 2.6 were of different design to the earlier cars and manufactured by Gallay.

There is no fan on the water pump pulley, but a thermostatically controlled electric fan is located in front of the radiator, this being mounted on a tubular cross member that is welded by way of brackets to the front body hoop that carries the bonnet hinges and radiator mountings. The thermostat itself is set in the bottom radiator tank.

EXHAUST SYSTEM (FORD)

Since the Ford engine's exhaust porting is on the opposite side to other engines fitted to Aces, the tail pipes are always on the left-hand side.

It is doubtful whether a normal Ford Zephyr manifold would have been fitted to an Ace. Two types of manifold have been encountered by the author. The first type comprises two cast iron manifolds, each covering three ports. A 'Y' steel pipe is bolted to these by means of triangular flanges, and leads downwards and rearwards to the oval silencer, out of which come the twin tail pipes. The second system, offered normally with the higher states of tune, comprised a pair of triple tubular manifolds convoluting under the bracing tube that runs from the scuttle hoop to the front suspension box on that side (owing to the greater height of the AC and Bristol engines, manifolds were able to pass over the top of the matching tube on the other side). These pipes lead into the same oval silencer with twin tail pipes.

CARBURETTORS & FUEL SYSTEM (FORD)

The standard carburettor for the MkII Zephyr engine was a downdraught Zenith 36 WIA, but normally the 2.6 Ace or Aceca was fitted with SU or Weber carburettors of the types specified earlier.

Petrol supply was by a variety of methods from car to car. some cars employed an AC/Delco pump fitted to the engine with an SU electric pump in the boot; the SU pump had a switch and warning light on the dashboard and was used for priming the carburettors before starting. Other cars had twin or single SU pumps in the boot with the mounting for the mechanical pump blanked off with a plate.

The petrol tank was of the same size, construction and finish as the earlier cars.

TRANSMISSION (FORD)

The clutch was the same diameter as that of the AC-engined Ace and a Moss gearbox was used. This was the gearbox that Jaguar used for the early 3.8-litre E-type, so in the Ace it is quite understressed and should give no trouble – but, in common with the the E-type, the change from first to second is accomplished either slowly or noisily.

Most 2.6 cars had Laycock de Normanville overdrive operating on third and top gears by means of an electric switch on the dashboard. The propshaft was the same as on other Aces and Acecas.

The iron gearbox casing and propshaft were finished in black, while the aluminium bell housing and overdrive were left in natural aluminium.

ELECTRICAL EQUIPMENT

Much of the electrical equipment used on these cars was common to all models in spite of the different engines and bodywork.

The dynamo on AC and Bristol engined cars was a Lucas C39 PV2. The Ace and Aceca 2.6 used a Lucas C40-1 with a drive at the rear for the revolution counter; the small reduction gearbox which comes between this and the drive cable is the same as on early Austin-Healey Sprites. The starter motor was a Lucas M45 on the AC engine and an M35G on the other two; the solenoid for these was a Lucas ST950.

Ignition coils were always by Lucas, as were the distributors – D6A on the AC engine, DXH6A on the Bristol and DM6A

All UK market Aces and Acecas were originally fitted with these Lucas P700 headlamps. Owners seeking to replace them might have opted for the Lucas Le Mans type, which had no tripod but had a 'Le Mans' logo moulded in the glass. The sidelights also served as flashing indicators.

This French registered Ace Bristol retains its Lucas 700 'Continental' headlamp units but the sidelights have been changed for an incorrect type at some time.

All cars with Lucas 542 rear lights had this DB10 relay switch mounted on the left hand inner wing. As with all Lucas equipment it is date stamped – this one 6.62.

The very earliest Aces had round rear lights, with subsidiary reflectors on the boot lid.

This style of rear light was used on all but the earliest Aces and some coil-sprung Cobras. The tubular mounting and grommets for the overrider are just visible. The two chrome coachbolts would not normally be present.

on the Zephyr. Original equipment sparking plugs were 14mm Lodge HN for the AC engine and 10mm KLG L.80 for the Bristol; specified plugs for the 2.6 Ace depended on state of tune.

The control box on AC and Bristol engined cars was a Lucas 37182 and on the 2.6 a Lucas RB106/Z; fuse boxes were Lucas type SF4.

Audible warning of approach was provided on most Aces and Acecas by a pair of Lucas WT614 horns. On some later cars, including the 2.6s, these were superseded by WT101 horns or even occasionally a pair of Bosch items. The Lucas windscreen wiper motor was a two-speed DR model.

AC and Bristol engined Aces equipped with heaters had Smiths units, while the 2.6 had Gallay equipment. The Aceca had two types of Smiths heater: the first type, F275, was superseded by F276 for the last 20 or so cars. The in-line thermoswitch on AC engined cars was manufactured by Otter Controls of Buxton. The original battery was a Lucas GTW 7A.

LAMPS

All lamps on Aces and Acecas were proprietary Lucas items used on other makes at various times.

Early AC-engined Aces used Lucas 589 sidelights, but all subsequent Aces used the larger Lucas 539 unit which doubled as the front flashing indicator. Headlights were Lucas P700s, and as these are now being re-manufactured corroded reflectors are not a problem. P700s look so much better than modern types, and are amazingly efficient when fitted with quartz halogen bulbs.

At the rear, early Aces had a small round light, Lucas 588, but quite soon the Lucas L542 rectangular rear light, which was to remain in use almost until the last of the Cobras (and was also used on mid-1950s Hillman Minxes), was adopted. Acecas, with their vestigial rear wings, used Lucas 549 lights, the lenses of which were common to many makes, from Triumph to Jaguar. On Aces and Acecas the red rear lamps did duty as stop, tail and trafficator lights by means of a Lucas DB10 relay. The number plate lamp used on all Aces (and Cobras) was a Lucas 467.

BODYWORK & BODY TRIM (ACE)

Underneath its sleek aluminium skin, the AC Ace has a multiplicity of tubes – most are ¾in steel tube – formed in a skeleton to support the body, to attach it to the chassis and at the same time give the whole car added rigidity and strength. The framework for the doors, bonnet and boot is also constructed in this way. Boot hinges were made up from the same tubing, but door and bonnet hinges were fabricated from various gauges of steel plate. The door hinge assembly (finished in body colour) also served to strengthen the general structure by joining the main scuttle hoop and door aperture tube. The entire framework was welded to the main chassis.

Inner wings were made of body gauge aluminium sheet, folded and cut to shape and attached with pop rivets. An arch was formed around the front suspension and had sections of black rubber sheet fastened around it by aluminium strips, again pop rivetted. The edges of the inner wings, where they came into contact with the main bodywork, were sealed with lengths of slotted, rectangular-section, sponge rubber. The bulkhead and footwells were of pop rivetted aluminium sheet, but on the Ace 2.6 this area was made of black pigmented fibreglass, in the same way as on the Aceca.

Body sections were formed on a wheeling machine from 18 gauge aluminium sheet, and were then welded together into large pieces, with constant checking and further shaping on wooden bucks, before being offered up to the framework. When a satisfactory shape and fit was achieved, the remaining seams were welded up and the surplus aluminium was formed around the tubes at the periphery of the body and pop rivetted into place; the wheel arches were given wired edges.

The tubular frames forming the doors, bonnet and boot had aluminium flanges

· ORIGINAL AC ACE AND COBRA ·

Part way through production of the 2.6 Ace the overrider specially manufactured for AC by Pyrene was introduced. All rear lights remained unaltered. Tubework and aluminium panels in the boot were sprayed silver. The boot lid is supported by a Wilmot Breeden sliding stay. The jack was by Shelley. The door hinges are correctly painted body colour.

All Aces had this type of bonnet hinge, some cars having the chassis number stamped thereon. The exact original type of rubber seal shown here is no longer available but a satisfactory substitute can be obtained. If your car has this type, re-use it if at all possible. It was called Stikastrip and was made by the now extinct firm of Clayton Wright. The method of rivetting the flange to the tubework to carry the returned edge of the bonnet can also be seen.

This type of door was used for all Aces and Cobras, the sides being a returned edge over a flange attached to the tubular framework and the top being curled over and pop rivetted. The door lock is screwed to a steel plate bracket welded to the tubework. Door hinges should be body colour.

36

ACE AND ACECA

The T handle (left) for opening the bonnet normally lived in the glove compartment along with the handbook.

attached to them with pop rivets. The aluminium skins were attached to these components by means of a returned edge. Black rectangular self-adhesive rubber sealing strip with a section of ½in by ¼in was used around the lips thus produced to give a snug fit and prevent chattering. This was stuck onto the doors themselves, but for the bonnet and boot it was attached to the body.

The front-hinged bonnet is held shut by budget locks with Wilmot Breeden chrome escutcheons; there was no particular place for the key, but it always seems to live in the glove compartment. The boot is secured with a lockable Wilmot Breeden chromium T-handle, number WB 7575, and is held open by a sliding, self-ratchet stay from the same manufacturer. Instead of this handle, very early AC-engined Aces had a budget lock to secure the boot lid identical to those used on the bonnet. All floor and interior panels are of aluminium sheet pop rivetted in place. The boot floor and aluminium bulkhead were made in the same way. All exposed panels and tube work in the boot were sprayed silver.

After a while the boot lid of the Ace was made shorter, so that it did not extend so far forwards into the rear deck. This was to allow the rear edge of the hood to be fastened further back. One of the reasons for this change was to try to stop rainwater running off the body under the edge of the hood.

The doors have no external handles and are secured with the locks mentioned in the trim section; each door also has a rubber-mounted rattle inhibitor.

The radiator grille is built up using anodised aluminium sections built into an ellipse of the same material. It is a push fit into the mouth of the bodywork and secured with screws. The AC and Bristol engined Aces have five horizontal bars and eight vertical ones, while the 2.6 Ace has four horizontal bars and 16 vertical ones. The provision for a starting handle was deleted for the Ford engined Ace.

Overriders of two types were fitted at front and rear. The first type differed only slightly from the second type which was fitted to some Standards and Austins. Both types were, in all probability, manufactured by Horvell. The later overriders would accept the twin tube bumpers if fitted, in which case they were attached by small bumper brackets made of strip steel, painted black and fastened by a pair of bolts at each side.

Only the first few Aces had a budget lock (top) for the boot lid.

A raised mounting for the Lucas 467 number plate lamp (above) was a feature of all Aces. This boot locking handle, by Wilmot Breeden, is correct for all cars.

All Aces prior to the 2.6 and all Acecas had this grille with five horizontal and eight vertical bars. This car has 'Le Mans' headlamps.

The 2.6 Ace had a much smaller air intake with four horizontal and sixteen vertical bars. The Italian-influenced body sculpturing running down each side under the headlamps was now gone.

ACE AND ACECA

On Ace and Ace Bristol the petrol filler cap was on the left hand wing. In order to let other motorists know what had just overtaken them Mr Charbonet the French importer had special plates made to hold the registration number at the rear.

The rear number plate of the Aceca (below) was carried in an illuminated box. If fitted, as they almost invariably were, with twin tube bumpers, this type of bracket would be employed. Rear lamps were Lucas 549, but the petrol filler and boot handle were the same as on the Ace.

For some reason, AC must have raided the parts bins at the Ford Motor Company or Rover in the early 1960s and come away with a job lot of overriders supplied to these manufacturers by Wilmot Breeden. AC proceeded to fit these to Greyhounds and then, turning them upside down, to the front of early 2.6 Aces. Later, some way through the production of the 2.6, AC had Pyrene specially make a pattern of overriders and this became the definitive AC overrider until the last of the Cobras. The mounting for these differed in that a pair of long bolts passed through the front cowl on either side encased by aluminium tubes of ¾in outside diameter, the holes in the bodywork being fitted with rubber grommets. These overriders were also fitted at the rear by the same method. To be frank, none of the above are very protective as Aces are easily dented front or rear; owners of all except the earliest Aces and 2.6 Aces can fit the twin tube bumpers that the factory offered as an extra.

For the American market there was an alternative design of chromium bumper. It resembled the normal type but the tubes were more widely spaced and had the ends turned together and welded up.

Windscreens on all the Aces were fully detachable and made by Elliott of Hendon. The chromed side rails fit into slots in the scuttle and are held in place by two bolts on each side up underneath the dashboard, the slots being sealed by rubber covered by a small rectangular aluminium plate secured by two screws. At first all windscreens were flat, but towards the end of the 1950s curved 'screens became optional. Since many owners realised that a curved 'screen cut down buffeting for both driver and passenger, some cars were retrospectively

The flat windscreen was more upright than the curved 'screen. All 'screens had the same chromium hooks to secure the overcentre catches of the hood. The small plate at the base of the frame should be secured by a pair of screws.

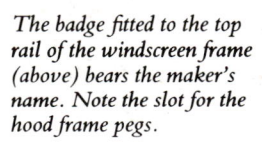

The badge fitted to the top rail of the windscreen frame (above) bears the maker's name. Note the slot for the hood frame pegs.

Better air penetration and less buffeting resulted from the new windscreen design. The aluminium plate is missing at the base of the frame, so water will enter here.

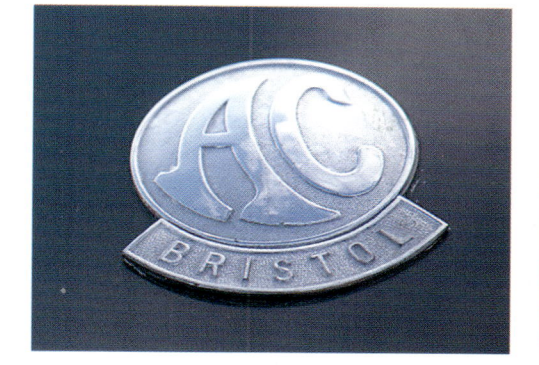

· ACE AND ACECA ·

Aces and Acecas fitted with the Bristol engine wore this badge.

For AC and Ford engined Aces and Acecas the same badge as had first been seen on the radiators of 1930s cars was still employed.

A chromium plated 'Monza' petrol filler cap was fitted to early Aces.

A beautifully preserved original interior such as this is a real rarity.

fitted with this type. The flat 'screen was available even into 2.6 production and at least one of these cars was fitted with one, although, in typical AC fashion, the usual curved 'screen was actually still listed as an optional extra.

As a matter of interest, wiper spindles and washer jets (if fitted) were mounted further to the rear on a car with a flat 'screen. It should be possible, therefore, by carefully examining the underside of the bodywork in this area to ascertain whether a car has been fitted with a curved screen at a later date.

Demisting vents, when they were fitted, were formed of aluminium sheet suitably shaped and screwed in place with a pair of chromed dome-headed screws, on top of slots in the bodywork.

On both AC and Ford engined Aces, there was a simple circular AC badge on both the nose and bootlid, but on the other model the word 'Bristol' appeared on a semi-circular extension to the lower part of the badge.

INTERIOR TRIM & WEATHER EQUIPMENT (ACE)

All three Ace models have similar interior trim. Although an Ace is built on the principles of a sports racing car, it is surprisingly snug and comfortable once you are seated, unless you are taller than average, in which case a lack of legroom is your lot, although this problem was remedied to some extent with larger footwells in later Aces.

The seats are of bucket type and peculiar to ACs, being of tubular construction with

There is no room for luggage behind the seats of the Ace, though this owner has managed to squeeze his tonneau cover in. The carpeted housing for the handbrake nestles between the seats.

The rear bulkhead on all Aces should be covered with this combination of leather and carpet on board.

The door pocket is held at the rear by the lock, and the lock strap is attached in the way shown here.

· ACE AND ACECA ·

This Ace Bristol has been retrimmed to the correct specification. The carpet wrapped round the scuttle hoop is a separate piece.

sheet aluminium panelling. Apart from the seat backs, which are covered with carpet, the entire seat is upholstered in leather over Dunlopillo; there are 14 pleats in the squab and eight in the cushion. There is provision for a certain amount of fore and aft adjustment by way of conventional notched seat runners, but movement rearwards is limited by the top of the seat coming into contact with the bodywork.

Behind the seats, the bulkhead is trimmed with a combination of carpet and leather, and at either side of this a small portion of the wheel arch intrudes into the cockpit and is also trimmed in leather. The insides of the door skins are covered with carpet, and a capacious door pocket is formed by leather being stretched between the tubes forming the door frame and attached by chrome self-tap screws and cup washers.

The door catches and strikers – of a type used on many pre-war and early post-war British sports cars, such as the MG T Series – were made by Wilmot Breeden and are no longer available, but replicas can be obtained from the AC factory and some other specialist suppliers. A leather strap, ½in wide, double stitched and made in the same leather as the upholsery, loops over the door catch knob and runs to the bracket supporting the central sidescreen socket. This strap should be used only for opening a door, not to pull on and slam as it will soon break. A leather door check strap is secured by two chromium self-tapping screws and cup washers at either end.

The inner sills are carpeted, as are the

The bracing tubes are covered in black leather.

43

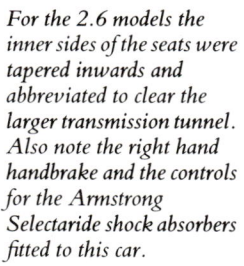

For the 2.6 models the inner sides of the seats were tapered inwards and abbreviated to clear the larger transmission tunnel. Also note the right hand handbrake and the controls for the Armstrong Selectaride shock absorbers fitted to this car.

footwells and transmission tunnel. A separate piece of carpet is used to wrap around the tubular scuttle hoop just in front of the door on either side. The carpets are bound with leather. The two bracing tubes that are visible protruding downwards from behind the dashboard at either side of the transmission tunnel are covered in leather. The transmission tunnel is rounded in section on the early models but rectangular on the 2.6.

Whereas most earlier Aces had a large central handbrake, the 2.6 Ace has a handbrake with leather gaiter on the right-hand side of the driver's seat. (Also peculiar to this model is the removable inspection cover, secured by chrome screws and covered in leather, midway along the transmission tunnel on the left-hand side.) Customers could specify a right-hand handbrake on earlier models and some were so fitted, although very rarely.

As far as the weather equipment is concerned, there are the following variations. Early cars have sidescreens with an almost semi-circular rear profile and the perspex section therein pivots upwards and forwards to open. The later sidescreens have sliding panels and are more angular. The frames of all types are made of fabricated steel covered in vinyl to match the hood, the sliding type having the runners shaped with plywood strip under this vinyl. Both types of sidescreen have a three-point socket fitting in the doors. There was a vinyl satchel to contain sidescreens when stowed in the boot.

The hood frame is extremely simple and consists of a single hoop with a subsidiary hoop hinged on it. When not in use, this frame pulls apart in the centre and is kept with hood and sidescreens in the boot. The

Both curved and flat 'screen Aces had these sidescreens (top and above) which pivotted up to open. The budget lock cover on the bonnet is in the open position ready to accept the T handle.

ACE AND ACECA

All short boot Aces had this hood profile but this car has the later sliding sidescreens.

Sidescreens were kept in this special envelope made of the same material as the hood. It has board stiffeners each end and the straps looped around tubes in the boot on either side to retain it on the shelf. On all Aces you would see the tubular hinges that project into the boot when closed. They have been removed from this car, which at the owner's request was fitted with external boot hinges when new.

The sidescreen envelope in its stowed position, and the spare wheel retained by the correct aluminium nut. The auxiliary electric petrol pump is just visible. The wiring loom is clipped to the diagonal tube.

earlier or 'long boot' Aces had a more vertical line to the rear of the hood if viewed in silhouette.

In order to erect the hood the following procedure is best adopted. Assemble the hood frame, keeping the two hoops together, and slot the ends of it into the chrome sockets attached to the bodywork just behind the doors. Unfold the hood material and drape it over the frame, placing the two-piece steel channel that is attached to the front of the hood over the top of the windscreen. At the same time, the two small, shouldered, pegs need to be introduced into the slot that runs along the top of the windscreen frame. Now place the loops of the chrome over-centre catches on the ends of this rail, over the hooks on the sides of the windscreen frame and tension this assembly with the levers – take care during this exercise as the hood fabric is easily torn between the two rails. Press down the 'lift the dot' fasteners, except the last three on either side, onto the studs in the rear deck, then from inside the car push the hinged hoop rearwards to tension the hood; two straps with poppers hold this hoop in place. Finally push down the remaining three fasteners on each side.

The hood material was the same as normally used on sports cars of this period, was either black or colour to tone with trim or paint. Unfortunately, this material cannot be precisely matched today. The rear window was in 'Vybak' or equivalent, and the section that fits around the sidescreens was finished with 'Furflex'.

A full-length tonneau cover was usually supplied, but is not listed as an option.

45

DASHBOARD & INSTRUMENTS
ACE

Aluminium sheet was used to fabricate the dashboard on the Ace and was covered in trim-coloured leather on early models without a cubbyhole lid and later cars with cubbyhole lids, including the 2.6. Some 2.6s had a black leather dash whatever the colour of the trim. The cubbyhole lid has a press-button catch with an integral lock; the inside of the compartment is carpeted and there is a double-stitched ½in wide leather check strap.

At the point where the steering column protrudes from the dashboard, the hole is elongated vertically to allow for adjustment of steering wheel height. Some cars have a small panel at this point, trimmed to match its surroundings and attached by two screws; this panel has to be removed if either column or dashboard has to be dismantled. The dashboard itself is attached to the scuttle at either end by one chrome screw and cup washer, and additional ones on the centre portion.

Instrumentation on the Ace was by Smiths and there is a generally standard layout for both AC and Bristol engined models which could be supplemented by the addition of switches for auxiliary functions such as driving lights, overdrive, heater, twin petrol pumps and so on. To either side of the steering column were the 5in speedometer (left) and rev counter (right). The speedometer had an inset electric clock, while the rev counter had a direction indicator telltale light at the bottom of the dial.

Directly above the steering column is the ignition or dynamo light, and in the centre of the dashboard the remainder of the instruments and switches are loosely arranged in a 'T' shape. Starting at the bottom, there is a Lucas PLC switch controlling headlights, sidelights and

A full tonneau cover (top) was normally supplied. As on most other sports cars the Ace's can be used with the passenger side still in place.

This is very likely the original hood (above). The sidescreens have been retrimmed with black vinyl – they would have matched the hood. To open the door on an Ace with the hood and sidescreeens erected one has to partially open the sidescreen to gain access to the interior door handle.

Early Aces did not have glove compartment lids. The leather should simply be turned over the rim, not piped and fixed with visible screws. The early type of check strap attached to the top of the door can just be made out. The dashboard should not be padded and the scuttle hoop should be carpeted.

ignition. Above this is the ammeter, and further up again is the oil pressure gauge. On the right of this is the water temperature gauge, and to the left is the petrol gauge. Below the petrol gauge is the panel switch, then the single speed windscreen wiper switch, and finally the starter button. All knobs and switches were black and all bezels chromium-plated.

By the later 1950s one could expect to find on an AC or Bristol engined car a windscreen washer button to the left of the wiper switch. On Bristol cars only, a manual advance and retard is found to the left of the starter button and a choke control to the right of and slightly below the PLC

The glove compartment lid on this untouched original interior is retained by the correct leather strap. When a heater was fitted, most Aces, except some late Bristols and 2.6s, had Smiths round heaters with small doors at the front.

ORIGINAL AC ACE AND COBRA

The old AC engine could just about cope with its increased rev limit but it was, after nearly forty years, at about the end of its development. The steering wheel centre incorporating indicator switch and horn push is retained by a small grub screw in the side of the steering wheel boss.

The dashboard should not be retained by Phillips screws (above) – otherwise all is correct on this Ace Bristol, including the absence of padding behind the leather covering.

The higher rev limit of the Bristol engine is clearly marked (right) and a KPH speedometer signifies that it was originally supplied to a country using that measurement. The oil temperature gauge was an optional extra.

48

Ace and Aceca

For the Ace 2.6 the clock was removed from the speedo and a separate one fitted on the left of the panel. The long headlamp flasher stalk is a period accessory but would not have been fitted as standard.

switch (this control was not necessary on AC engined cars as they had an electric choke).

In addition to these controls, there is a Lucas foot-operated dip switch to the left of the clutch pedal, and the centre of the steering wheel has a horn push and flashing indicator switch.

On the 2.6 Ace the layout is slightly different, as follows. The direction indicator warning lamp in the rev counter is replaced by two small chrome bezelled green lamps flanking the ignition warning light. A separate clock lives where the advance/retard control and/or windscreen washer button had previously been positioned. The two auxiliary driving lamp switch positions became a headlamp flasher (top) and a rheostat heater switch (bottom). Low down on the dashboard between the 130mph speedometer and steering column is the starter button. Depending on the car's specification, on the right-hand side of the rev counter are the following controls: the overdrive switch on a stalk, and below this an electric petrol pump switch with warning light to its left.

On the 2.6 model, the elliptical hole for the steering column is neatened up by a rectangular plate with chamfered edges, covered with fabric to match the dashboard and fixed with four chrome screws and cup washers.

All the above descriptions refer to right-hand drive cars.

BODY & BODY TRIM (ACECA)

The basic construction of the Aceca followed the same lines as the Ace in its utilisation of tubes. However, for the framework of the doors and tailgate the manufacturer chose to employ more traditional wooden frames. The front bulkhead, footwells and half bulkhead behind the seats were moulded in glass-fibre to give added insulation and sound

· ORIGINAL AC ACE AND COBRA ·

Although the Aceca derived directly from the Ace none of the body panels are interchangeable or even the same shape, the grille and nose being the only external evidence of its ancestry.

From the rear the coupé, like the Ace, presents a neat and uncluttered appearance.

ACE AND ACECA

The large tailgate encloses a spacious luggage compartment. The panels around the perspex rear window are covered in the same leather as the trim. The spare wheel cover has been removed.

The rear of the Aceca bonnet is louvred, and budget locks secure it. The washer jet was by Trico and the wipers on Aces, Acecas and Cobras were by Rainbow, since merged into the Trico group.

To provide ventilation without the need to open the main side windows the rear side windows were hinged.

deadening for the coupé bodywork. Fine-mesh aluminium stoneguards were fitted inside the wings.

For the tailgate, the same chromium locking handle and stay are used as on the Ace boot, but the heavier construction of the doors necessitated – and allowed for – conventional integral door catches with external chromium-plated push button door handles. There are fully retracting winding windows and opening quarter lights. For additional ventilation, the rear side windows can be opened a little, but the chromium catches only give two positions – ajar or closed. All the channel work for these windows is of chromium-plated brass.

Aceca windscreens came in two designs; the early ones have right-angle corners at the base, whereas the later type has all four corners rounded, supposedly to resist leaks better. A moulded perspex window is fitted to the tailgate, and below this is the illuminated rear number plate box fitted with a perspex cover held in place by a rubber sealing strip.

The bonnet is secured by budget locks. Just in front of these on all Aceca models are two sets of quadruple louvres.

Badges are as on the Ace. Although the prototype appeared at the 1954 Motor Show with 'ACECA' script at the rear and on the sides of the wings just in front of the screen pillar, this badging was dropped for production.

This Aceca Bristol was retrimmed by the factory many years ago and has now acquired a pleasing patina. The woodrim steering wheel is of an incorrect type and the wooden gearknob would have been frowned on by the factory. The speaker grille is in one of the correct positions for an Aceca, but the radio is of later manufacture.

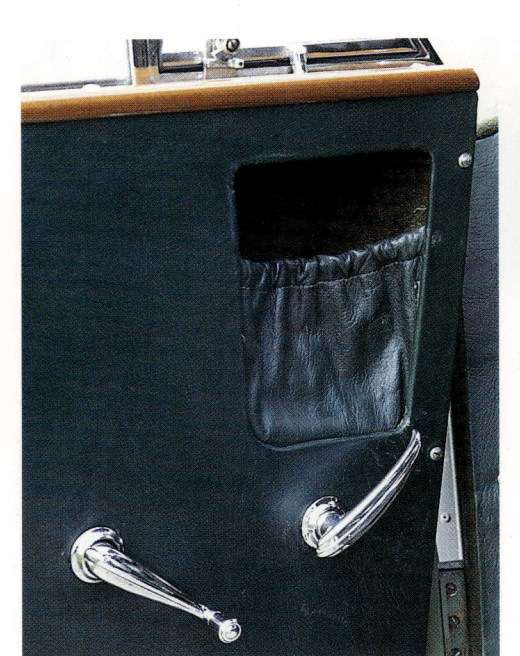

A small, awkward and rather useless pocket was provided in each of the Aceca's doors. The door trim and pocket were all in leather. The door handles are of the correct pattern and were fitted to some other cars of the period.

All Acecas seem to have been fitted with a pair of these emerald green perspex sun visors (right). The aluminium bracket for bracing and adjusting the steering column is evident here.

All Acecas had the same frontal aspect: the eight 2.6 Acecas did not have the smaller grille of their Ace counterpart.

INTERIOR TRIM (ACECA)

As befits its role as a little grand touring coupé, the Aceca is quite luxuriously trimmed throughout.

Until the late 1950s the seats were identical to the Ace's, but then the upholstered side rails enclosing the cushion ran back horizontally instead of curving gently upwards, presumably to improve accessibility. Adjustment is provided fore and aft, as in the Ace, but movement is somewhat restricted by the half bulkhead that separates the front and rear compartments. The front was fully carpeted, including footwells, bulkhead and transmission tunnel. The shape of the transmission tunnel and the leather gearlever gaiter differed depending on the type of gearbox fitted. Carpeting throughout was bound with leather.

Door trims were made of board covered in leather. A small rectangular door pocket provided below the quarterlight was carpeted within and had a gathered, elasticated keep over the opening; a larger pocket, of course, was not possible as it would have interfered with the retraction of the main window. There were walnut door cappings, and door handles and window winders were chromium-plated. A leather check strap, in the same colour as the trim,

The tool tray fits neatly into the wheel rim. This kit (although now in an AC Aceca) started off in an Aceca Bristol, as denoted by the special cranked spanner for rocker adjustment on these engines. The majority of the tools are not the original ones but their layout and sizes are correct.

was positioned at the base of each door.

The dashboard was trimmed in leather, except where burr walnut was used on the instrument panel and glove locker lid; the interior of this lid was lined in the same leather as the rest of the trim. Leather-covered panels adorned the windscreen pillars. Fitted above the doors were other panels with the same leather finish, underneath which the West of England cloth headlining, which was stuck directly to the roof, disappeared. All panels, door cappings and check straps were secured by chrome screws and cup washers. The original equipment sun visors were in a dark emerald semi-transparent perspex and had chromium fittings.

The rear compartment was carpeted both at the rear of the bulkhead and on the floor, including the spare wheel cover; the top of the bulkhead had a roll of leather to finish it. Leather covered all the rear compartment side panels and the interior panels of the tailgate.

The spare wheel cover was constructed of five-ply with a hand-hold cut into its one vertical side. In its centre was a deeply dished metal insert which was perforated to allow the fixing stud to protrude, an aluminium casting with four short ears screwing down onto this. Light brown flock was sprayed onto the interior of this panel; a circle of sorbo rubber was fixed in the centre to retain the tools in the tool tray, which fitted in the rim of the spare wheel. This tool tray was made of a sheet of three-ply with outlines of the tools cut out, and an additional sheet of three-ply to form a backing panel. The whole tray was flock sprayed in the same way as the spare wheel cover. The tools differed according to whether the car had a Bristol or AC engine.

The same cast aluminium nut is used to hold down the spare wheel cover as to retain the spare wheel on Aces and wire-wheel Cobras.

Dashboard & Instruments (Aceca)

Although it contains the same number and type of dials as the Ace, the Aceca dashboard is completely different in its construction and styling, and in addition has some different switches. As well as the familiar horn push and indicator switch in the centre of the steering wheel, directly in

· ORIGINAL AC ACE AND COBRA ·

This dashboard has the rather lighter burr walnut veneers commonly used for the Aceca. The surround to the original radio should also be veneered. The clock is a modern replacement. The tubular tailgate hinges are of the same construction as was later adopted for Cobra bonnet and boot hinges.

When new, Acecas would have been fitted with either the standard black steering wheel or the optional woodrim wheel fitted to the silver Ace Bristol seen on page 48. If neither of these can be obtained, any of the steering wheels fitted to the cars in this book would be a reasonable alternative.

front of the driver is a hooded panel finished in burr walnut veneer. On this panel are the same 5in speedometer with integral clock, and rev counter with indicator telltale, as used on the Ace. The ignition warning light is set between these two, and above it is the oil pressure gauge. On later cars the indicator warning light was replaced by two separate ones; these were positioned below the ignition light, leaving the rev counter containing a main beam lamp.

The remaining areas of the dashboard are covered in leather to match the trim. In the centre is a rectangular panel, retained by two chrome screws and cup washers, which contains (from left) petrol gauge, ammeter and water temperature gauge. There are five switches below these dials, only two of which had consistently the same function throughout the Aceca's life – ignition in the centre and starter button to the right.

Recessed into the main dashboard above this panel is a push-out semi-circular chromium ashtray; any single switches to the right and left of this would be for spot and fog lights. A car fitted with an overdrive had the operating switch to the right of the main dash panel within easy reach of the driver's index finger. Very often the lighting switch is in this vicinity, but on some cars it is to the left of the central panel. Wiper, panel light and other switches can be in such a variety of places that it is impossible to map them out exactly.

On the bulkhead, below and in front of the dashboard, is a subsidiary panel carrying the heater and air controls, their number depending on the complexity of the system fitted. On an Aceca Bristol, the choke and ignition advance/retard controls are sited in this panel. To each side of the bulkhead is a flap to control the flow of air to either the footwell or the windscreen. The dipswitch, Lucas type FS22, is on the rest for the left foot.

If a radio is fitted it should be beneath the glove locker. The downward bulge in the panel to allow for a radio is not one of AC's most sensible ideas, as it made an excellent obstacle for the passenger's knees.

The second type of Aceca seat had less curved sides. This car is fitted with the lightweight gearbox and overdrive, as the short gearlever shows. The gearlever gaiter should be green leather to match the trim, and the gearknob is incorrect. The owner has fitted an aluminium kick strip to the door frame.

The Aceca's speaker box between the seats is covered in the same leather as the seats and trim.

Optional Extras

Following were catalogued extras for the Ace and Aceca:

Second ignition coil.
Second petrol pump with duplicated fuel line from the tank.
Second spare wheel.
Bumpers – front and rear.
Screen washers.
Heater.
Demisters.
Radio.
Shield for petrol tank.
Shield for battery.
Aluminium fuel tank.
Extra fuel tanks.
Racing radiator cowl.
Oil cooler.
Oil temperature gauge.
Rear axle ratios of 3.64:1, 3.9:1 and 4.3:1.

For the Ace only these items were available:
Glass-fibre hardtop.
Racing screen.

From 1957, overdrive and disc brakes became an option on Bristol-engined cars, but overdrive was available earlier on the Moss gearbox of AC-engined variants.

On the Bristol-engined cars with 100D2 motors, compression could be increased to 9.5:1 by modification to the cylinder head.

Wire wheels of 15in were optional from around 1958, and at about the same time the curved windscreen became an option.

On the later AC and Bristol-engined Aces and Acecas, disc brakes and screen washers became standard. With the 2.6 Ace they were no longer listed as options.

Listed extras differing from other cars on the 2.6 Ace were as follows:
Engine tuned to stage 1, 2, 3 or 4.
Polished alloy rocker cover.

While the above were the only catalogued extras, owners could specify other equipment at the time of manufacture, so deviation from what appears to be standard trim is sometimes 'original'.

Colour Schemes

Factory sales brochures listed the following colours:

Body	Leather	Hood and Tonneau	Wheels
Black	Black		
Red	Red	Black	
Maroon	Maroon	Red	Silver
Bright Blue	Beige	Cream	Green
Beige	Grey	Red	Off-White
Grey/Blue	Grey		
Cream	Grey		

Many different combinations were employed by the factory, a number of which are listed below. Body colour comes before the leather colour in each case:

Middle Brunswick Green/Green
White/Black
White/Red
Svecia Red/Beige
Svecia Red/Cream
Gunmetal/Red
Dragonfly Blue/Red
Pacific Green/Red
Black/White
White/Red
Mist Green/Natural
Silver/Blue
Oxford Blue/Red
Heather Metaline/Black
Mist Green/Green
Vermilion/Beige
Mail Red/Black
Steel Blue Metaline/Red
Black Pearl/Red
Rouge Irise/Grey

The above is a representative list as a very large number of colour combinations was used on Aces and Acecas with AC and Bristol engines.

Contrasting piping was also occasionally employed on the seats; an example is chassis AE 22, which was painted ivory, had black leather with ivory piping and an ivory hood.

Carpets would normally match the trim, but not always. For example, Aceca number AEX 570 was painted Rouge Irise with grey leather and red carpet.

Wheels could be supplied in chrome but were normally painted.

As ever, many alternative colour combinations were used by the factory for the Ace RS 2.6. Since the production run was small these are listed in full, body colour coming before leather in each case:

White/Black
Svecia Red/Black
Black Pearl/Beige
White with Blue Stripe/Blue
Silver/Red
Black Pearl/Red
Bright Blue Metallic/Red
Steel Blue/Grey
White/Green
Cherry Red/Black
White/Red
Rouge Irise/Grey
Blue Metallic/Beige
Middle Blue/Black
Mist Green/Beige
Alvis Peony Red/Black
Vineyard Green/Green
Princess Blue/Red
Princess Blue/Blue
Vineyard Green/Black
Middle Blue/Red

The dashboard on the Ace RS 2.6 could be covered to match the interior or in black. Carpets normally would also match the trim. Although usually painted, wheels could be supplied chromed.

As there were only eight Aceca 2.6s made, their colours are listed below in order of chassis numbers.

Angel Blue/Beige
Vineyard Green/Beige
Rouge Irise/Beige
Rouge Irise/Black
Svecia Red/Black
Black Pearl/Grey
Princess Blue/Red
Black Pearl/Red

ACE (AC ENGINE) PRODUCTION AND EXPORT FIGURES

Of the 226 chassis allocated AE or AEX numbers, only 223 left the factory as AC-engined Aces. AE 56 became the prototype Aceca, AE 1172 was dismantled and returned to the stores, and AE 1191 became the Ace 2.6 prototype (RS5000).

The prototype Ace (Vin Davison's Tojeiro) did not have an AE number; the first was AE 01, the Motor Show chassis.

Production started at AE 22 (ex-works on 14 May 1954) and carried on consecutively until AE 108 (ex-works 13 January 1956) at which point Ace Bristols commenced manufacture and the chassis numbers became interspersed. The last AC Ace was AEX 1194, this leaving the works on 14 October 1960 bound for Canada. As with most AC models this was not actually the last car to leave the factory, AE 1190 being ex-works on 5 August 1963.

There were 124 cars built with AEX prefixes and 99 with AE prefixes.

AC Aces were shipped to the following countries:

Country	Number
USA	84
Canada	13
France	13
Venezuela	4
Spain	3
Switzerland	2
West Germany	2
Sweden	2
Bermuda	1
Cyprus	1
Australia	1
Portugal	1
Kuwait	1
Holland	1
US Forces Germany	1
RAF Germany	1

Early (upper) and later (lower) AC-engined Ace chassis plates, almost invariably found on top of the right-hand foot box.

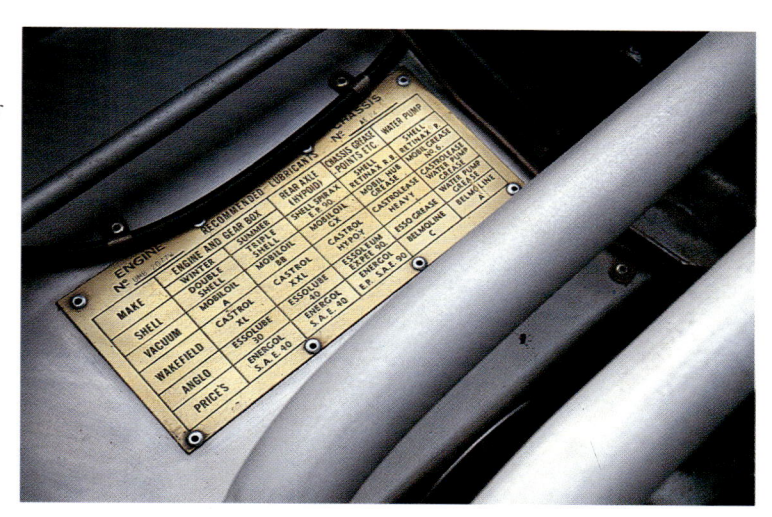

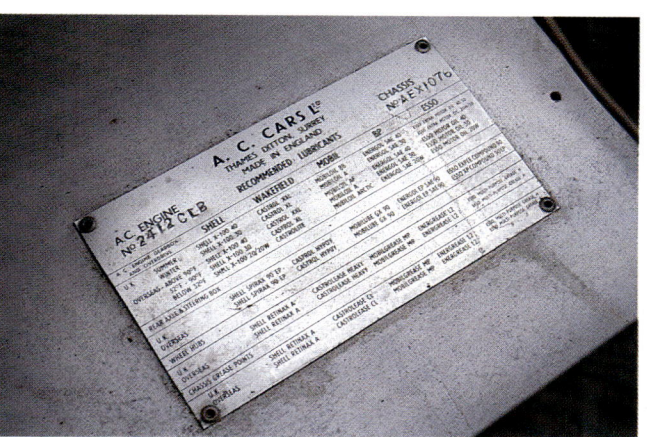

Sales year by year were as follows (these figures do not include chassis AE 01 or the prototype as no ex-works dates are given in the factory ledger):

Year	UK	Export	Country	
1954	18	5	Sweden	2
			USA	3
1955	39	23	Holland	1
			USA	13
			Canada	4
			Kuwait	1
			Portugal	1
			Venezuela	1
			Australia	1
			US Forces Germany	1
1956	6	38	Canada	2
			France	2
			USA	34
1957	7	14	Spain	2
			France	2
			Cyprus	1
			Switzerland	1
			USA	8
1958	7	14	USA	8
			Canada	4
			France	2
1959	4	22	USA	11
			France	3
			Canada	2
			Spain	1
			Venezuela	3
			Switzerland	1
			RAF Germany	1
1960	7	15	USA	7
			France	4
			Bermuda	1
			Germany	2
			Canada	1
1961	—	1	USA	1
1962	1	—		
1963	1	—		

The 1956 UK figure includes one US Forces sale. The 1959 figure includes one car to Jersey and one US Forces sale.

The following right-hand drive cars were exported: AE 25 to Sweden, AE 65 to Australia, AE 73 to Canada, AE 88 to Kuwait, AE 90 to the USA, AE 119 to the USA, AE 187 to the USA, AE 188 to France, AE 205 to the USA (this car was first fitted with an AC engine and then re-engined with Bristol Motor 100 D2 768 for the 1957 Le Mans), AE 206 to Cyprus, AE 1061 to Switzerland, AE 1062 to Jersey, AE 1136 to RAF Germany and AE 1137 to Bermuda.

The following left-hand drive cars were first dispatched to UK destinations: AEX 98 to US Forces UK, AEX 178 (written off during test), AEX 179 (allocated to the same customer as replacement for AEX 178) and AEX 219.

As a matter of interest, and to illustrate one of the quirks of the AC factory, AEX 1193 was despatched to Germany as a demonstrator on 16 December 1960!

The different engines fitted to AC Aces are listed below.

Chassis	Engine
P/Type & AE 01	Original engine numbers not known
AE 22 to AE 37	UMB 2043 to UMB 2089
AE 38	UMC 2094
AE 39 to AE 49	UMB 2096 to UMB 2120
AE 50	UMC 2121
AE 51 to AE 54	UMB 2123 to UMB 2115
AEX 55	UMC 2127
AE 56	UMB 2093
AEX 57 to AEX 58	UMC 2125 to UMC 2126
AEX 59 to AEX 60	CL 2140 to CL 2142
AEX 61	Not known
AE 62	UMC 2126
AE 63	UMB 2115
AE 64 to AE 65	UMC 2128 & UMC 2121
AE 66	CL 2185
AE 67 to AE 71	UMC 2129 to UMC 2137
AE 72 to AEX 146	CL 2143 to CL 2281
AEX 157 to AEX 220	CL 2211 to CL 2329
AEX 221	Not known
AE 412 to AEX 485	CL 2321 to CL 2376
AEX 1010 to AE 1016	CLB 2390 to CLB 2392
AEX 1035 to AEX 1037	CLB 2398 to CLB 2396
AEX 1047 to AEX 1062	CLB 2400 to CLB 2435
AEX 1075 to AEX 1084	CLB 2414 to CLB 2434
AEX 1105 to AE 1113	CLB 2427 to CLB 2439
AE 1136 to AEX 1144	CLB 2436 to CLB 2451
AE 1170 to AEX 1194	CLBN 2471 to CLBN 2476

ACECA (AC ENGINE) PRODUCTION AND EXPORT FIGURES

There were 155 chassis laid down as AC-engined Acecas but only 151 cars were made. Chassis AE 571 became BE 571 and was the first Aceca Bristol. Towards the end of production three chassis were made into Aceca 2.6 models: they were AEX 780 (to RSX 5501), AE 806 (to RS 5500) and AEX 815 (to RSX 5502).

Of the 151 cars, the first one (or prototype) was AEC 56, which was ex-works on 8 October 1954. In 1955, when production commenced, AE 499 was followed by AE 501, and then there was an unbroken run until AEX 570. Then, as Aceca Bristols began to be made as well, the numbers were interspersed, recognisable by their prefixes.

There were 72 cars made with AE prefix, 79 with AEX and 1 with AEC. Three cars with AE prefix were exported: AE 544 to Portugal, AE 538 to Belgium and AE 697 to Rhodesia. Two cars with AEX prefix remained in the UK: AEX 557 and AEX 796.

AC Acecas were shipped to the following countries:

USA	55
Canada	11
Portugal	5
France	4
Holland	1
Venezuela	1
Belgium	1
Switzerland	1
Spain	1
Rhodesia	1
US Forces Europe	1

Sales year by year were as follows:

Year	UK	Export	Country	
1954	1	—		
1955	29	16	USA	7
			Portugal	5
			Holland	1
			Canada	1
			Venezuela	1
			France	1
1956	12	15	USA	9
			Canada	2
			Belgium	1
			Switzerland	1
			France	1
			Spain	1
1957	8	7	USA	6
			Canada	1
1958	4	24	USA	16
			Canada	7
			Rhodesia	1
1959	4	9	USA	9
1960	8	8	USA	5
			France	2
			US Forces Europe	1
1961	3	—		
1962	2	—		
1963	1	—		

ACE BRISTOL PRODUCTION AND EXPORT FIGURES

Of all the AC sports cars prior to the Cobra, by far the largest number manufactured were Ace Bristols. In all 465 chassis were laid down. Two of these, BEX 1189 and BEX 1206, were re-allocated to become Ace 2.6 cars RXS 5001 and RSX 5002.

A total of 463 Ace Bristols were made as complete cars, breaking down into 100 BE and 363 BEX chassis. One of these cars, BEX 1198, had its engine removed before being sold on 18 October 1961. BEX 477 was supplied with no body to H. Pathey, the Swiss importer, on 24 July 1958.

The second car made, BE 117, went to France on 14 April 1956 and was fitted with a body by Chapron. One other car is recorded as having left the works with no engine and gearbox, this being BEX 327 on 19 June 1957, bound for the USA.

Of the 463 total, 91 cars were delivered in the UK and 372 were exported. The UK market took 84 cars with BE chassis and 7 with BEX.

Ace Bristols were shipped to the following countries:

USA	241
France	44
Venezuela	31
Switzerland	18
Canada	12
Hawaii	4
Rhodesia	3
Belgium	3
Singapore	1
Portugal	1
India	1
Hong Kong	1
Spain	1
Eire	1
St. Lucia	1
Austria	1
Lebanon	1
Colombia	1
West Germany	1

US Forces personnel in West Germany took two cars and those in France took two. A Royal Canadian Air Force man in France took one car.

Sales year by year were as follows:

Year	UK	Export	Country	
1956	11	51	USA	30
			Venezuela	11
			Canada	3
			France	2
			Switzerland	2
			Singapore	1
			Portugal	1
			Belgium	1
1957	26	129	USA	97
			France	9
			Venezuela	8
			Switzerland	4
			Hawaii	4
			Canada	1
			India	1
			Hong Kong	1
			Spain	1
			Eire	1
			St. Lucia	1
			Austria	1
1958	18	89	USA	51
			France	17
			Switzerland	6
			Canada	5
			Venezuela	4
			Rhodesia	2
			Lebanon	1
			Colombia	1
			Belgium	1
			US Forces France	1
1959	16	52	USA	34
			Venezuela	7
			France	6
			Switzerland	3
			Canada	2
1960	13	31	USA	20
			France	5
			Switzerland	2
			US Forces Germany	2
			Belgium	1
			Canada	1
1961	3	7	France	4
			US Forces France	1
			RCAF France	1
			Rhodesia	1
1962	2	2	USA	2
1963	2	6	USA	5
			Switzerland	1
1964	—	2	France	1
			Germany	1

In addition to the above, three cars are entered in the factory ledger with rather unlikely despatch dates: BEX 184, 2 August 1954, to the USA; BEX 334, 22 July 1954, to Venezuela; BEX 450, 28 April 1956, to the USA.

Chassis plate of Ace Bristol.

The Ace 2.6 chassis plate was a shoddy affair by any standards. The two rectangles above and below are actually pieces of painted-over sticky tape covering misdrilled holes or moulding defects in the glassfibre footbox. This manufacturing technique (!) was carried over to Cobras, on which white painted tape was used.

ACE BRISTOL ENGINE TYPES

The different types of engines fitted year by year are as follows (all years are cars ex-works):

1956	100C2	12
	100B2	1
	100D	48
	100D2	1
1957	100D	154
1958	100C2	1
	100D	33
	100D2S	1
	100D2	62
1959	110	1
	100D2	67
1960	100D	1
	100D2	43
1961	100D2	10
1962	100D2	4
1963	100D2	8
1964	100D2	2

BEX 184 and BEX 334 were fitted with 100D motors. BEX 450 was fitted with a 100D2 unit.

Only 12 cars are recorded as having been fitted with overdrive from new, but it is likely there were more.

ACECA BRISTOL PRODUCTION AND EXPORT FIGURES

A total of 170 Aceca Bristol chassis were laid down, but only 169 complete cars were made; chassis BEX 802 was stripped and returned to stores for spares. The first chassis, BE 571, left the factory on 16 July 1956 and was fitted with engine number 100D2 502. The last chassis; BE 819, was fitted with engine number 100D2 1141 and left the factory on 19 October 1962.

There were 88 cars with BE chassis prefixes and 81 cars with BEX prefixes.

Of these, 85 cars were delivered within the UK and 83 were exported. The destination of just one car, BEX 799, was not recorded.

UK purchasers took 79 BE chassis and 6 BEX chassis, while 74 BEX chassis and 9 BE chassis were exported.

Exported Aceca Bristols went to the following countries:

USA	45
France	11
Switzerland	7
Canada	5
Venezuela	5
Malaya	1
Rhodesia	1
Portugal	1
Hawaii	1
Belgium	1
Hong Kong	1
Australia	1
Canary Islands	1
Germany	1

Sales year by year were as follows:

Year	UK	Export	Country	
1956	6	8	Switzerland	1
			France	1
			Malaya	1
			Rhodesia	1
			USA	4
1957	16	19	Hong Kong	1
			Portugal	1
			Hawaii	1
			Belgium	1
			Canada	1
			Venezuela	2
			France	2
			USA	8
1958	20	26	Australia	1
			Switzerland	1
			Venezuela	2
			Canada	2
			France	6
			USA	14
1959	18	12	Venezuela	1
			Eire	1
			Canary Islands	1
			Germany	1
			USA	8
1960	17	15	Canada	1
			France	1
			Switzerland	2
			USA	11
1961	5	1	Canada	1
1962	2	1	Switzerland	1
1963	—	1	France	1

ACECA BRISTOL ENGINE TYPES

The different types of engines fitted year by year are as follows: (all years are cars ex-works):

Year			
1956	BE	100D	6
		100B2	3
	BEX	100D	2
		100B2	3
1957	BE	100D	12
		100D2	1
		100B2	1
	BEX	100D	18
		100B2	3
1958	BE	100D	5
		100D2	10
		100B2	6
	BEX	100D	12
		100D2	14
1959	BE	100D2	16
		100B2	3
	BEX	100D2	11
		100B2	1
1960	BE	100D2	16
		100B2	2
	BEX	100D2	14
1961	BE	100D2	3
		100B2	1
	BEX	100D2	2
1962	BE	100D2	2
	BEX	100D2	1
1963	BEX	100D2	1

The year of one car, BEX 799, is unknown, but was probably 1960.

Cars with the following engines were fitted with overdrive:

1956	BE	100B2	2
1957	BEX	100D	1
		100B2	1
1959	BE	100D	1
		100D2	2
		100B2	4
	BEX	100D2	2
		100B2	1
1959	BE	100D2	10
		100B2	2
	BEX	100D2	3
1960	BE	100D2	8
		100B	1
	BEX	100D2	5
1961	BEX	100D2	1
1962	BE	100D2	1

Oddly, in some factory sales literature, AC did not recommend overdrive in conjunction with the D series engines.

ACE RS 2.6 PRODUCTION AND EXPORT FIGURES

The following are some of the significant cars in the Ace RS 2.6 production run.

RS 5000 was the prototype using AE 1191 renumbered; this car also had the normal Ace bodywork and was ex-works on 16 March 1961.

RXS 5001 was the first export car, BEX 1189 renumbered. The RXS designation is inexplicable as further export cars carried RSX prefixes.

RSX 5002 was the Paris show car, BEX 1206 renumbered and ex-works on 2 October 1961.

RSX 5010 was the Geneva show car, ex-works on 9 March 1962.

RS 5016 was AC's demonstrator, ex-works on 4 March 1964.

RS 5036 was the last car, ex-works on 23 December 1963.

A total of 37 cars were made, as follows: RS chassis, 23; RSX chassis, 13; RXS chassis, 1.

Sales year by year were as follows:

Year	UK	Export	Country	
1961	5	3	France	3
1962	12	7	France	3
			Canada	2
			Switzerland	1
			USA	1
1963	8	1	Canada	1
1964	1	—		

The chassis figures appearing above are somewhat misleading as some cars having RSX numbers in the ledger were given RS numbers at the time of manufacture: for example, RS 5020 appears in the ledger as RSX 5020.

ACECA 2.6 PRODUCTION AND EXPORT FIGURES

Production of these cars was split equally, and so there were four cars carrying RS numbers and four with RSX numbers.

Sales year by year were as follows:

Year	UK	Export	Country	
1961	1	2	USA	1
			Spain	1
1962	4	1	France	1

The last car, RSX 5507, was apparently sold in England but may have been passing through an agent's hands. For uniformity, in all these records the first name, ex-works, in the factory ledger is taken as the destination even if probably temporary, except where the country of export is also given.

The first three Aceca 2.6 cars were constructed from re-allocated AC Acecas. Hence AE 806 became RS 5500, AEX 780 became RSX 5501 and AEX 815 became RSX 5502.

Leaf Sprung Cobra 260 and 289

CHASSIS

Since the Cobra was an evolution of the Ace theme, the first examples bore the most resemblance above and below the skin to the older model, especially the 2.6 variant.

The main chassis tubes were still of 3in diameter tubing and the 12-gauge wall thickness previously used only for the Aceca and 2.6 models was now standardised. These tubes were still placed 17in apart at their centres, as on previous models. Up to chassis no. CSX 2125 the front suspension tower was the same as on the Ace and Aceca, and except on very early cars the extra tube to mount the electric cooling fan was of square section. From chassis no. CSX 2126 and the introduction of rack and pinion steering, some important alterations were made. Naturally the steering idler bracket welded on the front of the tower was omitted, and two smaller brackets were welded on each side of the front of the tower to locate the new rack and pinion assembly. At the same time the tower itself was strengthened by being made of sheets of solid plate rather than plate having large trepanned perforations as on the Ace. Also the wishbone mounting brackets were repositioned. Previously they had been mounted on top of the chassis tubes – now, with the complete redesign of the front suspension, they were positioned on the chassis tubes below and outboard of their former locations.

An additional 3in tubular cross member was welded into the main chassis just ahead of the back suspension tower. Apart from adding strength, this was used as a mounting for the differential nose piece.

Since the Cobra differential was not built into the rear suspension tower as on the Ace, it became a separate unit similar to that of the Aceca. The rear suspension mounting used for the Aceca was perhaps not considered substantial enough, so for the Cobra a structure more like that of the Ace was decided upon, but with the sides rising at a steeper angle from the main chassis tubes to provide space within for mounting a complete differential casing. The differential unit was attached by rubber bushes on each side as well as the front mounting. The chassis outriggers either side of the new cross member carried the body subframe and were much more substantial. Additional square-section tubing, fish plates and webbing were all used around this rear suspension and final drive area.

Wishbone mountings were welded to the main frame as on previous cars. Shock absorbers were mounted in the same way front and back, although the construction of the rear mounting differed because of the revised layout in that area; now the rear shock absorbers were mounted forward of the drive shafts.

The central cross member had additional bracketing welded to it to provide a

Early Cobra chassis with Bishop Cam steering. The completed car, CSX 2063, left the works on 1 January 1963. The square-section tubes employed at the rear of the Cobra body frame and the additional framework and bracketry can be seen. The steering wheel is a slave item and Pirelli tyres would not have been fitted when the car was delivered to the customer by Shelby.

mounting for the handbrake, which now was sited just to the right of the transmission. All other outriggers were basically unaltered, and the 1½in diameter scuttle hoop remained the same.

After having the various body framework tubes welded to it, the whole structure was finished in black.

FRONT SUSPENSION

For the first Cobras, up to chassis CSX 2126, the front suspension was unchanged apart from the transverse spring becoming 39¼in long and now having 10 leaves. When the new steering was introduced, the fabricated uprights, which carried the king pins, were replaced by forged steel ones each having a cast steel top link secured to the spring in the same manner as before; a grease nipple is fitted to the spring eye pin. As with other transverse leaf-sprung ACs, the front and rear springs were wrapped with Drevo tape.

REAR SUSPENSION

Although the Cobra's 51in rear track was 1in wider than the six-cylinder cars, the rear spring was the same length at 41in between eye centres. One extra leaf was added to give eight in total and Armstrong shock absorbers were fitted all round. Occasionally Armstrong Selectarides were fitted to European cars from new, probably at a customer's request (COB 6005 was one such car).

The rear uprights were cast from malleable iron. The top of an upright was designed to fit directly onto the end of the leaf spring, while the bottom was machined to take a long pin to which the wishbone was attached.

STEERING

All the cars with the 4.2-litre engine and those with the 4.7-litre unit up to chassis number CSX 2125 continued to use the Ace/Aceca steering assembly. From then on a rack and pinion system was used; this shared many components with the type used on the MGB, but had a shorter pinion. It was manufactured by Cam Gears, gave 2⅞ turns of the wheel lock to lock, and was mounted at the front of the suspension tower.

This rack assembly was further modified at AC by shortening the track rods and then adding hexagonal adaptors to increase their overall length. The vertical links now used incorporated attachment points for the stub axles and forward-facing steering arms; this innovation considerably reduced the need for attention from the grease gun as only the top swivels required greasing, the handbook recommending this every 1000 miles.

The bottom ball pins were intended to give long service before attention was needed and could not be greased externally. However, in practice they gave poor service and tended to wear out quite quickly, the outer hard chrome surface on the ball pins becoming pitted and damaging the surface of the hemispheres. This would lead to considerable vertical play between the wishbone and the upright, and in extreme circumstances the ball pin could jump out of its location with predictably unpleasant results.

The steering column could no longer run in a straight line and so was now in two lengths with two universal joints. Although the steering wheel was still adjustable for height by means of the bracket attaching the column to the scuttle hoop, the provision for reach adjustment went with the change from worm and sector to rack and pinion.

The woodrim steering wheel that had been optional on Aces and Acecas became standard equipment on both 260 and 289 Cobras manufactured with Bishop Cam steering. Flashing indicator and horn controls were also of the old type and the steering was adjustable in the traditional manner. The absence of a trim panel surrounding the steering column where it emerges from the dashboard is correct.

For the rack and pinion steering Cobra a new dished steering wheel was produced, which was adjustable for height but not reach. Note that some of the small dials, although of the correct type, are transposed from the their original positions on this car.

Twin brake reservoirs (left) were introduced at chassis CSX 2165. An aluminium casting houses the cross shaft from which the accelerator pedal hangs. The trunking leads into the canister containing the cable-operated fresh air flap. The greasegun on this model is clipped to the bulkhead.

The handbrake lever (right) was always to the right of the transmission tunnel on Cobras; here it is in the 'on' position. The gear knob is of the first type fitted to these cars.

The steering rack (right) sits low down in front of the suspension tower. Note the heavy-section channel used to clamp the spring in place, and its tape wrapping. No fan blades are fitted, and the electric fan is mounted on the bar just visible in front of the radiator.

Rack and pinion cars had a new steering wheel, in aluminium with a laminated and riveted wood rim. It was quite deeply dished and had an AC motif in the centre where the horn push had previously been. Due to the depth of the dish it was not possible to press the frame in one operation during manufacture; instead the three spokes were sawn through in the middle and then bent by hand to the correct angle. An aluminium ring was fitted over the centre of the spokes to hold the AC badge and hide the gaps between the sawn ends.

Cobras produced with the worm and sector steering had both height and reach adjustment for the steering wheel, which was the aluminium and wood rimmed item previously fitted as an optional extra to Aces and Acecas. This type of wheel still had the stator tube running up through the column with horn push and indicator switch in the centre.

All steering columns, boxes, racks and track rods were finished in black.

BRAKES

Before the brake layout of the Cobra was finalised, at least one car was built with inboard disc brakes at the rear, but when the cars reached production stage there were outboard disc brakes all round. Up to chassis no. CSX 2124 the caliper was mounted at the front of the disc.

The front brakes used AC manufactured discs of 11 $^{11}/_{16}$in diameter and up to chassis CSX 2124 two-piston iron calipers were fitted, part no. GBB 48440 (l.h.)/GBB 48441 (r.h.). From then on three-piston type 16/3 calipers were fitted, of slightly varying types: part no. 64032714 (l.h.)/ 64032715 (r.h.) from chassis CSX 2125 until CSX 2164, and part no. 64032770 (l.h.)/64032771 (r.h.) from CSX 2165 on.

The rear brakes employed 10¾in discs, again made by AC, and Girling three-piston type 12/3 H calipers. This type of caliper incorporates a mechanism and small pads for the handbrake and is adjustable for wear; from chassis number CSX 2188 the handbrake was self-adjusting. Disc thickness was at first ½in at the front and ⅜in at the rear, but part way through production it was increased to ⅝in at the front and ½in at the rear – necessitating the fitting of a ⅛ spacer between the two halves of each caliper.

Master cylinders were of the CV type. From the first cars up to chassis CSX 2164, a single ¾in bore cylinder was employed. From CSX 2165, however, there was a pair of ⅝in bore cylinders, each with its own reservoir, one serving the front brakes and the other the rear ones. No brake servo was

The rear brake caliper on a leaf sprung Cobra. Aces and Cobras have this tubular stay for the rear wing.

fitted, which makes for a high pedal pressure. The handbrake is operated by a chromium-plated lever mounted to the right of the transmission tunnel on all models.

FINAL DRIVE

Hardy Spicer supplied the short propellor shaft. This was coupled to a Salisbury 4HU differential of the 'Powr-lok' limited slip type. As described in the chassis section, this differential was not built into the rear suspension tower as on the Aces but was a separate unit rather like that of the Aceca. It was held by three rubber-bushed mountings, one on either side of the differential and one on the nose piece; the side mountings were secured by 7in by ⅝in high tensile bolts passing through the A frame.

The most commonly fitted back axle ratio was 3.54:1 on cars with COB and COX chassis numbers, and also on CSX chassis up to 2069; from CSX 2070 the lower ratio of to 3.77:1 was most often used.

The driveshafts were made by Hardy Spicer. The rear hubs were more substantial than those on previous cars and ran in a pair of large, equal-sized ball bearings instead of the double outer row and single inner row of the Ace. During production the design of these hubs was modified. The first type had a machined step to space the outer oil seal, but later a radius was turned instead and a loose spacer fitted to relieve a possible stress and fracture point.

The wheel hub splines remained at 42mm. The oil capacity is 2½ pints.

WHEELS & TYRES

Dunlop 15in, 72-spoke, triple-laced wheels were standard equipment for the leaf-sprung Cobra. CSX chassis numbers up to 2159 had 5½in rims, then from 2160 to 2589 6in rims were used; COB and COX chassis numbers normally had 6in rims. Cars were supplied with silver-painted wire wheels as standard, chrome wire wheels and whitewalls becoming a popular option on the later rack and pinion cars.

As far as can be ascertained, the following tyres would have been fitted as original equipment, the choice of Goodyear being explained by the fact that Carroll Shelby was an agent for this make. On the early 260 cars 6.00/6.40×15 Goodyear Bluestreaks, T4 race tyres, or Motor Raceway Goodyears were fitted; later 260 and 289 cars had either 6.50/7.00×15 Goodyear Wingfoots or 7.35×15 Goodyear G8s. English cars usually wore Goodyears.

Wire wheels (above) with 5½in rims were standard on early cars. These are the correct chromium exhaust trims that could be fitted when new.

At chassis CSX 2160 wheels were increased to 6in width. The knock-on hub cap remained identical from the first Ace to the last wire-wheel Cobras.

ENGINE

The power unit fitted to the first Cobra was the largest of the new breed of lightweight V8 engines produced for the Ford Fairlane series. New casting techniques enabled an iron engine of this size, due to its thin walls, to weigh virtually the same as if the block and heads were of aluminium. This engine was considerably over-square with a bore and stroke of 96.5mm (3.80in) by 73mm (2.87in), and displaced 4261cc (260cu in).

LEAF SPRUNG COBRA 260 AND 289

This early 289 engine retains its standard cast iron intake and exhaust manifolds and Autolite 4-V 600CFM carburettor. Chromium plated rocker covers were normal at this period. The spun aluminium Harrison header tank that was fitted in conjunction with the aluminium radiator should be left unpainted. An interesting point of originality is that the green wire leading to the DB10 relay is almost invariably left out of the wiring loom, as on this car with its original loom.

The standard engine fitted to Ford models had hydraulic tappets. No attempt had been made to tune it, so it was a fairly lazy affair with power of around 165bhp at 4500rpm. Ford, warming to this new project and its sporting possibilities, was happy to uprate the engines supplied to Carroll Shelby, making a special run of 260 series with a more radical camshaft, solid tappets, larger porting and higher compression pistons. In this form the engine was publicised as giving 260bhp at 5800rpm, which one cannot help feeling was rather optimistic. Nevertheless, putting this motor in a car that had never before been propelled by anything giving much over 130bhp, except in the 2.6 Ace's most highly tuned forms, was bound to give exciting results.

As far as configuration was concerned this engine broke no new ground. The opposing banks of four cylinders made a 90° angle and the overhead valves were operated by pushrods from a single central camshaft. From this camshaft were driven the distributor and oil pump; the distributor rose vertically and emerged just in front of the inlet manifold, and the oil pump, located in the deepest part of the sump, was driven by a hexagonal shaft from the base of the distributor drive. This shaft can fail, so a good precaution is to replace it on every engine rebuild or even if the sump is removed. The canister type oil filter was behind the fuel pump on the left-hand side of the block.

The crankshaft was supported by five main bearings with journals of 2.2486in running in copper-lead alloy shell bearings; the big ends had journals of 2.1232in with the same bearing material. The substantial connecting rods were just over 5in long and had a gudgeon pin of a little under 1in which was a press fit in the small end. The cast aluminium pistons had two compression rings and one oil control ring. The cylinder heads were of cast iron, and a cast iron intake manifold sat in the vee between the two heads.

Engine compartments are sometimes mildly modified by owners. Although retaining its original motor this car is non-standard in some respects such as the spark enhancer on top of the coil, modified pipework for the header tank and an extra expansion tank, and non-standard exhaust manifolds. The engine block and bellhousing should of course not be painted red. When replacing the inner wings the owner has chosen not to adopt AC's practice of fitting rubber sheeting, attached with aluminium pop rivetted strip, around the spring cut-out.

65

This early car still retains its original Harrison aluminium radiator. Just visible to the rear of the spring clamps are the blades of the mechanical fan.

At this time Ford had seen fit to dispense with such things as rocker shafts for many of its overhead valve engines and that fitted to the Cobra was one of these, each rocker being universally mounted. A certain amount of sideways movement was inevitable, but, unlike some English Ford engines so equipped, these V8s seem to give no trouble.

Chromium-plated pressed-steel rocker covers were standard up to chassis 2200. Shelby cast aluminium covers were optional from chassis 2180 and became almost universally employed from 2201.

The 289 engine evolved out of the 260 because more power was required, the larger capacity being reached by increasing the bore to 4in. Ford produced a 'High Performance' version of the 289 engine, and this was the one that Shelby fitted to Cobras.

The 'High Performance' block incorporated more substantial main bearing caps than either the 260 or standard 289 versions. The crankshaft was cast from a better quality high nodular iron, which gave greater strength and flexibility. The forged steel connecting rods incorporated ⅜in bolts instead of the 5/16in size used for the 260 and normal 289, but the gudgeon pins remained unaltered.

There were larger inlet and exhaust valves, and the rocker studs were screwed rather than pressed into the cylinder heads, this feature being one way of distinguishing the 'Hipo 289' engine, as it became known, from the ordinary 260 and 289 engines. The camshaft was uprated and the valve springs had an additional damper spring. Solid cam followers were fitted instead of the standard 289's hydraulic ones.

All these features combined to give the engine more power and it was advertised as producing 271bhp at 6000rpm and 312lb ft of torque at 3400rpm. Virtually every part of the High Performance engine could be tuned or uprated to give even more power, and indeed Shelby was quick to do this for his racing cars. Many racing parts then became available to customers, engines modified in this way giving as much as 400bhp.

Standard finish for this engine was black, then mid-blue starting with 1965-specification engines.

COOLING SYSTEM

The first 260 Cobras were fitted with the same Gallay radiator as the 2.6 Ace used. At least one other pattern of radiator was tried on these early cars before Harrison aluminium crossflow radiators, as used on Chevrolet Corvettes, were employed for a while; the spun aluminium header tanks for these were also made by Harrison. These radiators did not last long and very few still exist in useable condition.

Finally, to resolve the Cobra's radiator problem Ford arranged, on Shelby's behalf, for the McCord Radiator company to manufacture a crossflow radiator along with its own remote header tank. Water was circulated by an aluminium Autolite pump and electric fans of the various types mentioned in the electrical equipment section were fitted.

In order to aid cooling during the initial running-in period, fan blades from the Ford Falcon six-cylinder engine were bolted to the water pump pulley, but these could be removed after 5000-6000 miles.

EXHAUST SYSTEM

Special cast iron Y-shaped manifolds, two for each bank of cylinders, were made for the Cobra in England and shipped to Shelby American with the car. Although these manifolds would be considered fairly restrictive today, at the time they were quite innovative in that the exhaust gases did not combine into one pipe until a distance of some 18in from the exhaust ports.

Exhausts exit just outboard of the overriders on either side. The chromium exhaust trims turn in very slightly at their ends.

A separate exhaust pipe and silencer are fitted on each side and the tailpipes emerge at the rear just outboard of the overriders.

CARBURETTORS & FUEL SYSTEM

A four-barrel Autolite carburettor, rated at 480cfm, is fitted and topped by a circular chromium air cleaner of 14in diameter with a disposable element. Also fitted were Holley 4-BBC carburettors rated at up to 715cfm. The mechanical fuel pump, operated by the camshaft, is an Autolite component and draws fuel from the 15 gallon tank in the boot.

TRANSMISSION

Some very early 260 Cobras were fitted with a four-speed Ford gearbox in an iron casing, but the Borg Warner T10 four-speed unit was used on all subsequent cars. This Borg Warner gearbox had an aluminium casing, which has received criticism for its lack of strength. However, in normal road use it is perfectly satisfactory, breakages occurring only occasionally when abused or raced. It has the advantage of being much lighter than its Ford counterpart.

Three different sets of ratios were fitted to road Cobras with this gearbox. There is no way of telling which cars were supplied with which gear ratio set, but the majority started out with the wider ratio 'L' set with ratios of 2.36:1, 1.76:1, 1.41:1 and 1:1. These were quite adequate for everyday use, but a rarer and more desirable 'M' or Sebring set gave very close ratios of 2.36:1, 1.62:1, 1.20:1 and 1:1. Today the 'M' set is much more desirable when cars are used for racing – the percentage drop in engine revs between third and top for each ratio set being as follows: 29% with the 'L' set, and only 17% with the 'M' set!

These two gear sets used Ford input shafts with a 11/16in by 10 spline, which mated to a 10½in Ford clutch plate contained in a coil sprung type clutch assembly.

The chromium gaiter retaining ring displays its origins with the FoMoCo logo. The T handle is lifted up in order to select reverse gear. Later series leaf sprung cars were fitted with this type of gearknob.

White pigmented glassfibre footwells were used from very early on. Above the accelerator mechanism and attached to the aluminium bulkhead are on the left the Lucas SF4 fuse box and on the right the Ford regulator fitted in conjunction with the Ford dynamo.

The other gear set used in this 'box was sourced from General Motors and known as the 'K' set. In this case the input shaft has a 1⅛in by 10 spline necessitating a GM 10½in clutch plate to match. The ratios for these gears are 2.20:1, 1.64:1, 1.31:1 and 1:1; as can be seen, bottom gear is rather higher.

All the gears were made of high nickel alloy steel, forged and heat treated to SAE 9310, making them a very superior product indeed. The 'M' and 'K' set gears are virtually unobtainable today, and command high prices as a result. Borg Warner transmissions in good condition are highly prized by their owners today due to the difficulty of obtaining replacement parts. Worn out transmissions have often been replaced by the Ford 'toploader' type – more readily available, but not original equipment.

The gearchange is operated by external rods and levers. The gearlever is short and straight, with a spring-loaded T-handle to enable reverse gear to be engaged.

A C-4 automatic gearbox was offered as an option for the CSX series Cobras and some 30 cars were so fitted, all of these being late ones.

ELECTRICAL EQUIPMENT

The dynamo was a Lucas C40-1 and had a rev counter drive from the rear through a reduction box; this drive was fitted also to Mk1 and Mk2 Austin-Healey Sprites and the Ace 2.6. Ford supplied the starter motor, the distributor (C40F-12127-A) and the coil (FAC 12029-A). The sparking plugs were 18mm Autolite BF32s. Both the control box (RB106/2) and fuse box (SF4) were by Lucas.

Twin-tone Lucas horns of model WT101 were used, part number 69090A being the high note and 69087A the low note. The twin-speed windscreen wiper motor was also a Lucas item, model DR3; the date of manufacture is stamped on these motors (as it is on some other electrical equipment), enabling the fanatic to tell if a replacement has been fitted.

At first Smiths supplied the electric engine cooling fan. The earliest type was mounted ahead of the radiator and was type ES.2379/4, but this was superseded from chassis number CSX 2080 by a type PES.2626 fan mounted behind the radiator. After chassis number CSX 2167, the fan became a Lucas model 3GM (with larger blades) and reverted to its old position in front of the radiator. Cars with COB and COX chassis numbers would always have been fitted with the Lucas fan. The original equipment battery was a Lucas FRT 9A on these cars.

US specification cars had Lucas dynamos and starters up to chassis CSX 2070, and from then on used Ford items, the dynamo being C40F-10000-A and the starter motor C30F-11001-A. Lastly, from chassis CSX 2201 Ford C5AF-10300-D alternators were used. Control boxes used with the Ford generators were type C2AF-10505-A for the dynamo and type C5AF-10316A for the alternator. US cars had negative earth and European cars had positive earth.

Those readers familiar with Ford parts coding may have asked themselves why apparent impossibilities occurred in the manufacture of these cars, the answer being that they did not: the 'rogue' parts being the later type fitted.

To explain to the uninitiated, a prefix C5, for instance, shows the part to be first released in 1965 (C for the decade and 5 for the year). The last letter of the complete number indicates how many times the part had been altered from its first design (A showed an unaltered design, B one alteration, and so on). An alternator C5AF-10300-D, therefore, would be the later type.

LAMPS

Headlamps for US cars were Lucas sealed beam units, the number being SZA20. For

· LEAF SPRUNG COBRA 260 AND 289 ·

Cars with COB chassis numbers would have been fitted with these Lucas P700 headlight units and 539 sidelights. The aluminium sheet air dam visible under the number plate was found many years ago at the factory by the owner of this car, who was told that it had been used experimentally.

England and Europe a variety of lamps were available, but strictly P700 Lucas light units should be used. Otherwise the lights were unaltered from the Ace – Lucas 539 sidelights, Lucas 542 rear lamps and a Lucas 467 number plate lamp.

BODYWORK & BODY TRIM

In its method of construction and basic shape, the Cobra followed a gradual evolution of the Ace body shape. The framework was once again largely built up of ¾in steel tubing, incorporating the 1½in scuttle hoop and a 1in hoop beneath the rear deck, the whole being welded to the chassis and painted black. Door, bonnet and boot frames were all mounted on fabricated hinges, as on the Ace except that the bonnet hinges were now tubular fabrications similar to those for the boot. The aluminium panels were formed in the same way and usually by the same craftsmen as had made bodies for the six-cylinder cars.

At first the changes necessary for the Cobra compared with its immediate predecessor, the 2.6, were quite small. The 2.6's lower bonnet and nose, which had been made possible by the short-stroke engine, easily accommodated the V8.

The distinctively shaped wheel arches of the 260 and 289 models were present from the beginning. In the eyes of many people, including the author, these cars display an understated elegance that was lost in the vulgar excesses of the coil-sprung cars required by the rather large section tyres fitted to the 427 version. There were, in fact, two types of wheel arch on these cars: early on in the 289 series, at chassis number CSX 2160, the width of the arch was increased slightly, due to the increase in rim width from 5½in to 6in. At around the same time side vents appeared in the front wings behind the wheel arches to assist dissipation of heat from the engine compartment.

For a good while the Wilmot Breeden budget locks that had been fitted since the

Rear lights were still the Lucas 542 units used since the early days of the Ace and also fitted to the 1950s Hillman Minx. Was it a coincidence that the Hillman stand was next to AC's at the 1953 Motor Show?
Only cars with COB and COX chassis numbers had the diestamped AC badge on the boot lid, which was shorter at the bottom to provide a deeper valance and at its front edge to allow room for the fuel filler. The exhaust pipes on this car are non-standard.

69

Side vents first began to appear on the leaf sprung Cobra at the same time as the slightly larger wheel arch flares, but there was no exact changeover point. The exhaust is a non-standard four-branch racing type.

first Aces were used to secure the bonnet. Then these were replaced by a pair of chromium handles by the same maker. This was a good deal less neat but save fiddling with the key; if any competition work was envisaged, precious seconds could be saved.

The black glass-fibre footwells of the 2.6 Ace now became pigmented with white to reflect the heat, although some of the very first few CSX cars did retain the old black colouring.

Doors were the same as on the Ace and had identical Wilmot Breeden door catches. As mentioned before, replica catches are available, but they sometimes do not have the original manufacturer's motif on the bracket that holds the striker. In cases where this bracket is not actually broken at the screw holes, it can be used again by fitting the new striker to it. The only disadvantage with this solution is that these original pieces do not take kindly to being rechromed, so the weathered chrome would at first clash with the new.

Apart from the wheel arches, the rear bodywork and boot lid were similar to the Ace, but not identical. The Cobra boot lid is shorter at the top to give a little more rear deck space to incorporate the central fuel filler, and also at the bottom to give a deeper and stronger body valance. The vertical portion of the boot skin swells out more than on the Ace and the number plate light is partially inset.

The fabricated internal boot hinges, Wilmot Breeden sliding stay and locking chromium handle were also as on the Ace. The petrol tank was no longer under the boot floor so the spare wheel could be recessed, this whole portion being moulded in the same pigmented glass-fibre as the footwells.

Black rubber sealing strip of ½in by ¼in section with adhesive on one side was still used to seal door, bonnet and boot apertures.

The windscreen followed the same

Cobras had square section tubing for some of the rear framework which, although painted black at first, was sprayed silver, along with the wiring loom, in the boot area. The spare wheel sits in its correct white glassfibre well, and the original 'Shelley' jack is in place. The aluminium bulkhead in the region of the filler neck carries creases seen on all cars. The panels are pop rivetted in place.

· LEAF SPRUNG COBRA 260 AND 289 ·

The overriders were mounted by means of long bolts enclosed in aluminium tubes passing through holes in the body protected by rubber grommets. These and various other rubber seals used on AC cars were normally supplied by Clayton Wright or, sometimes, the Hertfordshire Rubber Company. The grille assembly is recessed into the nacelle and fixed in place by self tap screws through its rim.

The grille is made up of two different sections of anodised aluminium, the shapes of which are apparent here. The overriders are bolted to the central chromium hoop.

The 'short' boot lid was necessary to allow for the petrol filler. Sixteen 'lift the dot' studs retained the hood on all Aces and Cobras. The rear bumper kinks out to clear the boot handle but opening and closing the boot is still awkward.

design as the curved 'screen fitted to the last of the Aces and was still made by Elliott, as all AC's sports 'screens had been since the two- and four-seaters of the mid 1930s, although a good number of screens were also made by Beclawat owing to increased demand once production got under way. For the owner wishing to take part in speed events, this 'screen was completely, and fairly swiftly, detachable merely by undoing the two bolts on either side behind the dashboard and sliding the whole assembly up and off, remembering first also to release at the centre of the 'screen the small chromium angle bracket which was held to the scuttle top by two screws. The lower edge of the 'screen was sealed by 1½in wide rubber weather strip. Demisting vents were fitted only if cars had heaters, which were optional on CSX cars but standard on European COB and COX Mk2s.

The very first Cobras were fitted with the early Ace 2.6 type of overriders, but the

71

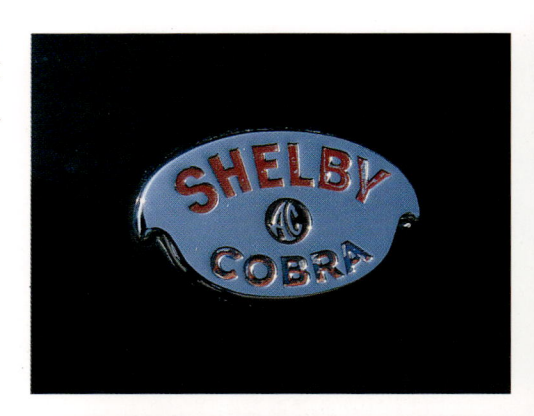

This badge was used from the first car to chassis CSX 2054, normally on cars completed by Ed Hugas or Tasca Ford.

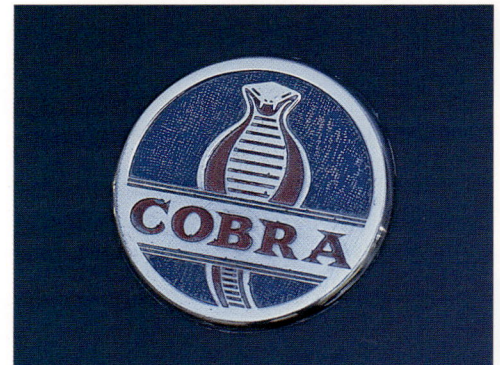

This is the second type of badge used, variously nicknamed 'flat head' or 'smiling' Cobra. It can be found on many early CSX cars and some of the first COX and COB series.

Carroll Shellby finally settled on this design of badge for the majority of leaf sprung and coil sprung Cobras.

CSX series cars had either this or the later badge on the boot. The number plate lamp was partially recessed.

This badge (below) was carried on all COX and COB series cars at the rear.

later 2.6 type made specially for AC by Pyrene was almost immediately standardized for both front and rear until the end of Cobra production. At the front these were united by a chromium hoop that followed the outline of the radiator nacelle and was welded to brackets which bolted to the overriders. These in turn were bolted to triangulated tubular outriggers that formed part of the body frame, the bolts being sleeved with ¾in aluminium tubes and the holes in the bodywork having rubber grommets.

At the rear there was a tubular chromium bumper similar to the optional one offered in the US on the old Aces, but the Cobra type differed in kinking rearwards just inside each overrider and then running parallel. This assembly was attached to the inner tubework in the same way as at the front.

Lastly, we come to badges – a veritable minefield! As far as can be deduced, the following changes are near the correct sequence. Up to chassis CSX 2054, there were elongated 'Shelby AC Cobra' motifs front and rear; there were exceptions, such as the AC factory demonstrator (CSX 2030), but certainly most of the early cars completed on the East Coast at Ed Hugas' Pittsburgh dealership in this serial number range had this style of badge when new. From CSX 2055 to CSX 2132, the so called 'flat-headed' Cobra emblems were fitted, these also appearing on a few early COB and COX cars. At around chassis CSX 2133, the final design of badge was fitted. On US cars these badges were at the front and rear of the car, but on European cars there was a large die-stamped and chromed AC motif at the rear on the boot lid.

All CSX cars carried the rectangular 'Powered by Ford' badge on each front wing, and some – but not all – European cars were similarly fitted.

INTERIOR TRIM & WEATHER EQUIPMENT

As far as creature comforts are concerned, the Cobra does not have many. But what it does have, like its predecessors, is simple, functional and of good quality materials.

· LEAF SPRUNG COBRA 260 AND 289 ·

Exactly as it was when delivered to its first owner in May 1963 – only the gentle patination showing its age. This type of seat belt was only fitted to US Cobras. Seat belts were by either Ray Brown or Impact, and had 'CS' stitched on the webbing. These early Cobra seats were also used on a very few of the last 2.6 Aces.

The second Cobra seat was only subtly changed from the previous one, the external difference being the gradually reduced side support – in a car that needed it more than the Ace! Under the leather the aluminium seat pan had now become a Pirelli trampoline.

The seats of this restored car are a little too fully upholstered.

Cobra windscreens share these chrome hooks to attach the hood clips with all Aces.

The hood frame is first erected with the two bows vertical. The rear one is pushed backwards to this position when the hood itself is fastened.

The original equipment hood and sidescreens are beautifully preserved on this car (right). Replacement items never attain the same fit and look as this. After budget locks for the bonnet were dispensed with some cars were fitted with the 'tear drop' handles seen here before the definitive bonnet handles were adopted.

There were few changes for the Cobra compared with the last few 2.6 Aces, which themselves evolved from previous Aces. The transmission tunnel was rectangular in section as on the 2.6, but more bulky towards the front, thus narrowing the footwells. Carpeting was again used on the insides of the door skins, inner sills, footwells, transmission tunnel and seat backs; on areas other than the doors and seats it was leather bound. Carpet was normally black but could be ordered in other colours, with black or trim colour binding. Due to reduced boot space (because of the repositioned petrol tank), the sidescreens were now stored in the space behind the seats, behind a curtain of elasticated vinyl.

As production of the Cobra progressed, the seats were altered slightly so that the small curved side pieces all but disappeared; the cushions still had eight pleats, as on the

The hood fabric just clears the rubber grommet for the filler neck (above). The petrol cap was a 'Ceandess'. The stitching on this original hood has faded a little but was originally brown rather than black.

LEAF SPRUNG COBRA 260 AND 289

Ace, but the squabs now had only 10. Early Cobra seats shared the same aluminium skinned frame as the Aces, but later this gave way to a frame incorporating a Pirelli-made rubber trampoline for the seat base.

The leather door pockets, pull straps for door latches and check straps were all as on the Ace. The hood frame and hood were also identical, still being fastened with over-centre catches at either side of the windscreen and 16 'lift the dot' fasteners at the rear. Consequently, the procedure for erecting the hood is the same as described earlier for the Ace.

DASHBOARD & INSTRUMENTS

The general appearance of the Cobra's dashboard is similar to the last of the Aces, but it does in fact have many detail differences.

Apart from the first one or two cars which used 2.6 Ace 5in main instruments, both the speedometer and rev counter were of 4in diameter, the former being calibrated to 160mph and the latter (containing a main beam warning light) to 10,000rpm. These dials were manufactured by Smiths, as were all the gauges fitted to cars with COB and COX chassis numbers and US specification cars CSX 2000 to 2200. The exceptions were quite a number of CSX cars fitted with a Rotunda revolution counter, manufactured by Faria. From chassis number CSX 2201, US cars were fitted

The rear panel of the sidescreen slides forward for hand signals or ventilation.

Sidescreens are stowed behind an elasticated curtain at the rear of the seats. The bulkhead would have been covered in black vinyl from new rather than carpet.

Cars can be driven without sidescreens but to indulge in real speed they should be fitted. Although the hood balloons and creaks quite alarmingly, and the noise is appalling, speeds of well over 120mph are quite possible without dire consequences.

The Rotunda rev counter looks odd alongside the Smith instruments but is in fact original equipment on some early cars. It was fitted intermittently – the first documented car having one being CSX 2057 and the last CSX 2122. In addition, some cars from chassis CSX 2130 until 2200 were fitted with Sun rev counters.

Cold air circulation for the cockpit is controlled by means of two knobs, one on each side of the dashboard. The stalk controls the headlamps.

This car, chassis CSX 2306, ex-works on 30 January 1964, has the Stewart Warner instruments and Ford Galaxie clock. Switches also came from Ford production cars. On CSX cars with this steering wheel there is a Cobra motif in the centre. Somebody with a fear of getting lost has fitted a compass.

with Stewart Warner gauges as a matter of course, but some earlier CSX cars may have had the Smiths equipment replaced by Stewart Warner items at the Shelby factory (or vice versa by American owners who preferred Smiths instruments).

The Stewart Warner speedo and rev counter were of 3½in diameter, calibrated to 160mph and 8000rpm respectively. The ignition warning light was directly above the steering column and was flanked by a pair of direction indicator warning lights.

The smaller gauges were arranged in an inverted triangle. The lower gauge was an electric clock, which was normally by Smiths but a number of the cars with Stewart Warner equipment used a totally inappropriate clock from the 1962 Ford Galaxie. To the right of this was the ignition switch and to the left the switch for headlights and sidelights; directly above this latter switch was the rheostat for the panel lamps and to the left of this was a similar one for the heater. The two-speed windscreen wiper switch lived above the ignition switch.

Above the clock were the petrol gauge (left) and oil pressure gauge (right), reading to 100psi. Above these, from the left, were the ammeter, oil temperature and water temperature gauges.

To the right of the rev counter was the dipswitch and next to it the electric screenwasher. At the extreme end of the panel on each side, where it curls forward slightly, is a knob for operating the fresh air vents. Lastly, on the steering column is the stalk for the indicators and the horn.

The dashboard itself is made from aluminium sheet with a formed lip on the lower edge, this edge dropping down slightly in the centre portion. The whole is covered in black leather, including the glove locker lid (which is piped). This lid is fitted with a lock and is carpeted internally in black; the inside face is covered in black Rexine and has a ½in wide black leather check strap. The dashboard is fixed by five chromium screws and cup washers – one at each end onto the 1½in scuttle hoop and the other three above and slightly to the left of the ignition light, ammeter and glovebox lock. The above description refers to a right-hand drive car.

US 260 & 289 Cobra
Optional Extras

The following were catalogued as options by Shelby American:

Chromium air cleaner.
Aluminium rocker covers.
Chromium bumper bars.
Chromium exhaust trims.
Adjustable wind deflectors.
Tinted sun visors.
Heater.
Seat belts.
Whitewall tyres.
Aluminium 4v intake manifold.
Chromium luggage rack.
External rearview mirror.
Radio.
Hardtop.

In addition Shelby offered the following racing options:

9 quart Aviad sump.
Oil cooler.
2 × 4v intake manifold.
3 × 2v intake manifold.
1 × 4v intake manifold.
Competition exhaust system.
Dual coil ignition.
Spalding 'Flamethrower' magneto.
Large capacity radiator.
Aluminium radiator.
Aluminium crankshaft and water pump pulleys.
Aluminium engine block.
Aluminium cylinder heads.
High compression pistons.
Engle competition pushrods.
Differential oil cooler.
Four Weber twin choke carburettors and manifold.
Bonnet scoop for above.
Front brake air scoops.
Rear brake air scoops.
Aluminium brake calipers.
Twin master cylinders.
Cold air box and intake.
Extra bonnet vents.
Undertray.
17 gallon fuel tank.
37 gallon aluminium fuel tank.
Electric petrol pump.
Larger diameter petrol filler.
Front anti-roll bar.
Rear anti-roll bar.
Competition springs.
Koni adjustable shock absorbers.
Steering bracket (pre rack and pinion).
Rollover bar.
Competition wire wheels.
Alloy wheels, hubs and wheel arch extensions.
Close ratio gearbox.
Competition seats.
Competition windscreen.
Radiator stoneguard.
Competition lights.

US 260 & 289 Cobra
Colour Schemes

Since these cars were made under contract for Carroll Shelby, private customer involvement in the construction was virtually absent and the range of colours employed was reduced.

By far the most widely used colours were red with black interior or white with red interior, particularly early on.

The first car, CSX 2000, was shipped unpainted. From then until CSX 2017 all cars were white or red. CSX 2018 was the first car in black with black leather, the next being CSX 2029 and then two small runs of CSX 2056 to CSX 2061 and CSX 2071 to CSX 2076. Two more black cars, CSX 2069 and CSX 2070, were produced immediately before the last run but these had red leather. Before these only one white car departed slightly from normal practice in having dark red leather.

Other colours used are listed below with the chassis number on which they first appeared:

Bright Blue	Black	CSX 2105
Princess Blue	Red	CSX 2108
Vineyard Green	Black	CSX 2112
Vineyard Green	Beige	CSX 2119
Blue Metaline	Black	CSX 2125
Silver	Red	CSX 2159
Svecia Red	Black	CSX 2165
Rouge Irise	Black	CSX 2168
Silver	Black	CSX 2279

At CSX 2522 a special ICI low-bake paint was used for the first time, the car being painted white with red leather.

Racing cars and Le Mans replicas were despatched in primer or unpainted with black leather interiors. The only exceptions were the two factory Le Mans cars for 1963. These were respectively British Racing Green with Black leather (CS 2131) and White with Blue Stripes and Black leather (CSX 2142).

The dashboards were finished in black leather and carpets were trim colour or black. Wheels were either painted or chromium.

European Cobra 289
Colour Schemes

Broadly speaking the choice of colours for this series of cars was the same as that for the CSX production already running, as follows:

Rouge Irise/Black
Red/Black
White/Red
Vineyard Green/Beige
Bright Blue/Black
Black/Black
White/Black
Princess Blue/Red
Opaline Green/Black
Svecia Red/Black

Dashboards were finished with black leather and carpets in trim colour or black.

Wheels could either be painted or chromed.

US 260 & 289 Cobra
Production Figures

All these cars were constructed under contract by AC cars for Carroll Shelby. Almost all of them were sent direct to the USA by sea or air from the factory; two destinations were used. The numbers made and destinations were as follows:

CSX 2000–CSX 2074
75 4.2-litre cars.
Air to Los Angeles	4
Boat to Los Angeles	53
Air to New York	1
Boat to New York	16
Retained by AC Cars (CS 2030)	1

CSX 2075–CSX 2125
51 4.7-litre cars.
Boat to Los Angeles	37
Boat to New York	14

CSX 2126–CSX 2589
460 4.7-litre cars with rack and pinion steering.
Air to Los Angeles (including first rack and pinion prototype CSX 2126 and four chassis to be built as Daytona coupés: CSX 2286, CSX 2287, CSX 2299 and CSX 2300).	8
Boat to Los Angeles	438
Boat to New York	14

In addition to the above the following cars were sent elsewhere: CS 2130, CS 2131, CSX 2142 (UK, racing cars); CSX 2451 (air to Turin, 9ft wheelbase chassis only); CSX 2601, 2602 (air to Milan, chassis only, to be built as Daytona coupés).

The following numbers of roadster Cobras left the factory month by month. This list includes all racing cars both designated as such by the factory and those converted by Shelby, but does not include thre three cars kept in the UK (CSX 2130, CS 2131 and CSX 2142).

Year	Month	Monthly total	Annual total
1962	January	1	
	July	5	
	August	8	
	September	4	
	October	18	
	November	17	
	December	8	61
1963	January	20	
	February	13	
	March	14	
	April	17	
	May	8	
	June	7	
	July	25	
	August	6	
	September	19	
	October	15	
	November	34	
	December	33	211
1964	January	32	
	February	37	
	March	32	
	April	42	
	May	33	
	June	36	
	July	40	
	August	31	
	September	22	
	October	3	
	November	2	310

During the production run some cars left the AC factory specifically designated as racing cars, and they are as follows:

- CS 2130 – Le Mans prototype, John Willment Racing Team. Silverstone GT 1963 driven by Jopp (4th OA).
- CS 2131 – AC factory Le Mans car 1963 driven by Bolton/Sanderson (7th).
- CSX 2136 – Le Mans replica. Elkhart Lake USRRC 1963 driven by Bondurant/Macdonald (4th OA, 1st GT).
- CSX 2137 – Le Mans replica. Elkhart Lake USRRC 1963 driven by Johnson/Spencer (6th OA, 2nd GT).
- CSX 2138 – Le Mans replica. Castle Rock USRRC 1963 driven by Macdonald (8th OA, 2nd GT).
- CSX 2142 – USA Le Mans car 1963 driven by Hugas/Jopp (retired).
- CSX 2154 – Le Mans replica.
- CSX 2155 – Le Mans replica. Daytona FIA 1964 driven by Hitchcock/Tchicotuba/Schlesser (10th OA, 8th GT).
- CSX 2159 – First race car with wide rear wings.
- CSX 2260 – Race car with wide rear wings. Daytona FIA 1964 driven by Schlesser/Guichet (DNF).
- CSX 2301 – Race car with wide rear wings. Sebring 1964, driven by Spencer/Bondurant (5th).
- CSX 2323 – Race car with wide rear wings, Targa Florio 1964 driven by Gurney/Grant (8th OA, 2nd GT).
- CSX 2345 – Race car with wide rear wings, Targa Florio 1964 driven by Hill/Bondurant (DNF).
- CSX 2385 – Race car with wide rear wings.
- CSX 2409 – Race car with wide rear wings.
- CSX 2431 – Race car with wide rear wings, Watkins Glen 1964, Miles (1st).
- CSX 2458 – Race car with wide rear wings.
- CSX 2459 – Race car with wide rear wings.
- CSX 2488 – Race car with wide rear wings. Elkhart Lake USRRC driven by Johnson/Leslie (DNF).
- CSX 2494 – Race car with wide rear wings.
- CSX 2513 – Race car with wide rear wings. Bridgehampton Double 500 1964 (7th OA, 3rd GT).
- CSX 2514 – Race car with wide rear wings.
- CSX 2557 – Bridgehampton Double 500 1964 (DNF).
- CSX 2558 – Bridgehampton Double 500 1964 (DNF).

In addition the following chassis were built up as Daytona coupés:

- CSX 2286 – Le Mans 1965 (Gurney/Grant DNF).
- CSX 2287 – Daytona 1964 (MacDonald/Holbert DNF).
- CSX 2299 – Le Mans 1964 (Gurney/Bondurant, 4th).
- CSX 2300 – Daytona 1965 (Leslie/Grant, 6th).
- CSX 2601 – Daytona 1965 (Johnson/Payne DNF).
- CSX 2602 – Daytona 1965 (Muther/Timanus, 4th).

Race results given refer to the first race of any importance entered.

Chassis plate of a European leaf sprung Cobra. CSX cars up to chassis 2201 did not normally have chassis plates, with the exception of some very early cars, which had a plate similar to that of the Ace 2.6 but giving only the chassis number.

COBRA 289 PRODUCTION AND EXPORT FIGURES

Chassis numbers of this series started at COX 6001 and ended at COX 6062. Only 60 cars were built, chassis numbers 6052 and 6056 simply having 'reserved for USA' against them in the factory ledger. The first of these two is said to have been used to rebuild COB 6040 after a severe crash when almost new. Of the 60 cars built there were 42 with COB chassis numbers (UK cars) and 18 with COX (export cars).

Sales year by year were as follows:

Year	UK	Export	Country	
1963	1	3	France	3
1964	31	8	France	2
			Switzerland	4
			Canada	1
			Australia	1
1965	8	7	USA	2
			Switzerland	1
			Portugal	1
			Sweden	1
			Germany	1
			Greece	1
1966	2	—		

Of the above, two COB cars, 6059 and 6060, were exported in 1965. Two COX cars, 6016 and 6017, were sold in the UK in 1964.

427 Cobra and AC 289

Possibly the first coil sprung Cobra chassis in the AC showroom in Thames Ditton, with a late CSX leaf sprung car, unpainted and with inhibitor on the chrome, waiting for shipment by sea to Los Angeles.

CHASSIS

With the second distinct model of Cobra, it was decided at last to dispense with the transverse leaf springs that had served so well since the first Ace was introduced at the 1953 London Motor Show. AC and Shelby were quite happy to use the resources of the Ford Design Department, and under the guidance of Klaus Arning, who had been responsible for much of the GT40 chassis work, a totally new coil spring suspension was drawn up.

Twin parallel tubes were still used, but these had grown to 4in diameter in 12 gauge steel and were now more widely spaced, at 22in. There were four cross members of the same material: one in between the front suspension uprights, one beneath the motor, one carrying the gearbox mounting and one in front of the differential. This obviously made the basic structure much stronger.

A tubular scuttle hoop remained, with bracing tubes running down and forward to the front suspension assembly, but this was a completely different construction from all earlier Aces and Cobras. It was built up from 2in diameter tubes, with a pair of verticals either side rising from the main chassis and having perforated webbing between them. Linking these uprights was sturdy X-bracing also formed of 2in tubes, the suspension mountings being lugs welded to the main chassis tubes and sub-structure frame.

At the rear, two further tubes rose from each main chassis member and were united by another tube welded horizontally to their upper extremities. In addition, there was a pair of horizontal cross bracing tubes at the top, the rear one having two 45° ¾in tubes returning down to its corresponding vertical. This assembly was in the main made up of 2in tubes and all the various lugs necessary to attach the suspension components were of fabricated and welded sheet steel.

As before, tube ends were closed where necessary with welded discs; the rear chassis, however, was closed by a steel channel cross-piece with three perforations. The various outriggers and tubes forming support and framework for the body were welded to the main chassis, the finish of which was, as always, black.

FRONT SUSPENSION

Double wishbones of unequal length, fabricated from tube, were employed, those at the top being U-shaped and the lower ones V-shaped. Wishbone bushings were of bonded rubber and greaseless, only racing versions having bronze bushes; racing and S/C versions also had an anti-roll bar.

The coil springs had a diameter of 4½in, a wire diameter of fractionally over ½in and 10 coils. They enclosed telescopic shock absorbers by Armstrong, one of the firms to which AC had remained faithful over the years.

Suspension parts had the same black finish as the chassis, except for the shock absorbers which were in their manufacturer's colours.

REAR SUSPENSION

Unequal length wishbones and trailing arms, once again fabricated from tube, were used at the rear. Suspension uprights (cum hub carriers) were again of cast iron, the lower wishbone pin being clamped in the upright.

The coil springs had the same diameter and wire diameter, but only eight coils; they also enclosed Armstrong telescopic dampers. Suspension was set to give the wheels 2° of negative camber, but the camber, castor and toe-in of the rear wheels was fully adjustable by means of rose joints. This was an advantage for those who wished to use their cars for purposes other than boulevard cruising, as it made a wide range of handling characteristics easily available. The S/C model incorporated an anti-roll bar at the rear. Track for all coil-sprung cars is 54in at front and rear.

Both front and rear suspension had anti-dive and anti-squat characteristics which helped to make the coil-sprung Cobra a softer, less responsive car than the old leaf-sprung version, although all-round roadholding was superior.

STEERING

The same steering rack was fitted to this version of the Cobra, and attached to the front of the framework that carried the front suspension. Swivel pins linked the top and bottom wishbones to the uprights. As before, the steering arms faced forwards (owing to the rack position) and bent inwards to clear the increased width of the wheels fitted to this model. This also meant that the hexagonal adaptors for the steering rack were shorter than before. The steering again gave 2⅞ turns of the wheel from lock to lock.

The steering wheel remained the same for the coil sprung Cobra, the 427 variant having a Cobra badge in the centre.

The AC 289 retained the AC badge used on the horn push of the previous model. Black pearl paintwork with maroon interior was this car's original colour scheme.

The following settings are correct for this model: wheel camber, nil; wheel toe-in on rim, 1⁄16in; castor angle, 3°; king pin inclination, 11°.

From the rack, the steering made its way rearwards with a split column having two universal joints. The column was suspended, as on previous models, from the scuttle hoop and was adjustable for height at this point. The dished aluminium, wood-rim wheel was identical to that on the later edition of the leaf-sprung Cobra.

Steering parts were painted black except for the natural finish of the cast aluminium bracket holding the steering column below the scuttle hoop.

BRAKES

Girling disc brakes were still fitted all round. The front discs had a diameter of 11 11⁄16in with caliper type 16/3 and the rear ones a diameter of 10¾in with caliper type 12/3 H. The disc thickness was ⅝in front and ½in rear. The racing and S/C models used Girling aluminium two-piston calipers, type CR at the front and ORA at the rear. It is possible that these have subsequently found their way onto some road cars. Discs on racing and S/C models were of larger diameter, but also thinner.

Even with the vastly increased power of the 427, neither Shelby nor AC saw any need to fit a servo to the braking system, so consequently the pedal pressure was, as with all Cobras, fairly high.

FINAL DRIVE

The Salisbury 4HU differential assembly, which had already proved itself well able to withstand the power of earlier racing Cobras, continued to be used for these cars. At 3.54:1, the rear axle ratio reverted to that employed on the very earliest USA specification Cobras and all European leaf-sprung Cobras, although a 3.31:1 ratio was available. After Chassis COB 6120, AC 289s were fitted with the 3.31:1 ratio. The differential was again mounted at two points on the main casing and at the nosepiece on the rearmost of the 4in chassis cross members.

Drive shafts continued to be supplied by Hardy Spicer. These were the same type as used on the leaf-sprung cars, but during production they were modified to incorporate larger universal joints and yokes which in turn necessitated larger holes in the rear suspension tower to accommodate them. The short splined shaft that passed through the new type of suspension upright ran on a pair of taper roller bearings, the shaft having two diameters at this point for strength. The inner bearing and outer bearing had inside diameters of 1½in and 1⅝in respectively.

Wheel location was now of two distinct types: 427 Cobras used the peg drive variety with six driving pegs while the European AC 289 continued to use 42mm splined hubs. At least one 427 car, chassis CSX 3150, is recorded as having left the factory with wire wheels but certainly peg drive wheels were normal on this model.

Spinners for the aluminium wheels were of the centreless three-eared variety, the ears being long and dished outwards; their open ends necessitated the fitting of aluminium hub plugs. Some spinners were forged in aluminium, some in steel. Cars with wire wheels still had the traditional two-eared knock-ons with an inscribed AC logo.

WHEELS & TYRES

Several different types of magnesium alloy wheels were used on the 427 Cobra. Most of the first run of homologation cars, chassis numbers CSX 3001 to CSX 3055, were equipped with six-spoke FIA-type Hallibrand wheels, although some of the

Peg drive Hallibrand aluminium wheels, three-eared knock ons and an aluminium blanking plug for the centre are all correct for the S/C 427 and some roadgoing cars.

These are the Sunburst wheels specially made for the 427 Cobra because of difficulty in obtaining the Hallibrand variety.

Wire wheels with 42mm hubs continued to be used on the AC 289.

This 427 side-oiler motor has been later fitted with a 1966 'Police Interceptor' medium rise aluminium intake manifold, but it looks just like the correct 1965 part.

Some AC 289s were fitted with a dynamo. Aluminium heater pipes are joined to heater hose to pass through the bulkhead. The glass SF2 washer bottle sits in its correct position, perilously close to one of the exhaust manifolds. In shadow above the bellhousing are a pair of brake servoes fitted by the factory for the first owner. Shelby Cobra aluminium rocker covers were never standard on European Cobras.

later cars in this series had GT40 pattern wheels. The true road cars from chassis number CSX 3101 had 10-spoke 'Sunburst' wheels, but some cars between chassis numbers CSX 3125 and CSX 3157 were sold with GT40 style wheels of 7½in width front and rear.

Rim size for the road cars was 7½ × 15in, fitted with 8.15 × 15in Goodyear Blue Dot tyres; in the middle of production some cars were fitted with 9½in rear tyres. This may have been done just after delivery to try to better fill the vast wheel arches. 427 S/C cars were equipped as standard with 7½ × 15in front wheels and 9½ × 15in rears; these were fitted with 9.90 × 15in and 11.90 × 15in Speedway Special tyres. These wheels were of magnesium alloy and generally left unpainted. European AC 289 cars had 6 × 15in chrome or painted wire wheels fitted with 185 × 15 Dunlop SP41HR tyres.

ENGINE

The ancestry of the 427 and 428 engines fitted to Cobras goes back to 1958, the first motors of this series being of 332 and 352cu in. These engines are of Y block or extended skirt type and have thick wall construction. Weighing over 700lbs, they are considerably heavier than the 260 or 289 motors.

Although three types of this engine were fitted to the Cobra, many of the dimensions remained the same. All are of conventional basic construction with oversquare bore and stroke, plain main bearing crankshaft and pushrod overhead valves.

The 427 motor, from which the car took its name, came in two versions – 'side oiler' and 'top oiler'. The 'side oiler' fed oil directly to the crankshaft from the pump, while the 'top oiler' supplied the camshaft followers and oil filter before the crankshaft. The 'top oiler' 427 proved in competition to be a reliable and relatively raceworthy engine, but as Ford's GT40 development progressed and engines became even more highly stressed the lubrication system revealed shortcomings, especially in long-distance races. As a result, the 'side oiler' block engine was evolved.

Comparatively few 'side oiler' motors were fitted as original equipment to 'street' 427 Cobras, but they were certainly fitted to both Competition and Semi-Competition models. Some even had the sometimes troublesome aluminium heads, which were prone to gasket problems owing to the different expansion rates of the aluminium head and iron block.

The 'side oiler' motor can be recognised externally by the oil gallery running along the lower left-hand side of the block casting and by the core plugs being a screw-in type (on the 'top oiler' they are the press-in variety).

Both 427 variants fitted to the Cobra had cross-bolted main bearing caps on the centre three of the five bearing crankshaft; the heads of these bolts identify both 427 types externally from lesser FE engines. All FE crankshafts had five main bearings with journals of 2.74in and big ends of 2.43in. Up until 1965 all crankshafts were cast iron, but from 1965 to 1967 the 427 engine could be fitted with a cross-drilled steel crankshaft known as the 'Le Mans'. The connecting rods are just under 6½in long and come in two varieties – normal FE 13/32in nut and bolt for the iron crank and 'Le Mans' 7/16in capscrew type for the steel crank. Bore and stroke are 4.23in by 3.78in. Aluminium slipper-type pistons were fitted, giving a compression ratio of 10.4:1 with flat top pistons or 12.4:1 with raised crown pistons; these are only nominal ratios as they varied according to the cylinder heads used.

The cylinder heads are cast iron and of the 'low rise' type. 'Medium rise' and 'high rise' heads were available, but they are unlikely to have been supplied by Shelby in street cars. The latter two types of head had machined combustion chambers and had to be matched to their respective inlet manifolds.

The camshaft followers are solid; although hydraulic followers were offered in 1968 these would be incorrect for a Cobra. The valves were operated by conventional rockers on a shaft. Rocker covers were made of chromium-plated pressed steel and held down by five screws through the flange.

'Low rise' heads were normally fitted with a dual plane twin carburettor inlet manifold. Many combinations of cylinder heads and manifolds, of course can be fitted on these engines, but in the absence of any further data from the period it can be safely assumed that the above specification was usually adhered to.

When he experienced difficulty in obtaining 427 engines, Shelby began to fit the 428 'Special Police Interceptor' engine into roadgoing 427 Cobras. This was still an FE series motor and was very similar to the 427, but it lacked the cross-bolted main bearings and had hydraulic camshaft followers (although some specification sheets state otherwise). While the 428 engine's cubic capacity was fractionally greater than the 427's, it was not merely a matter of a larger bore. The crankshaft throws were increased to give a stroke of 3.98in while the bores were actually smaller at 4.13in.

It is tempting to think that Shelby began to fit the 428 engine because it was less than half the price of a 427, but as far as can be determined 427s returned for some later

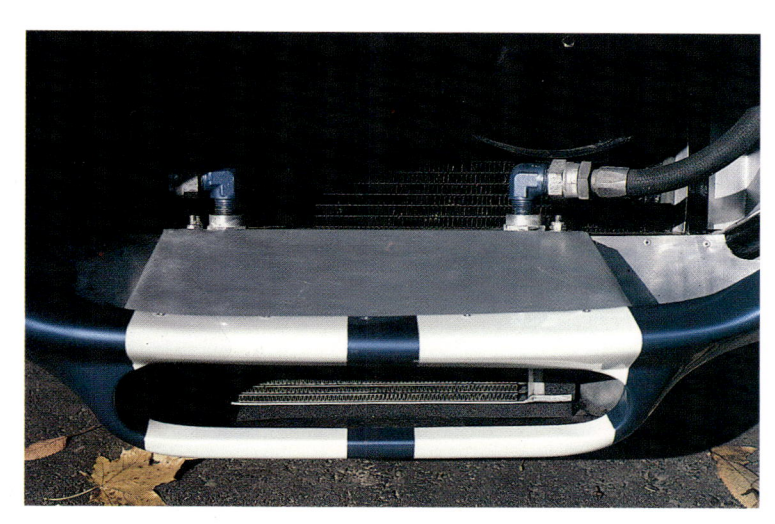

S/C 427 Cobras were fitted with oil coolers. This car has the original pipes and fittings.

Exhaust pipes for road cars swept upwards over the drive shafts on either side and then down to exit as shown. Chrome trims were a popular option.

cars. Alternator and starter were located on the right-hand side of the block and were painted with Ford blue engine lacquer, as were the sump and water pump.

COOLING SYSTEM

At first McCord, which had manufactured cooling system equipment for the earlier cars, supplied radiators and header tanks for the 427; the capacity was a little larger at 5 US gallons.

Later on Serck of England manufactured the radiator, this being a six-row, cross-flow, D-type core. The header tank was from a Canadian Ford, but the entry pipe was reversed to enable it to be fitted more conveniently to the radiator top hose. The standard Ford water pump was retained but without fan blades; an electric fan was fitted in front of the radiator. Twin fans were listed and were certainly fitted where circumstances deemed it necessary, but a single fan was fitted to the vast majority of cars. The finish for all these items was black.

EXHAUST SYSTEM

Exhaust manifolds for some of the first roadgoing 427s were from 1963/4 Ford 390 engines. After a short time Carroll Shelby arranged for special cast iron manifolds to be made in England. These led into a single pipe on each side with straight-through silencer, and then to tailpipes which curved over the driveshafts before exiting at the rear. Only the racing and S/C cars had individual manifolds and a side exhaust, although a very few customers had their road cars fitted with this system by dealers.

CARBURETTORS & FUEL SYSTEM

Two Holley 600CFM 4V carburettors were fitted to all roadgoing Cobras. These had rather small primary jets which rendered the car quite docile at the first depression of

· ORIGINAL AC ACE AND COBRA ·

Only the S/C 427 (and actual racing cars) had side exhausts as standard. They should be finished in this manner, not chrome plated.

S/C Cobras had a large aluminium Monza type filler cap recessed into the rear wing. Normal road cars continued to use the 'Ceandess' filler cap used on Aces and leaf sprung Cobras.

the accelerator pedal, but bringing in the sizeable secondary jets had completely the reverse effect.

A pair of chromium 8in diameter air cleaners surmounted the carburettors, the rear one being slightly higher owing to the dual plane manifold. An Autolite mechanical fuel pump fed petrol from the 18 US gallon steel saddle tank mounted under the boot well.

TRANSMISSION

The clutch was a Ford 11½in plate, coil spring unit operated hydraulically by a CV cylinder.

The gearbox was a standard Ford 'toploader' four-speed with cast iron casing, which rendered it very heavy but very strong. The name 'toploader' was given to this type of 'box because assembly or dismantling was carried out through the top of the casing. The gears were wider and heavier than on the T10 gearbox used in earlier Cobras, making the gear change slightly slower. Although two sets of ratios for this gearbox were available from Ford, only the close set was used; the ratios were 2.32:1, 1.69:1, 1.29:1 and 1:1.

The gearchange linkage was altered from the earlier cars to a standard Ford four-speed linkage and gearlever. The lever was mounted backwards, so that it curved upwards and then forwards.

Automatic transmission was probably not fitted to more than four cars, two of these being the twin Paxton supercharged cars, chassis CSX 3015 and 3303, that Shelby built for himself and a customer. The gearbox used was a C-6.

Hardy Spicer continued to supply the propellor shafts for both the 427 and 289.

ENGINE (289)

This engine was essentially the same as that fitted to the leaf sprung Cobras except that it had a J type engine block. This differed from the B block fitted to the earlier cars in that it had a six-bolt bellhousing (instead of five).

COOLING SYSTEM (289)

A Serck radiator was fitted in conjunction with the header tank used on the 289s.

84

This type of gearlever is peculiar to the 427 Cobra.

Exhaust System (289)

Cast iron manifolds and downpipes were the same as on previous 289 Cobras, but the connecting pipes to the silencers were longer, to compensate for the forward placing of the engine in the chassis compared with the 289 leaf sprung roadsters. Silencers and tailpipes were the same as on 427 street cars.

Transmission (289)

The AC 289 was fitted with the Borg Warner T10 aluminium casing gearbox. L or M gear sets were used, K sets being by this time not available.

Electrical Equipment

Much of the electrical equipment used on the 427 Cobra and AC 289 was common to all Cobras, so only the differences are discussed here.

Two types of Autolite alternators were used, one being the C6AF-10300D. But on the AC 289, certainly for the UK market, the C40 dynamo was still fitted. Starter motors were also by Autolite, a three-bolt type for the 427 and a two-bolt type (C6AF-11001) for the AC 289.

Autolite also supplied the distributor and coil. The control box was usually Autolite type C5AF-10316A, except on the AC 289

Autolite regulators were used on the 427, as was this type of Trico washer bottle. Some chassis numbers were scribed and some stamped – no mention of AC cars!

· ORIGINAL AC ACE AND COBRA ·

Extremely wide rear wings were used on the majority of 427s. Lucas 549 rear lamps were also fitted to most cars. The filler cap that had served on the majority of previous models was beginning to look a little lost on this car. Exhaust pipes on the 427 exit slightly further outboard than on the leaf sprung cars.

No overriders were fitted to the S/C Cobras. In their place were quick-acting jack brackets. The roll over bar is also correct for this model only. The extra rear wheel arch lip was peculiar to the S/C. Note the original Shelby American manufacturer's licence plate with 1965 date sticker.

Sidelights were incorporated in the headlights, so the lamps below served only as indicators and had amber lenses.

427 COBRA AND AC 289

where it was still a Lucas RB106/2. Two types of then-current Lucas fuseboxes were used. Twin Lucas H9 horns with high and low note were used for the AC 289 and the 427, replacing the bulky Windtone horns previously employed.

The Lucas windscreen wiper motor was a two-speed DR3. The electric cooling fans were still supplied by Lucas, but the heaters were specially made by Smiths. Negative earth was used for the 427 and late examples of the AC 289, but early AC 289s were positive earth. An Autolite battery was fitted to 427s and a Lucas type FRLT9A to AC 289s.

LAMPS

Lucas sealed beam headlights with integral sidelights were fitted to 427s and sealed beam headlights without sidelights were used on AC 289s. The sidelights on 289 cars were still Lucas type 539 units; these had amber lenses on the 427 and were employed as direction indicators. On later 427s from

The first few AC 289s had this rear light arrangement (above), later cars normally reverted to the Lucas 549 rear lamps. These cars had the narrower of the two rear wing types used for the 427. This first AC 289 was fitted with various items by the factory and specified by the original owner, including sidelights and rear lamps, which are not found on subsequent cars in this series.

Apart from the fact that the headlamp units were Continental or English, the front lamps of the AC 289 were exactly the same as on the 427.

This is a Beclawat windscreen, although there is no visible difference apart from the badge. Wind wings were always an optional extra. Once this type of bonnet handle was standardised quite early in leaf spring production it was used for all remaining Cobras.

around chassis number CSX 3201, these direction indicators were changed to type RB 682s. At the same time, the rear lights, which had hitherto been type Lucas 542, were altered to RB 692s; below them was a type RER 31 reflector of the same size. The AC 289 was either fitted with Lucas 542 rear lamp units or twin rear lamps. All cars had Lucas 467 number plate lamps.

BODYWORK & BODY TRIM

The body construction methods employed for the 427 Cobra and AC 289 were exactly the same as for the Aces and Cobras that came before them, but during production there were variations in aspects of the overall shape.

Before AC created the body bucks for the 427, it produced two cars, CSX 3001 and CSX 3002, with reworked FIA type bodies from the earlier cars. These two, and all cars up to chassis number CSX 3053 (apart from CSX 3027, which left the factory as a racing chassis without a body), were built as competition cars in order to homologate this model for FIA events, but by the time the regulation number of cars should have been completed, in April 1965, only 52 were finished.

As a result, the racing cars were able to compete only in SCCA amateur racing, which meant that Shelby was left with a rather large number of apparently unsaleable competition 427 Cobras, only about 16 having been purchased. The remaining unpainted cars lay out in the open (with some on blocks due to an aluminium wheel shortage) by Shelby's hangar at Los Angeles airport. Upon seeing this forlorn line of cars, a Shelby eastern sales representative named Charles Beidler

All but the last 427s and all AC 289s had white glassfibre boot floors (above). Only the pair of side hatches for access to the rear lamps were in black. Boot hinges for Cobras were tubular, the same construction as the Aceca. Luggage space by this time was minimal.

It was still necessary to have a kinked rear bumper to give clearance for the boot handle.

Cold air intakes for the cockpit are within the radiator nacelle at each side, not trunked from the ovals inboard of the indicators as might be expected. The overrider supports should be in bare aluminium and their rubber grommets are missing. Normally the lower bar of the bumper hoop would be of elliptical shape. The chrome trim on the air splitter is correct for the 289 and 427.

All 427s carried this badge on their flanks (left). US market leaf sprung cars and some European models had a similar badge in the same place reading 'Powered by Ford'.

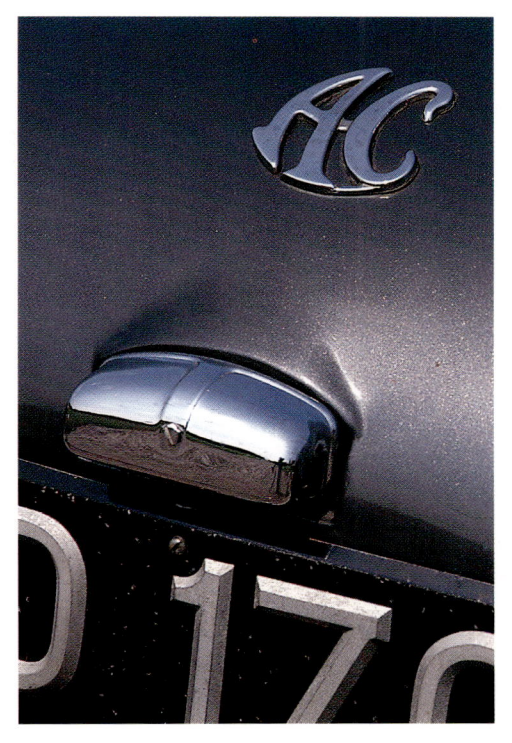

The shape of the area around the number plate lamp on the boot of Cobras seems to have been inconsistent but the lamp remained the same – a Lucas 467. A diestamped AC badge continued to be used on the boot of the AC 289.

suggested that with a few modifications they could be turned into really exciting road cars, and so was born the fabled 427 Cobra S/C (Semi-Competition).

The main visual differences between the S/C model and the roadgoing 427 were lips around the wheel arches of the large flared rear wings, a glass-fibre air scoop attached to the bonnet with rivets, a rollover hoop and the lack of mesh for the air intakes inboard of the sidelights. Of course, it is quite simple to dress up a normal 427 Cobra to give the appearance of an S/C model, but only 31 cars were sold by Shelby to this specification.

Cobra 427 road cars started at chassis number CSX 3101, the prototype which left the AC factory on 2 April 1965. Two other development cars were sent over from the factory on 22 April 1965, these being CSX 3118 and CSX 3120.

The immediate difference that strikes the eye is the bulkier appearance of the 427 Cobras. Although the length of the body was not altered, the larger radiator intake and increased wheel arch flares at front and rear combine to give the whole car a different character from its leaf-sprung forebears.

Two distinct types of rear wing were used. Those up to chassis CSX 3124 had large flares, then at chassis CSX 3125 a narrower rear wing was introduced. After chassis CSX 3158, however, it was decided to return to the earlier design, this being retained for the rest of production. The probable reason for this is that the first few road cars used up unwanted homologation style bodies. When these were finished, AC narrowed the rear wings, only to have to return to the wide type again as customers wanted this style – even though it looks odd with the narrower wheels.

The enlarged air intake no longer carried a grille. Instead there was just a single chromium bar running horizontally across the opening, this trimming the front of an air splitter which curved downwards

If seat belts were fitted to the AC 289 they were of this type. The bottom of the dashboard followed the same contour as on the leaf sprung cars in order to incorporate the clock.

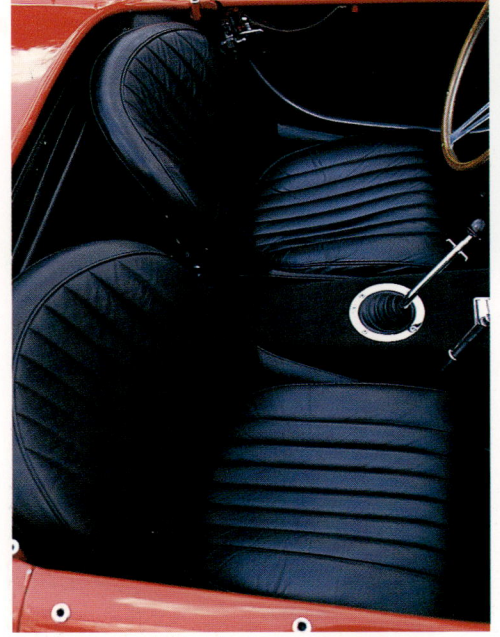

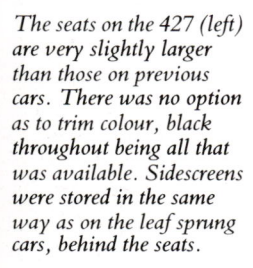

The seats on the 427 (left) are very slightly larger than those on previous cars. There was no option as to trim colour, black throughout being all that was available. Sidescreens were stored in the same way as on the leaf sprung cars, behind the seats.

A polished aluminium trim adorned the door sills on both 427 and AC 289. Moulded black glassfibre leather-grained hinge trims had been available since some way through leaf sprung Cobra production.

slightly towards the rear. The same overriders were used but had remodelled chromium tubes to encompass the larger nacelle. On either side of this, inboard of the sidelights, were two vertical intakes which were backed with aluminium mesh. Underneath the radiator opening was another intake for an oil cooler, but as this item was not fitted to road cars it was dispensed with after some 200 had been built. Rear bumpers and overriders were the same as those fitted to earlier Cobras.

All hinged panels and the tubework to support them were constructed in exactly the same fashion as before, albeit with some different dimensions. Hinges and rubber sealing strips were unchanged. Windscreens were manufactured by Elliott and Beclawat. The same mounting was used with its facility for complete removal if desired.

The white glass-fibre floor boot and spare wheel tray were changed to black on late 427s and all AC 289s, but the glass-fibre footwells remained in white throughout production.

The AC 289 wore the narrow wheel arch bodywork that was used for a short time on the larger engined car, and in all other respects, apart from badging, was bodily the same. There were Cobra badges at front and rear on the 427, but for the 289 the type of AC badge first fitted to the boot lid of the European leaf-sprung Cobras was used. The larger car carried '427 Cobra' rectangles on the sides of the front wings.

· 427 COBRA AND AC 289 ·

There was no glove compartment in the dashboard of the S/C Cobra. Instruments were also rearranged as shown.

INTERIOR TRIM & WEATHER EQUIPMENT

The interiors of both of these cars were the same as the Cobra that immediately preceded them except that the seats of the 427 were fractionally larger. Apart from a very few AC 289s, all cars now had black leather trim.

Hoods and sidescreens were also the same type, but both the hood and optional hard-top had a slightly different shape where they fitted over the rear deck and wings, due to the altered body contours in that area.

DASHBOARD & INSTRUMENTS

The layout and method of construction were almost identical to the previous model, the only differences occurring on the 427.

The 427 dashboard panel was straight at its bottom edge and there was no clock. The 427 speedometer read to 180mph. The rev counter was driven electrically on the 427 and was calibrated to 8000rpm. On the AC 289 the rev counter was driven off the dynamo mechanically and read to 10,000rpm. However, when an alternator was fitted, an electrically driven rev counter calibrated to 8000rpm was used. The 289's speedometer read to 160mph. A Smiths electric clock was fitted only to the AC 289.

An anti-clockwise speedometer is fitted to the S/C and some early road 427s. The fuel pressure gauge is also a legacy of the car's first-intended use.

The dash panel was straight at its bottom edge on all 427 cars. No clock was fitted, and this later type of Lucas ammeter was correct for the 427.

91

427 Cobra Competition Specifications

Engine
Aluminium cylinder heads.
Large capacity Aviad sump.
12.4:1 compression ratio.
Medium or high riser manifold with 4V Holley carburettor.
Remote oil filter.
Oil cooler.
No fans for cooling.
Two aircraft type 'Rebat 35a' batteries behind passenger seat.
Tuned length tubular exhausts exiting through side of body – no silencing.

Brakes
Quick-change pad racing calipers.
Fluid reservoirs on left-hand inner wing.
Glass-fibre brake scoops and rear ducting.

Wheels and Tyres
6½ and 8½in six-spoke FIA magnesium wheels on early cars.
7½ and 9½in Hallibrands later.
9.90 × 15 and 11.90 × 15 Goodyear Speedway Specials.

Fuel
42 US gallon aluminium tank.
4in diameter quick-action filler cap, frenched in rear wing.
Mechanical fuel pump with twin Stewart Warner 240-A electric pumps in boot.

Suspension
Front and rear anti-roll bars.
Bronze suspension bushes.

Instrumentation
Smiths rev counter.
Oil pressure and water temperature gauges in front of driver.
Other gauges including speedometer on the right.
No glove compartment.

Bodywork
Large wheelarch flares.
Oil cooler intake below radiator nacelle.
Glass-fibre scoop rivetted to bonnet.
Front half of bonnet rivetted to tubular frame.
Roll bar mounted at three points.
Quick-action jacking points front and rear.
Boot panelled in aluminium.
No door pockets.
Optional racing screen and glass-fibre driver's seat.

427 Cobra Semi Competition Specifications

Engine
Large capacity Aviad sump.
10.4:1 compression ratio.
Medium riser manifold with two 4v Holley carburettors (some with one 4v Holley carburettor).
Remote oil filter.
Oil cooler.
Electric fan, thermostatically controlled.
Two aircraft type 'Rebat 35a' batteries behind passenger seat.
Tuned length tubular exhausts exiting through side of body – integral silencers.

Brakes
Quick-change pad racing calipers.
Fluid reservoirs on left-hand side inner wing.
Glass-fibre brake scoops and rear ducting.

Wheels and Tyres
7½ and 9½in Hallibrands.
8.15 × 15 Goodyear 'Blue Dot', front.
11.40 × 15 Goodyear 'Speedway Specials' or 11.40 × 15 Firestone 'Indy Specials' } rear.

Fuel
42 US gallon aluminium tank.
4in diameter quick-action filler cap, frenched in rear wing.
Mechanical fuel pump with twin Stewart Warner 240-A electric pumps in boot.

Suspension
Rubber suspension bushes.
Front and rear anti-roll bars.

Instrumentation
Smiths rev counter.
Oil pressure and water temperature gauges in front of driver.
Other gauges including speedometer on the right.
No glove compartment.

Bodywork
Large wheelarch flares, rear with extra lip.
Oil cooler intake below radiator nacelle.
Glass-fibre scoop rivetted to bonnet, with integral aluminium plenum.
Front half of bonnet rivetted to tubular frame.
Roll bar, mounted at three points.
Quick-action jacking points front and rear.
Boot panelled in aluminium.
No door pockets.

427 Cobra Colour Schemes

A reduced range of colours was used for these cars. They are listed along with the chassis number when first used:

Red	Black	CSX 3102
Blue	Black	CSX 3105
Green	Black	CSX 3106
Black	Black	CSX 3109
Grey	Black	CSX 3112
Silver Grey	Black	CSX 3113
White	Black	CSX 3116
Vineyard Green	Black	CSX 3153

Dashboard and carpets were black.

The first series of 427 cars, CSX 3001 to CSX 3063, were not painted by the factory. Of the second series sent out with bodies, only two were unpainted but with black leather; these were CSX 3101 and CSX 3127.

427 Cobra Production Figures

These cars were constructed under contract for Carroll Shelby by the AC factory in the same way as the US leaf-sprung Cobras; again almost all of them were sent to the USA.

Below is a list of all roadsters that left the AC factory bound for the USA, the first 52 being homologation cars:

Year	Month	Monthly total	Annual total
1964	October	2	2
1965	January	20	
	February	25	
	March	5	
	April	5	
	May	20	
	June	20	
	July	7	
	August	8	
	September	17	
	October	3	
	November	16	
	December	4	150
1966	January	15	
	February	12	
	March	11	
	April	10	
	May	10	
	June	22	
	July	16	
	September	10	
	October	1	
	November	25	
	December	22	154

In addition to the above, 10 further chassis numbers were listed:

CSX 3027 13 January 1965, Ford Advanced Vehicles for Harold Radford (chassis).
CSB 3054 11 February 1965, Ford Advanced Vehicles for Harold Radford (rhd chassis).
CSX 3055 24 March 1965, Ford Advanced Vehicles for Harold Radford (chassis).
CSX 3063 1 June 1965, Ghia, Italy (96in wheelbase chassis).
CSX 3150 8 December 1965, Ford Advanced Vehicles, Slough (then Brussels motor show).
CSX 3217 14 February 1966, Ford Advanced Vehicles, Slough.
CSX 3222 14 February 1966, Ford Advanced Vehicles, Slough.
CSX 3301 9 January 1966, Ford Advanced Vehicles, Slough.
CSX 3359 no details, just 'Hex Motors' November 1971!
CSX 3360 no details.

AC 289 Colour Schemes

The following colours were used for the European coil-sprung cars:

Pearl Black/Maroon
Metallic Chrome Sand/Black
Pacific Green/Green
Dark Blue/Black
White/Black
Red/Black
Guardsman Blue/Black
Blue/Black
Vineyard Green/Black
Bright Blue Metaline/Black
Pacific Green/Black
Black/Black

Coloured leather was used sporadically but in the main these late cars, along with their larger engined relations, used black leather.

The dashboard was covered in black leather and carpets would match the trim or be in black. Normally chromium wheels were used on these cars but it was possible to specify painted ones.

AC 289 Production and Export Figures

There were 27 chassis numbers assigned for the AC 289 Sports, as the factory designated them.

The chassis numbers ran from COB 6101, leaving the factory on 27 June 1966, to COX 6127 (this car described in the factory ledger as 'chassis, parts supplied loose' leaving the factory on 15 July 1968. This last car, and the chassis number immediately preceding it (which was exported to the USA with no engine), were the only AC 289 Sports to leave the factory incomplete.

COB 6106 was the factory demonstrator. It was 'ex-works' on 19 May 1967, but as it was registered for the road in 1965 it may well have been the first car completed.

A total of 27 cars were made, six of which were exported. Of the remaining 21 cars, 20 were sold in the UK. One car (COX 6108) carries no completion date or destination in the factory ledger, so does not appear in the yearly sales figures, which are as follows:

Year	UK	Export	Country	
1966	10	1	Switzerland	1
1967	6	2	USA	1
			Belgium	1
1968	3	3	USA	2
			Channel Islands	1
1969	1	—		

Buying Guide

As the years go by, ACs, along with many of their contemporaries, are being restored to what is termed 'concours' condition, where a degree of shininess and perfection undreamed of by the manufacturer is achieved. Attrition naturally means that the stock of unrestored cars declines with the passing of time, but there are owners who unfortunately choose to improve cars from good condition to a 'concours' state. The truly original car is fast becoming a real rarity.

Any owner can do as he likes, of course, but I would urge caution before embarking on the restoration of a perfectly good original car. ACs in poor or unoriginal condition are still be be found, and these make a much better – and probably cheaper – basis for sympathetic improvement. I do not much care for concours cars, partially due to their sterility, but I fully recognise that there are many cars which badly need loving attention because they have been neglected or modified. My only plea is this: if you plan to restore an Ace, Aceca or Cobra, please carry out the work to original standards and specifications wherever possible. Do not rechrome for the sake of it, polish every aluminium casting to a mirror finish or discard perfectly good, but slightly worn, upholstery and trim if they were fitted to the car when new.

As far as the different ACs dealt with in this book are concerned, there are points to look for on individual models, but in no cases are faults terminal and they should be relatively inexpensive, in view of the cars' values, to correct.

Chassis and body flexing can cause Aces and Cobras to develop body cracks, which usually manifest themselves between the rear wheel arches and door shut faces, on the bodywork adjacent to the doors and vertically in the sills. Such cracks are not a cause for undue concern as they do not mean that the car is about to fall to pieces! Repair in these areas is best left to professionals, unless you are a skilled aluminium welder and former, as it entails cutting out the affected areas and letting in new sections of the correct gauge sheet aluminium.

Bubbles in the paint around the headlamps are a sure sign that there is corrosion in these areas; again this is not structural and repair is a matter of replacing the affected metal. This corrosion is caused by the aluminium bodywork having an electrolytic reaction with the steel headlamp bowl when subjected to damp, and can occasionally occur elsewhere where the aluminium is in contact with steel.

The steel tube around which the bottom of the sill is formed and fastened can rust, but replacement – a matter of welding in a length of correct section tubing and re-fixing the sill in place with pop rivets – is fairly simple. If the aluminium is corroded as well, it will need replacing as necessary. Outriggers can rust but are equally likely to have been deformed by incorrect jacking; either way, they can be replaced quite easily.

The Aceca's main Achilles heel is corrosion of the body suppporting framework around the rear suspension. This is sometimes difficult or even impossible to see without some dismantling of the car. Probably the safest course is to expect the worst unless recent work has been done in this area by someone who knows what he is doing and there are bills and possibly photographs to support this. The wooden door frames on these coupés do distort and sag a little with age, and even rot, which can show if the bottom rear corner of the door 'hangs out' when closed.

Due to the fact that these bodies were handmade and every car differs in some small respect from any other it is not possible to buy replacement body parts as it is for mass-produced cars such as Jaguars and Austin-Healeys. Repairs to or replacement of sections therefore really are to be entrusted to a proven and reputable specialist; this need not cost a prohibitive amount due to the inherent simplicity of the coachwork; a repaired or even completely new body shell for an Ace would, for instance, be far less time consuming and therefore less expensive than that for a Jaguar XK140 roadster.

A quirk of Cobra production is that one of the parts stamped with the chassis number is the boot latch. This is only bolted to the boot lid and so is easily swapped from car to car and could be attached to a vehicle not made by AC to give it credibility. This is the boot latch from COB 6048, actually fitted to COB 6020 – but there's a simple explanation: both cars have the same owner, who inadvertently mixed the parts. Consider the consequences if the car changed hands in this state!

Suspension and steering are of course subject to wear as on all cars – one of the first signs of worn suspension is quite often rear end steering, as described in the main text.

Mechanical condition is important of course, but many components, including parts for the AC engine, are now being remanufactured by the AC factory. Their inventory is being expanded all the time so it is impossible to give a list of the many parts now re-available for the different models.

The AC engine has a long life and is troublefree if treated with the respect which its years deserve; the wet liner engine does not appreciate being allowed to overheat drastically and will very likely blow its cylinder head gasket in consequence. Even with radiator inhibitors block corrosion will eventually become a problem (as it has with pre-war engines of this type) but modern welding techniques make some repair possible and in the fullness of time I feel sure that, for a price, replacement aluminium cylinder blocks will become available.

The Bristol engines fitted as original equipment were, except in certain circumstances, not to the same specification as those fitted to Bristol cars, so it would be second best to fit a motor from this source should the original motor be missing or totally beyond repair. A 100D2 Bristol engine would be very difficult to find, expensive and very costly to recondition. A properly built up Bristol engine is, however, a beautiful piece of engineering that will last for a very long time and give great satisfaction in its going.

At the time of writing both engines and parts are still relatively easy to acquire for the Ford Zephyr-engined Aces and Acecas, but the Rubery Owen-manufactured aluminium cylinder heads fitted to many of these cars are very difficult to find and original type valves and guides are almost non-existent. In common with other Ford short-stroke motors, pistons do have a limited life but rebuilding, certainly to a mild state of tune, should present no problems.

Parts to rebuild the various V8 engines found in Cobras are readily available but such items as the blocks for both HP 289 and 427 side oiler are becoming difficult; their desirability and relatively low production being the main reasons. Out of the huge number of 289 engines made by Ford under 20,000 were genuine High Performance units, and of course the majority of these were used for cars other than Cobras.

Many ACs, often Aces and Acecas, have been fitted with non-original engines over the years. This has usually been done after the original engine has suffered a mechanical calamity or simply to improve performance. Before buying one of these cars with the intention of refitting an original specification motor it should be borne in mind that AC, Bristol and some V8 engines are increasingly rare.

Aces fitted with alternative power units, especially V8s, often have also had bodywork modifications to make them visually similar to Cobras. While it would be unlikely for anyone with some knowledge to mistake one for the other, to reverse the combination of modifications back to original specification would be a lengthy, difficult and expensive project. If you wish to own a car to original specification these factors might make it wiser to pay the likely premium for an unmodified example.

Provided that any car that you consider buying is driveable, do try it out. However, you may find it disappointing: the legendary precise handling of the Ace may actually seem to be vague, and the supposedly brutal Cobra will probably turn out to be woolly and quite tractable. All models definitely improve upon long and close acquaintance, but you will have to be the owner to find this out for yourself.

Whoever long ago coined the phrase *caveat emptor* must have been thinking ahead to the world in which we now live. Each car manufactured by the AC factory was given a chassis number, an identity which referred to that car and that car only. It is up to the intending owner of a car to satisfy himself as to the continuous history of a vehicle. Any interruptions should be viewed with grave suspicion, the degree of originality acceptable to the individual being the deciding factor. Some Cobras, and doubtless in the future Aces, have been sucked into the twilight vortex of being reduced to nothing and then re-created from just that or perhaps a piece of tube, a door or some registration papers. What credibility would be given, I wonder, to a two square-inch piece of canvas torn from an original painting by Rembrandt, attached to some fresh canvas and repainted in the same style by someone else many years later? No gallery or serious collector would give it consideration if they knew the true facts. Don't be too despondent, though, there are still many cars with a perfectly respectable provenance to be found.

One thing that struck me while studying the old factory ledger in the preparation of this book was that various names cropped up repeatedly as people bought their second or even third AC in succession. Marque loyalty is not a trait exclusive to AC, but certainly many owners tend to stay faithful, sometimes for the majority of their motoring lives. Bearing testimony to this are two brothers who, at the time of writing, still own cars they bought before the war. Several Aces have been in single ownership for over 30 years and Cobras owned for 20 years or more are not uncommon. Once acquired, ACs are very often kept.

Owing to this loyalty and the rarity of the various models, there are seldom many cars on the market at any one time. If you want an AC Ace, Aceca or Cobra and can find a real one, buy it if you can. You will not regret it.

· ADDRESSES ·

Clubs

AC Owners Club Ltd
Membership Secretary: B. C. Clark, The Flint Barn, Upper Wootton, nr Basingstoke, Hants RG26 5TH.
Australian centre: Geoff Dowdle, 35 Leopold St, Croydon Park 2133, NSW.
French centre: G. Maitre, 14 Rue Larrey, 75005 Paris.
Dutch Centre: C. P. Louwen, Heeswyk 2, 3417 GR Montfoort.
German centre: Dr Rolf Versen, 11AM Inzerfeld 53, D-41 Duisberg.
Swiss centre: C. Vogele, Rebhalde 40, CH 8640 Rapperswil.
US centres, East: T. Bowman, 8637 Sylvan Drive, Melbourne, Fla 32904.
West: J. Feldman, 11955 S.W. Faircrest St, Portland, Oregon 97225.

Shelby American Automobile Club
PO Box 788, Sharon, CT 06069, USA.

Specialists

While a large number of specialists exist for cars like Jaguars or MGs which were made in considerable numbers, production of AC cars was so small that no such facilities are available to the AC owner. The best advice I can offer to a new owner is either to contact the relevant club official or to talk to another owner. In either case unprejudiced advice can be obtained about whether parts and expertise are available and where.

The prime source of parts is the AC factory, whose inventory of parts for Aces, Acecas and Cobras is constantly being expanded as demand warrants their remanufacture. The factory address is

AC Cars
Vickers Drive
Brooklands Industrial Park
Weybridge
Surrey   KT13 0YU.

The following small list may also be of some assistance:

Bristol engine rebuilds and parts
TT Workshops
127 Engineer Road
West Wilts Trading Estate
Westbury
Wilts   BA13 4JW

Lamps and electrical equipment
Holden Vintage and Classic Ltd
43B Hartlebury Trading Estate
Hartlebury
Kidderminster
Worcs   DY10 4JB

Leather
Conolly Brothers
Wandle Bank
Wimbledon
London   SW19 1DW

Trimming supplies
Edgware Motor Accessories
94 High Street
Edgware
Middx

Rubber extrusions and sealing strip
C.O.H. Baines
9 Park Road
Tunbridge Wells
Kent   TB4 9JP

Wire wheel rebuilds and supply
Motor Wheel Services
Jeddo Road
Shepherds Bush
London   W12 9ED

Brake and instrument drive cables
Speedy Cables
The Mews
St Paul Street
Islington
Londoin   N1 7BU

Instrument repairs
Thomas Richfield
4 Broadstone Place
Baker Street
London   W1H 4AL